ERWIN RAMSDELL GOODENOUGH:
A PERSONAL PILGRIMAGE

SOCIETY OF BIBLICAL LITERATURE
BIBLICAL SCHOLARSHIP IN NORTH AMERICA

Kent Harold Richards, Editor

ROBERT S. ECCLES

ERWIN RAMSDELL GOODENOUGH
A Personal Pilgrimage

Scholars Press
Chico, California

SOCIETY OF BIBLICAL LITERATURE
CENTENNIAL PUBLICATIONS

Editorial Board

The Society of Biblical Literature gratefully acknowledges a grant from the National Endowment for the Humanities to underwrite certain editorial and research expenses of the Centennial Publications Series. Published results and interpretations do not necessarily represent the view of the Endowment.

Library of Congress Cataloging in Publication Data

Eccles, Robert S., 1911–
 Erwin Ramsdell Goodenough, a personal pilgrimage.

 (Biblical scholarship in North America / Society of Biblical Literature)
 "A bibliography of the writings of Erwin Ramsdell Goodenough by A. Thomas Kraabel": p.
 Includes index.
 1. Goodenough, Erwin Ramsdell, 1893–1965. I. Title.
II. Series: Biblical scholarship in North America.
BL43.G66E25 1985   291'.092'4   85–10918
ISBN 0-89130-907-1 (alk. paper)
ISBN 0-89130-908-X (pbk. : alk. paper)

Printed in the United States of America
on acid-free paper

ERWIN RAMSDELL GOODENOUGH
Yale University Archives, Yale University Library

To the blessed memory of Samuel Sandmel:
scholar, teacher, mentor, friend.

*Ecce quam bonum et quam iucundum
habitare fratres in unum.*
Ps 133:1

CONTENTS

PREFACE

It was a great honor for me to be invited to write the book on Erwin R. Goodenough for the subseries Biblical Scholarship in North America for the Society of Biblical Literature Centennial Publications series. I was a pupil of Goodenough in the mid-forties at Yale. Like many other students, I was stimulated and had the whole new world of Hellenistic studies opened up to me in his famous seminar. Later he was to guide me through the writing of my doctoral dissertation. How could I have dreamed when I was his student that I might some day be given the responsibility of writing the volume to represent him in a series commissioned by the Society of Biblical Literature, the society that over long years he served both as journal editor and president? Writing this small volume has given me the opportunity to try to honor my teacher to whom I owe so much.

It was the late Samuel Sandmel who first suggested to me that I might be asked to do this writing. Professor Kent Harold Richards extended the invitation from the editorial committee of the SBL. I am grateful to both of them. I also owe great thanks to many others who have assisted me in bringing this volume to completion: to Cynthia G. Goodenough for her permission to publish materials from her late husband's papers; to Judith A. Schiff and her staff at the Yale Archives for their kindness in assisting me in the summer of 1981 in the consultation of Goodenough's papers, and permission to publish selections from these papers; to E. J. Brill, publishers, and Professor Jacob Neusner of Brown University, and to Dean A. Thomas Kraabel of Luther College to reprint the latter's bibliography of Goodenough's publications, which originally appeared in the memorial volume to Goodenough, *Religions in Antiquity*; to Professor Robert A. Calhoun of Yale for permission to quote from his unpublished *Lectures in the History of Christian Doctrine* (New Haven, 1948); to the Society of Biblical Literature for a research grant; to DePauw University for full use of its facilities, in particular to its excellent library; to Dean Eldon Jay Epp of Case Western Reserve University who served as my editor, who assisted me greatly with his advice and encouragement, especially with his painstaking attention to my manuscript; and to Ms. Maxine Davies, who typed the manuscript in its final form.

Above all I thank my wife Kathryn for her unfailing interest in and support of my labors, and her forbearance during the many hours of many days over the past four years when I have been preoccupied with the research and writing of this book.

Greencastle, Indiana
25 August 1983

INTRODUCTION

Erwin Ramsdell Goodenough is distinguished as the American scholar of the twentieth century who has made the richest contribution to our understanding of the influence of Hellenism on Judaism and early Christianity. He was first led into these studies by his analysis of the theology of Justin Martyr, which he found to be marked by Hellenistic Jewish influences best exemplified in the writings of Philo Judaeus. Goodenough found in Philo the primary exemplar of Hellenistic Judaism, although this Judaism was richly varied and Philo was not its exclusive spokesman. The study of Justin Martyr also aroused Goodenough's interest in religious symbolism, which finally bore fruit in his major work on Jewish symbols in the Greco-Roman world.

Goodenough intended to speak primarily through his scholarship, yet in his writings he has left enough clues to the development of his own religious consciousness that some attention must be given to his own religious thought. The best scholarship is informed by the strong, even passionate, concern of the scholar for the ultimate significance of his research. For Goodenough, scholarship was a sacrament, and toward the end of his life he considered his personal religion to be of sufficient interest to others to write a brief spiritual biography and summation of his religious thought.

The present volume introduces the work of one who was reared in pietistic Methodist fundamentalism and who in his youth responded to the call to the ministry and began to serve in the parish. Shortly thereafter he was drawn into the even more compelling world of historical scholarship in religion. As a scholar Goodenough eventually found it necessary to question and finally to abandon the traditional orthodoxies of his upbringing. Because of certain poignant personal experiences he ultimately abandoned institutional religion. Nevertheless from many statements in his scholarly work it is evident that he never abandoned the ultimate values of religion, whether these were to be found in Christianity, in mystical Hellenism, or in Hellenistic Judaism. His scholarship must ultimately be judged by its cogency, but to gain a full understanding of Goodenough it is necessary to be aware that the force behind his scholarship was not only a brilliant mind endlessly fascinated by the phenomena of religion but also a spirit always sensitive to the values of religion—who found scholarship itself to be a sacrament.

As a profound scholar himself, Goodenough was demanding of his students. Anyone who studied under his guidance gained not only knowledge of the field of study but also understanding of the nature of scholarship itself. If some of his students did not themselves become scholars in the full sense of the word, they at least through him had rich opportunity to know what scholarship is. They have been better teachers, better writers, and above all have been enabled through his inspiration to live a richer life of the mind.

1

A BIOGRAPHICAL SUMMARY

The significance of an individual is determined by whatever defines his life. Erwin Goodenough was defined by his scholarship. One of his students who knew him the most intimately said, "I have never known a scholar quite so content with scholarship as Erwin."[1] Goodenough was impelled to scholarship by a desire not only to know and understand historical facts but also to find answers to ultimate questions of human existence. Toward the end of his life he wrote a small book summing up the religious insights that he had gained from a lifetime of scholarship in the history of religion.[2] Its first chapter is a brief autobiography which traces the route that took Goodenough into a life of scholarship.

He was born 24 October 1893 in Brooklyn, New York. He describes at length the powerful influence his parents exerted upon him. His father practiced law. Goodenough remembered him as a committed exemplar of the Puritan ethic of industry and hard work. He permitted himself little or no recreation and practiced many useful manual skills at home. He was severe in manner yet exercised his authority, whether at home or in the large Sunday school of which he was superintendent, with only the utterance of quiet words. Goodenough understood this severity as the result of his father's severity with himself. For example, he was attracted to pretty women, but he relentlessly submerged any thought of flirtation.

Erwin saw in his father "bitterness and repressed aggression" (*Mature Faith*, p. 5), yet he was notable for his deeds of kindness. The father's religion and character were inseparable, yet his God appeared to be not a threatening God but a kindly God. Goodenough confessed of his father, "To me as a boy his taciturnity, his unrelaxing work, his severity, made him an unapproachable, unknown superman, the sort of father indeed from which gods are made. From him I learned many values—

[1] Samuel Sandmel, "An Appreciation," in *Religions in Antiquity: Essays in Memory of Erwin Ramsdell Goodenough* (ed. J. Neusner; Studies in the History of Religion–Supplements to *Numen*, 14; Leiden: Brill, 1968) 5.
[2] Goodenough, *Toward a Mature Faith* (Englewood Cliffs, NJ: Prentice-Hall, 1955); reissued as a Yale Paperbound, New Haven: Yale University Press, 1961.

more than I shall ever myself understand" (*Mature Faith*, p. 6). With such a father Erwin turned to his mother, who was always able to satisfy his need for warmth. Her warmth and sympathy were sustained by her vivid faith in God's goodness, and she could pray with complete assurance, "Thy will be done." Her faith made such a deep impression that throughout his life Erwin continued to find in that same prayer the deepest comfort in times of trouble.

Out of this background Goodenough discovered that God took on the severity of the father and Jesus the feminine warmth of the mother. In spite of the beard with which Jesus is commonly portrayed, he became for Goodenough primarily a feminine figure representing the love he experienced with his mother. The presence of this Jesus at school could protect him from the bullying of other boys. His emotional development was late, and other boys considered him to be a sissy. In spite of his resentment at being picked on, he was taught that to fight back was a sin and that he must forgive his enemies. He says, "If repressed resentment, tears, and an illusion of forgiveness were my releases, my compensation was in my mother, and in religion" (*Mature Faith*, p. 9). These recollections show the important place that psychological analysis had in Goodenough's later thought.

The old-fashioned Methodist tradition in which all the Goodenough children were nurtured had profound influence on Erwin. Its Calvinist ethic produced a legalism as strict as that of orthodox Judaism. Sunday was devoted to faithful attendance at several church services. Recreation was not permitted. Only sacred music might be played on the piano. Goodenough considered that his family deserved the reputation of being pious prigs, and this made all the more difficult his relations with other boys. He observed that this was precisely the "pharisaism" that Jesus denounced. Yet Goodenough recognized lasting values that derived from this way of life. It was an excellent schooling in individualism. All the Goodenough children assumed their father's pattern of incessant work. Erwin, however, found that his lifelong inner compulsion to work was accompanied by a sense of joy in the creativity of work.

The other side of the Methodism of Goodenough's childhood was "its love of free emotional expression of one's love of God and Christ" (*Mature Faith*, p. 12). He recalled the thrill of the hymn singing, the hand clapping, and the shouts of praise. The songs were primarily passionate love songs expressing an only slightly veiled eroticism. These experiences prepared him later to understand the appeal that reproductive symbols and cult acts have had in religions of civilizations with fewer repressions than our own. He came later to understand that what other religions were doing through symbol and ritual he and his fellow Methodists were doing directly in immediate expression, shocked though they would have been at the setting up before them of a religious image.

Goodenough saw in his religious background one facet of the nineteenth-century world, a world seen as a place of order, and basically good. Yet it was a world of illusion in which the dark forces of human evil that were manifested in World War I became incomprehensible. He held no nostalgia for it.

The second greatest religious influence upon young Erwin was through his Uncle Charlie, an elderly relative whom he visited every summer after he became fifteen. In a long life of hard work on the family farm, the old man's only distinction was his seeking after and achievement of ecstatic religious experiences. When he was past seventy, Uncle Charlie's sole proposal of marriage was refused. Goodenough remarked, "So all his life he turned his intense sexuality likewise into his religious experience, as many of the greatest mystics have done" (*Mature Faith*, p. 16). Uncle Charlie divided all Christians into those who had been only "converted," and those who had been "sanctified" and had received the "second blessing." Like mystics from Philo of Alexandria onward, this contrast was represented in allegory. For Uncle Charlie as well as for Philo the migration of the Israelites to the promised land represented departure from the world of sin under God's leadership. However, neither the migrant Israelite nor the migrant soul could be rescued from the cycle of lapse, repentance, and reinstatement except through "death," the death of self-assertion.

Goodenough reported that although his parents were never sanctified, he and his sisters were. He later interpreted this experience in Freudian terms as the "death" of the "self," which is only the suppression of the id putting one in danger of approach to schizophrenia. The high point of this period in his life was an experience of religious ecstasy during a religious revival. He learned from Uncle Charlie what Freud would call the surrender of the id to the ego-ideal, the abandonment of gratifying physical desires in favor of conforming to the standards of society, ethics, and God so as to be accepted by our environment as proper. These experiences were of great advantage to Goodenough in his later studies of ecstatic religious experiences, whether those cultivated by the Dionysiacs or the old rabbis at the feast of Tabernacles. When later in Platonism he met the distinction between mere opinion in the physical world and the true knowledge accessible only through the vision of the ideal world he felt perfectly at home. Only with this attitude is the change of fertility religions into mystery religions comprehensible.

He entered Hamilton College in Clinton, New York, in 1911. His work in languages, mathematics, and literature was exacting, but it provided him with no stimulus for "intellectual or social ranging" (*Mature Faith*, p. 22). He tried in vain to seem to be "one of the boys," but he lived primarily in religion, music—he was college organist for three years—and in literature. Finally, in a course in Shakespeare he made the new discovery of the critical approach to literature. He said that quite unknown to himself he had found his *metier*, and with his professor's encouragement he planned to go on in the field of literature. The summer of 1914 was marked by a profound religious experience in which he went through agonies of guilt for certain peccadilloes. In the midst of this turmoil he decided to enter the ministry, and this appeared to resolve the crisis. He planned to take a Ph.D. in English to satisfy his intellectual drive, but the ministry would be the emotional expression of his life. Only later in his life of scholarship did he discover that these two drives could be coordinated.

In 1915, after receiving his B.A. from Hamilton, he did a summer's work in English at Columbia and then in the fall enrolled in Drew Theological Seminary. After one year he transferred to Garrett Biblical Institute in Evanston, Illinois, and received the S.T.B. in 1917. In the fall of that year he was married to Helen M. Lewis. During summers and weekends while he was at Garrett he pastored a small Methodist church in Crescent City, Illinois, which he describes as "a little parish in a village on the great corn plain of Illinois" (*Mature Faith*, p. 25). He discovered that he was a very effective preacher, but after the second year did not know what he was talking about. Years later he wrote in a letter to an older pastor friend of that period words of appreciation for "the beauty that you put into the lives of the young minister and his wife who more than twenty years ago were for a little time in Crescent City."[3]

In seminary Goodenough had the greatest enthusiasm for courses in analysis of Christian history and doctrine. His interest now shifted from analysis of Shakespeare's plays to the problem of the origin and nature of religion. He found himself to be an empiricist, thinking in terms of documents and evidence. He felt the need of more facts about Christian origins, and so moved on to study at Harvard as a graduate student. He studied under some of the greatest American scholars of the time: Ephraim Emerton, George Foot Moore, James Ropes, George LaPiana, Kirsopp Lake, F. C. Conybeare, and Charles Gullick. Harvard became a major turning point in his intellectual and spiritual life. In that atmosphere of empiricism he found that no one cared what he believed, "but cared tremendously that I be able to justify by evidence anything I said about historical fact" (*Mature Faith*, p. 26). He discovered the difference between verifiable fact and the theory that endeavors to explain it. Discovery of the scientific world was a great illumination for him. At the same time he observed astutely that the scientist as much as the historian

---

[3] Unpublished letter of 22 April 1927 to the Reverend Christian Helmsreich upon the celebration of his fiftieth year in the ministry (Archives of Yale University; Erwin R. Goodenough Papers, Yale University). Used by permission.

deals with faith, that is, unverifiable suppositions. Yet he expressed optimism in the scientific methods characteristic of the times. "All the movement of history and chemistry has been to try to abolish the world of faith and to substitute for it complete knowledge of the universe and of ourselves as facts" (*Mature Faith*, p. 27).

He felt the impact of his new orientation only gradually. As he lost the old faiths he felt that he was never without protection, never without the orientation of a scholar who through his active search could find new positions in whose value he could have faith. At Harvard and later at Oxford he came into a new life. At Oxford he spent most of his time reading in the Bodleian Library and writing his dissertation. The most important thing that three years in England and on the Continent did for him was to isolate him from his parents, the Methodist Church, and from immediate obligations to persons representing his old orientation. But enough of the old loyalties remained that he became fully ordained as a Methodist minister in Paris. He made his transition without friction and found satisfaction in making new and mature friendships.

Goodenough had hoped for a teaching position in a seminary in America; but upon his return he was found to be theologically too far to the left, and no seminary would hire him. At this crucial moment he was offered an instructorship in history at Yale. The year was 1923, and Goodenough was thirty years old. Beyond this point in *Toward a Mature Faith* he offers no further autobiography except for a brief summary. He says that in his developing academic career he had come to feel that he "slowly transformed what was best from my whole heritage into a pattern which seemed to me to make some sense for living in the new age" (*Mature Faith*, p. 32).[4]

On 14 October 1957, ten days before his sixty-fourth birthday, Goodenough wrote a letter to the Reverend Russel G. Nye of Des Moines, Iowa, explaining why he would be unable to attend the fortieth reunion of his class at Drew Theological Seminary. It reflects his wry humor, and since it contains such an excellent biographical sketch of his career it is appropriate to reproduce it in its entirety.[5]

> Dear Nye:
>   It would be good to join you at Drew for the reunion, but June is so busy for us academicians that I cannot plan to attend. This is a bit of a substitute to greet you all and wish you well.

---

[4] The present author recalls a conversation with Goodenough in which he said that he had originally intended to entitle his book *What is Worth Saving from Christianity*, but his publisher prevailed upon him to adopt *Toward a Mature Faith* as a more positive and acceptable alternative.

[5] Unpublished letter from the Archives of Yale University; Erwin R. Goodenough Papers, Yale University Library. Used by permission.

Much of the time at reunions is given to reporting on our lives since graduation, so I give the following outline:

After my shocking defection from Drew at the end of the first year I graduated at Garrett, then went to Harvard Divinity School. I had a touch of TB at the end of the first semester, and was out for a year and a half, then back for the year 1919/20 at Harvard. Thence to Oxford, where I took the D. Phil., as they call it there, in 1923. I had hoped to teach in a theological school on my return, but I was by this time too far left for any but a few schools to want me, and they were full, so I fortunately got an instructorship at Yale in 1923, to teach history. I went up from that, through the usual *cursus honorum*, to become Professor of the History of Religion in 1934. By this time I was in five departments, the original of what Harvard calls a "University Professor," without the title, salary, or honor that Harvard gives the title, but with all the academic freedom. I have taught what I pleased in various lines, and in general had a very happy teaching experience.

My real interest, however, has always been in writing, and now as I write Vol IX of my *Jewish Symbols in the Greco-Roman Period* I am actually doing my seventeenth volume, with three or more printed as articles. I trust every member of the class has read them all!

The personal life has been extremely rich. I was married the September after I left Drew, and had a family of four children.[6] The eldest of these is Associate Professor of Anthropology at the University of Pennsylvania, the second is head of a group of research physicists working on the big calculating machines at M.I.T., the third is in business, and the fourth, a girl, happily married and combining teaching with bringing up three small boys. There are ten grandchildren to date. In 1941 I was divorced from my first wife and married again.[7] By this marriage I have two lovely children, a girl 14 and boy 13. My wife took her Ph.D. at Yale in Child psychology a year ago, and is doing fine work at the Gessell [sic] Institute of Child Psychology, and writing books herself. She has not caught up to me yet, but soon will have done so.

I am now 64, and was written up in a newspaper in Israel last summer, when I read a paper at a Conference, as "the Aged Scholar." Since I am probably one of the youngest in the class, you see where that puts the rest of you.

So that is my Cursus Vitae. The warmest possible greetings to you all.

Five years later, in 1962, Goodenough's second marriage was ended by divorce after twenty years. On 11 May 1963 he was married to Cynthia Brooks Goss, and his correspondence of that time indicates that it was a very rewarding relationship. Only two years later his death occurred on 20 May 1965. He was in his seventy-second year.

[6] He was married 5 September 1916, to Helem Miriam Lewis. Children of this marriage were Ward Hunt, John Bannister, James Hinchman, and Hester Vanneman.

[7] He was married 20 January 1942 to Evelyn Ivy Wiltshire. The children of this marriage were Ursula Wiltshire and Daniel Adino.

Goodenough was a man of strong and sensitive feelings, and he could express himself pungently. At the same time he was a man who made deep and warm friendships, as indicated in letters to friends and colleagues. This is also reflected in their letters to him. He was a generous man. This is shown in his frequent letters of thanks and appreciation for favors done to him, and for the work of others. His generosity appears also in his thoughtful letters of recommendation of students and colleagues, in his generous support of colleagues, and in his acceptance of different points of view. He was generous with his time and thought in relation to his students, and he very graciously accepted ideas of students that might not agree with his own. He was conscientious almost to an extreme in his supervision of doctoral students assigned to him, and he treated them as younger colleagues.

Goodenough had long and warm connections with the Jewish community and with Jewish scholars. In addition to being a very productive scholar himself he spent much time and energy in university affairs and in the affairs of learned societies. His correspondence reflects his activities in the American-Israel Society, the American Council of Learned Societies, the Association for the Scientific Study of Religion, and the Society of Biblical Literature, which he served for a time as president and at another time as editor of the society's *Journal of Biblical Literature*.

FIRST RESEARCH:
JUSTIN MARTYR AND PHILO

Goodenough's first published scholarly work was his doctoral dissertation, "The Theology of Justin Martyr."[1] Thirty years later in the introduction to his work on Jewish symbols he explained what had aroused his interest in Justin:

> I suggested at the end of the dissertation that the hellenization of Christianity had been made possible because Jews in the pagan world had opened doors through which pagan notions had come into their Judaism; that when such Jews became Christians these notions were already at home in their minds as a part of their Judaism itself, and so at once became part of their Christianity. To investigate the possibilities of this hypothesis has been the concern of all my subsequent investigations.[2]

Thus, his study of Justin was the first step in the scholarly program that he set for himself from the beginning of his career, the writing of the history of early Christianity. He chose to investigate Justin because of his transitional position in early Christianity. Justin was the first to use conceptions and phrases more fully developed by later theologians. But it was first necessary to trace these elements to their sources before their true significance in second-century Christian theology could be known.

Goodenough begins by surveying the philosophical environment of Justin. Earlier thinkers had tried to arrive at a sense of the wholeness of reality and phenomena in terms of some primal element: water, fire, or some other material principle. A surprising number of pre-Socratic fragments call the primal form of matter *theos*.

The Pythagorean doctrine of number and the Platonic doctrine of forms offered a new departure in human thought. Aristotle argues against Plato that for the forms to be able to affect matter there had to be an efficient cause. In later writings Plato developed such a concept. For him the

---

[1] Goodenough, *The Theology of Justin Martyr* (Jena: Frommann, 1923; reprinted, Amsterdam: Philo Press, 1968).

[2] Goodenough, *Jewish Symbols in the Greco-Roman Period* (12 vols.; Bollingen Series, 37; New York: Pantheon, 1953–65) 1. 6.

divine *nous* became the efficient principle as well as Universal Intelligence permeating all things. Goodenough said that whatever contribution Plato made to the later Logos doctrine must be found in his remarks about the *nous*. The Stoics identified the *pneuma* with reason, the Logos, as the basic principle of reality. No use of the term Logos by the Stoics has been more misunderstood than the *logos spermatikos*, the "spermatic principle," which in strictly Stoic thought always had a theological significance. For Justin Martyr it came to represent a cosmological entity. Goodenough considers only Platonism among later philosophical schools, since it was the one that most influenced Christianity. He says, "In such an atmosphere the Divine *Nous* or Logos . . . became personalities in a sort of philosophical theogony which graduated down to the most insignificant demons. Such was the popular philosophical environment of Justin, a welter of crude superstitions expressed in myth and snatches of philosophical terminology" (*Justin Martyr*, p. 32).

Palestinian Judaism had lost influence over Christianity by Justin's time. Influence came rather from Hellenistic Judaism, notably through the thought of Paul, who made the tremendous discovery that Jesus, the man of history, could be identified with the Logos of Hellenistic Judaism. The writings of Philo of Alexandria give us the best picture of the thought of this school.

Of the various schools of philosophy, Justin shows best acquaintance with Platonism. He expounds his understanding of Platonism in a conversation with an Old Man. At a certain point in the conversation, Justin admits to being over his depth. The Old Man then explains to him how "the Prophets more ancient than the philosophers gave men the truth because it had been revealed to them by the Holy Spirit, and that they had been followed by Christ, the supreme revelation of Truth" (*Justin Martyr*, p. 71). On the Old Man's recommendation Justin searches out the new school of philosophy, Christianity, and soon adopts it as his own. We know little of Justin's life as a Christian. According to the best scholarly judgment only the *First* and *Second Apology* and the *Dialogue with Trypho* can be accepted as genuine works of Justin.

In his third chapter Goodenough presents his most distinctive contribution to the study of Justin's theology, the identification of Hellenistic Judaism as the most decisive influence on Justin's thought. This resulted from Justin's need to answer the sneers of the philosophers that Christianity was not worthy of an intelligent man's consideration. In defense against this charge he employs the arguments of the Greek Jewish apologetic. Just as Hellenistic Jews could claim that Greek philosophers obtained their ideas from Moses and the Hebrew scriptures, so likewise could Justin claim that teachings common both to Judaism and to Christianity were the sources of much in Greek philosophy. He found the basis for this in Jewish scripture, which for him was superseded only by the teachings of Jesus. This reflects the influence of Hellenistic Judaism as exemplified in Philo.

If Justin accepts the claim that scripture is the true philosophy basic to Christianity, how is he to refute the claim of nonbelievers that Christ is "still a novelty and his doctrines the product of an unphilosophical mind?" (*Justin Martyr*, p. 110). He does this by claiming that Christ was the incarnation of the one Universal Mind, True Reason. Goodenough explained Justin's argument: "Whoever has striven to lead a life according to reason has lived according to Christ, and has been, however unconsciously, a Christian . . . ; [therefore] Christianity is not a novelty, it is as old as the universe, as old as truth" (p. 110).

In Justin's scriptural interpretations there is no evidence that he ever made a careful study of Philo's writings. However, as Goodenough showed in his later studies, though Philo may be the most eloquent and prolific spokesman for philosophical Hellenistic Judaism, he was by no means the only one. It is unnecessary, therefore, to prove that Justin was directly influenced by Philo to argue that for him Hellenistic Judaism was a powerful resource. Early Christianity seems to have been uncritical in its doctrine of God and expressed its views about God in traditional devotional terms derived from the synagogue. In answering Jewish or pagan attacks on Christianity, Justin attempts to speak philosophically about God. He emphasizes most the *transcendence* of God, thus rejecting the Stoic view of God's immanence, also denying Stoic views by insisting that God is *unchangeable* and *eternal*. Justin thus conceives of God in the manner of Philo. For Justin God is the One who transcends space and time, yet inconsistently Justin argues that God has *location* and remains in his place, "wherever that may be" (*Justin Martyr*, p. 126). Goodenough traces this inconsistency directly to the Philonic tradition. Other ways that Justin describes God are also traceable to the Philonic tradition: that God is *formless, unbegotten, nameless*, and *ineffable*. If Justin is sometimes infelicitous in the use of Philonic categories, we must remember that his aim was not philosophical or critical but practical and apologetic. He was primarily a Christian attempting to use philosophical terminology to defend the faith.

In his fifth chapter Goodenough explains how the concept of the Logos served the philosophers of the late Hellenistic period as a link connecting a transcendent Absolute with the world and humanity. The Logos idea served Christians in another way. When Christians began to teach Christ as superhuman—a gross offense to Jews who could not countenance the idea of more than one God—Hellenistic Jewish thinking solved that problem "by the brilliant stroke of identifying Christ with the Logos" (*Justin Martyr*, p. 140).

In the writings of Justin the doctrine of the Christian Logos is in a very uncertain state. Instead of the Logos of God, Justin prefers to speak of a Second God. There must be two Gods, one who *remains* in heaven, and one who *appears* in theophanies. Justin develops the argument in Philonic terms. He describes the Logos as unbegotten, but, to avoid the implication that the Logos has existence independent of the Father, Justin also uses the figure of emanation. So there are two Gods but only one source. Yet, lest this image suggest diminution of the source by the constant outflow of the Logos, Justin also resorts to another figure, the kindling of one fire from another. Fires may be two in number, but they are alike in essential character. Philo had expounded both of these figures, beams of light and fire from fire, to illustrate how God's power is disseminated.

Although in many points there is the closest similarity between Justin's and Philo's speculations, Justin fails to penetrate Philo's deeper thought. Justin was not a pioneer in interpreting Christ in terms of the Logos. Hellenistic Christianity had long "been working the mine of Greek Judaism to explain Christianity in philosophic language" (*Justin Martyr*, p. 175). Goodenough's demonstration of Philonic influence upon Justin has been recognized by other scholars. His distinguished Yale colleague, Robert Lowry Calhoun, observed that when Justin moves away from the doctrines of God and the Logos in which Hellenistic Jewish formulations had assisted him, that is into the specifically Christian area of thought, "the detail and originality of his affirmation thins out."[3] The influence of Hellenistic Judaism was not merely incidental to the formulation of Justin's thought but crucial to it.

In his conclusion Goodenough ascribes to Justin the true and gentle spirit of sainthood, but declares that he was in no sense a philosopher. He was primarily a traditionalist whose chief desire was to explain Christianity as he had learned it. It is doubtful that Justin added anything to Christianity at all apart from possibly the application of the theology of the Spermatic Logos concept. "In brief, the Christianity which Justin has described, with its foundation of primitive Palestinian Judaistic beliefs, was almost entirely dependent for theory upon a Hellenistic Judaistic tradition which had been running in through the doors opened by St. Paul, and by the authors of the Epistle to the Hebrews and of the Fourth Gospel" (*Justin Martyr*, p. 294).

Goodenough's interest in Philo is clear in his study of Justin. That Philo quickly came to the center of Goodenough's attention is demonstrated in his 1926 article, "Philo in Public Life."[4] In 1932 he published

---

[3] Calhoun, *Lectures on the History of Christian Doctrine*, Yale Divinity School, 1948 (unpublished; for private circulation only). Used by permission.
[4] Goodenough, "Philo in Public Life," *Journal of Egyptian Archaeology* 12 (1926) 77–79.

"A Neo-Pythagorean Source in Philo Judaeus," which is a clear fore-runner of his later Philo studies.[5] Goodenough traces to Pythagorean theory Philo's exposition of Genesis 15:10, "He divided them in the middle and laid them opposite each other" ("Neo-Pythagorean Source," p. 117). Philo discusses equality in God's creation of the world, which was established through the instrumentality of the Logos Cutter; he claims that Moses recognized the universality of this principle, which is everywhere at the bottom of Jewish laws. Philo tries to fit into the Torah a definite conception of the Logos and the creation of equality.

In later Pythagorean theory matter is divisible only down to the atom. But atoms so conceived differ from those of Democritus, for whom atoms are the prime reality. Like the Pythagoreans, and unlike the Stoics, Philo rejects any materialism in deity. For Philo God did not create matter. Philo is thoroughly Pythagorean in his idea of creation as the application of the number system and also in his understanding of creation as a bisection of primal matter.

According to Goodenough, when Philo calls the principle of cosmic harmony the Logos he goes beyond anything found in Pythagoreanism. Other Pythagorean influence on Philo appears in his view that the material universe is made of a series of entities related to each other by arithmetical and proportional equality and also in his use of the term "Logos Cutter." Goodenough remarks, "Philo is certainly not the only Jew of his civilization who is trying to reconcile Jewish Scripture with Greek ideas" ("Neo-Pythagorean Source," p. 152).

In "Philo's Exposition of the Law and his De Vita Mosis"[6] Goodenough makes a comparative study of two of Philo's treatises. De vita Mosis had previously been classified with other writings of Philo addressing apologetic arguments to Gentiles. But Goodenough finds it to be different from other apologies since it shows no concern for attacks on Jews by Gentiles. Rather, it addresses interested outsiders with an elementary introduction to Judaism. Moreover, the Exposition of the Law refers to De vita Mosis as representing an integral part of the argument of the Exposition.

Rejecting earlier critical opinion Goodenough concludes that the two treatises are in some sense related to each other as are Luke and Acts. In disagreement with other scholars, he concludes that the Exposition is best to be understood as written for Gentiles, which explains the similarities between it and De vita Mosis. The latter is addressed to the sympathetic outsider interested in learning more about Judaism. If that should

---

[5] Goodenough, "A Neo-Pythagorean Source in Philo Judaeus," *Yale Classical Studies* 3 (1932) 115–64.

[6] Goodenough, "Philo's Exposition of the Law and his De Vita Mosis," *Harvard Theological Review* 26 (1933) 109–26.

awaken further interest, the reader might wish to go on to the detailed exposition of the Pentateuch in the *Exposition*. Both treatises show evidence of the nature of Jewish propaganda among Gentiles that is much more important than had previously been recognized.

The article shows the contrast between Philo's two representations of Joseph. In the *Exposition* Joseph appears as an admirable political leader. In a writing intended for Gentiles this would give a model to be emulated by their own political leaders. In the *Allegory* Joseph is depicted "as a politician analogous to the Roman prefect, but as a despicable creature, a threat to all that is noble in Judaism or in nature" ("Philo's Exposition," p. 116). The *Allegory*, written for Jews alone, could thus express in a veiled manner Philo's hatred of Roman domination. Goodenough would develop this point later in his *Politics of Philo*. Also revealing the intended Gentile audience of the *Exposition*, one of its parts, *On the Special Laws*, shows the practical harmony of the Jewish law with Gentile jurisprudence. This is the central topic of Goodenough's earlier *Jewish Jurisprudence in Egypt*. Two years after the present article appeared, Goodenough published *By Light, Light*, in which he gives a full exposition of Philo's manner of addressing some of his writings strictly to Jews, and others to Gentiles, seeking to commend to the latter the merits of Judaism in a form that they could understand and accept.

3

PHILO:
POLITICAL PHILOSOPHER AND POLITICIAN

Philo was occupied with two kinds of concerns, the practical concerns of politics and law, and the theoretical concerns of religion and philosophy. The first he engaged in out of necessity and duty. The second he engaged in by preference and delight. Goodenough's earliest studies of Philo were of the man of politics and law. In 1928 he published his essay "The Political Philosophy of Hellenistic Kingship,"[1] which bears not only upon Philo's politics as it relates to the civil state but also upon his philosophy of kingship, which he sees exemplified in Moses, the great mystagogue of the Jewish mystery. Essentially this essay touches on the full range of Goodenough's interests in Philo.

In the essay Goodenough observes that in the Hellenistic period disillusionment with the city-state and democracy led to the search for a better model for the civil state. The image of Cyrus, the great king, provided the model. Alexander opened the Greek world to oriental and Egyptian concepts of rulership, which exercised great influence on the developing concept of Hellenistic kingship—namely (1) the king himself is animate or embodied law, he is justice itself; (2) the king is related to the state as God is related to the universe; (3) the king is modeled after God himself and has divine qualities; (4) the king is empowered by God and guided by the divine Logos.

By the close of the fifth century B.C. the city-state began to fail to satisfy the political needs of the Greeks. Their sense of failure led them to seek some basis of government other than democracy. Although democracy was the ideal model, even Plato became skeptical that it could ever serve as the basis for practical government. Even the model of the philosopher-king held out no greater promise. Consequently the Greeks were drawn increasingly to the model of kingship as exhibited in the great Cyrus.

As the attraction of rule by kings increased, a political philosophy of

---

[1] Goodenough, "The Political Philosophy of Hellenistic Kingship," *Yale Classical Studies* 1 (1928) 55–102.

kingship arose in the Hellenistic world. Isocrates applies to politics the theories of kingship that had been expressed by Socrates, Plato, and Zenophon. He sees in Philip the saving principle that enables him to bring harmony to Greece when the rivalries of the cities had run their course. He recognizes the popular belief that kings are equal to gods, at least in powers. Isocrates declares that the king should be a model to others in virtue and show his true kingliness in ruling over himself. With the advent of Alexander, Greece was opened to oriental and Egyptian political and religious conceptions that influenced the philosophy of kingship that developed among the Greeks.

Archytus of Tarentum makes an interesting distinction between the inanimate or written law and the animate (*empsychos*) law, which is the king. This concept underwent extensive development in other writers. Archytus states that the king must not only show understanding and power in his rule, but he must also show benevolence toward his subjects, keeping close to the law so as to do nothing except what is in their interests. Most important of all: the king himself is not only the embodiment of the law to his subjects, but therein is representation of the law of the gods, to which all civil law must conform. Plato argues that it is best not when simply laws govern, but when some royal man with political wisdom gives law adapted to each individual case, giving direct commands to others. In a Pythagorean fragment the king is himself said to be the law. Parallel to this, Isocrates argues that in monarchy the most powerful law is the disposition (*tropos*) of the king. Aristotle argues that no man is worthy to govern his fellow citizens except one who completely surpasses them in virtue. Such a man may be regarded as a god among men. Rather than being subject to law, he himself is a law. Since Aristotle, like Plato, is skeptical that such a man will ever be found, he dismisses royalty as an impossibility. Where could Aristotle have derived the concept of such an ideal ruler since he himself rejects the whole conception as visionary? Goodenough thinks that the source must be found among a people who actually claim to be ruled by such a person.

In a fragment from Diotogenes identified as Pythagorean, the author argues that the king himself is animate law (*nomos empsychos*): he is justice itself. The duties of the king are threefold: leadership in war, justice, and religious leadership—functions of the state recognized since Homer. Diotogenes develops a Platonic conception of the close connection between law (*nomos*) and mind (*nous*). The true statesman is such by virtue of his supreme *nous*, which saves the city. Plato would object that such a king would be divine rather than human, yet this is precisely the conception of kingship that Diotogenes accepts. The king in performing his role in the kingdom acts just as God does in his leadership and command of the universe. The king is related to the state just as God is related to the world. Goodenough emphasizes the Pythagorean character of this section. The metamorphosis of the king into deity is all summed up in the fact that he is animate law. Justice is the virtue of virtues. The king, having justice in himself, is able to infuse it into the entire state, making harmony out of its various parts. Majesty and graciousness are also attributes of kingship. In sum, royalty is an imitation of divinity.

A fragment on kingship attributed to Ecphantus claims that when God fashions the king he employs himself as an archetype. The king is a copy of the higher king, and he appears to his subjects as though he were light. The earthly king has a unique quality, which is like that of a god, for his soul is sent down to him from a higher realm than the souls of ordinary men. In the theology of the reform of Ikhnaton of Egypt the king is represented as an emanation of the sun god, Aton.

A prime function of the king is to put his subjects into harmony with the universe. Goodenough sees evidence of Persian influence on Ecphantus, who calls the king not only "father" and "shepherd," but also a "law" to his subjects. Not only in Persia but also in India the religious character of the king makes him the animate constitution of the state. In another fragment Ecphantus teaches that those who accept the logos of the king have goodness infused into their natures in the manner of growth of excellence from implanted seeds. This is the Stoic doctrine of the *logos spermatikos*, which plays an important part in the thought of Philo later on. Ecphantus goes beyond Stoicism in transferring the *logos spermatikos* from God to the king. The supreme function of the king is to infuse into man a new power enabling him to live spontaneously by divine law rather than by the compulsion and injustice of written codes.

A very similar concept of the function of kingship is expressed in the pseudo-Aristotelean "Letter to Alexander" and also in 3 Macc 6:24. Justin takes for granted the same philosophy of kingship. Important for dating the idea of the king as animate law is a fragment *On Kingship* of Musonius, a Stoic of the first century A.D., which suggests that by then the idea was already one of great antiquity. Finally Plutarch, like the others, speaks of the law that is animate in the king, namely, the Logos which dwells within him, protecting him and never leaving his soul without guidance. Philo of Alexandria used the same symbolism. Plutarch also represented God as radiating his force and power into the universe like the sun. Likewise the king in the state is an emanation of this divine radiance.

The greater the king the greater his need for the guidance of the Logos, which comes through following the road of philosophy. The Stoics taught that the true king is the product of philosophy and virtue. The official titles of rulers of the Hellenistic period—"protector," "illustrious," "benefactor"—suggest that this philosophy of royalty was also the official philosophy of the state. While Greek thinking was quite early influenced by the conception of the king himself as the state, the *nomos empsychos*, only in the Hellenistic age did it exercise great influence, as demonstrated in imperial Roman political thought and practice, and in later European political thought almost to modern times.

In 1929, the year after the publication of his article on Hellenistic kingship and the same year as the appearance of his volume on Jewish courts in Egypt, Goodenough published "Kingship in Early Israel."[2] His interest in kingship now extends to kingship in ancient Israel, and he finds underlying presuppositions similar to that of Hellenistic kingship: the king is supreme lawgiver to his people because he is the incarnate law; the king receives power as a gift from God, and the king is related to the state in the same way that God is related to the world; the king as a copy of the higher king appears to his subjects as light, and he demonstrates the qualities of graciousness and beauty of form. The concept of the ideal king was not originally Greek but probably came into the Greek world from Babylonia by way of Persia. Goodenough professes to be the first scholar to show that the idea of the king as incarnate law was clearly grasped in Babylonia. Gudea, the early shepherd king, professes a heart of such purity that it sends forth beams of light as the day. The solar origin of justice was common in ancient Babylonia.

In Neo-Babylonia the kingly idea remains the same. Marduk chooses Nebuchadnezzar to be the true shepherd of his people. The king's justice is not his own but is a gift of the gods. Just as in the Greek concept, the Babylonian king was the incarnation of the god's commands. In both realms kingship was conceived of in sun symbolism.

A Hebrew philosophy of kingship long antedates actual royalty in Israel. Philo recognizes that the Moses legend expresses ideas of royalty. Philo also notes that the legend of the baby Moses preserved in an ark of bulrushes in the Nile is closely akin to the birth legend of Sargon and that this represents the relation of the ruler to the Stream. For Philo, Moses' apprenticeship as a shepherd is another image of royalty. Exod 18:13–27, the narrative of Moses' being overburdened by the duty to hear cases, shows Moses to be the sole source of law to his people. Goodenough finds in this a similarity to the incarnate law conception of both Hellenistic and Babylonian kingship. Philo comments on Num 11:11–15, the cry of the people for food and Moses' complaint to Yahweh because of his overburden of leadership. This means that Moses as sole possesser of Yahweh's spirit has been Israel's sole ruler. When Moses shared some of his spirit with the seventy elders, it is not a direct gift of Yahweh's spirit but rather a transfer from Moses to the elders. Rulership and the gift of Yahweh's spirit were synonymous.

[2] Goodenough, "Kingship in Early Israel," *Journal of Biblical Literature* 48 (1929) 169–205.

Philo's interpretation of Moses as king is significant for understanding the ancient Hebrew view of kingship. Moses' kingship appears in several ways: his beauty of form, his training in science and magic, his experience as a shepherd. Because he was incarnate law he had mystic power over the elements. Philo sees in Moses the ideal ruler. Even though nowhere in the Pentateuch is Moses called king, Philo's interpretation of Moses' office comes close to the intention of the E source. The JE material in Joshua and Judges shows the same viewpoint. The very name of Joshua—"Preserver," or "Savior"—suggests one of the functions of the divinely endowed ruler. The narrative of the judges makes still clearer the meaning of rulership. Goodenough notes that the judge-ruler-savior makes no claim of personal social preeminence, for his personal contribution is his loyalty to Yahweh. Otherwise his office is identical with royalty, and in his proper function he is essentially the incarnate law in making and administering law.

Israel's demand for a king in 1 Samuel stems from the fact that Samuel succeeds in all functions of a judge save one, for he does not serve Israel as savior against their enemies. The people demand a king who will serve this need (1 Sam 8:5, 20; 9:17). In spite of the initial objection by some in Israel that Yahweh cannot be their king in the old sense if the person of the human king intervenes, nevertheless the full account of the establishment of Israelite kingship shows that the foundation of the royal office is an act of Yahweh. In spite of his objections Samuel tells the people that Yahweh will tolerate the new order and continue to bless Israel on one condition, that the king will always be obedient to the voice of Yahweh (1 Sam 12:14–15). Like the judges before him, the king must be the spirit-filled and spirit-led link between Yahweh and his people. Goodenough says, "This conception of the royal office, which is in all points in agreement with the oriental monarchy, is the criterion consistently applied to royalty thereafter" ("Kingship," p. 187).

The rejection of Saul must be understood in the light of this conception. Saul, in preempting the right to offer sacrifice in Samuel's place, is in effect forcing himself on Yahweh, thus repudiating his total dependence on Yahweh for his powers of kingship. His penalty is to suffer the withdrawal of Yahweh's spirit (1 Sam 16:14). It is significant that David even before Saul's death came into possession of the royal symbols, a piece of Saul's robe, his spear, and Saul's jug of water, possibly a symbol of the divine stream. Following Saul's death David acquires the crown and the royal bracelet, which in Assyrian and Babylonian theories of kingship appears to symbolize the incarnate law. David's military conquests are recognized as the work of Yahweh (2 Sam 5:12), and his role as a shepherd is recognized (2 Sam 7:8). With it comes the promise that Yahweh will establish David's house as a permanent dynasty. David's rule is characterized by its justice and righteousness, and to David is attributed universal wisdom. This further identifies him with the incarnate law. This character of David's kingship is illustrated in the preexilic psalm in 2 Sam 23:1–7, and the same is attributed to Solomon in 1 Kgs 3:4–13. The continuance of the royal symbolism after Solomon's time is described in the crowning of Joash (2 Kgs 11:5–12).

The royal psalms offer another important source for the Hebrew concept of kingship. Goodenough agrees with Gunkel and Kittel that these psalms are of preexilic origin rather than postexilic idealizations. Especially Psalms 45, 72, and 110 celebrate the elements of Old Testament kingship. Most notably, Psalm 72 demonstrates this in the prayer that Yahweh will make the king incarnate law.

During and after the exile the older idea of rulership in Israel underwent a radical change. The Jews had now become the people of the covenant. In earlier times the inspired ruler was himself Israel's covenant with God. Now in the absence of such an embodied law, the covenant came to be a revealed and priest-guarded code. This is clearly shown in the Deuteronomic theory of kingship. Rather than being himself the incarnate law, the king in order to rule with justice is himself to be guided by the written law of the Levitical priesthood (Deut 17:14–20). Yet the old concept of the king as embodied law was not abandoned. Goodenough finds this idea transposed into the later Jewish messianic expectations, the passionate hope that still in the future such an ideal ruler would come.

The persistence of these exalted concepts of royalty from ancient Babylonian times to Imperial Rome, even in the face of the great adversities that people actually experienced at the hand of their rulers, can be accounted for simply because such belief made life more hopeful and happy for the believer.

> The belief that the king is God's representative on earth with more than human powers, and that he is particularly God's agent of salvation by bringing divine justice into the world and making it apply to human needs, this has from ancient times until the most recent periods of human history been a belief cherished only less passionately than that in God himself and his love. ("Kingship," p. 205)

In his next work, *The Jurisprudence of the Jewish Courts in Egypt*,[3] Goodenough turns from Philo's theoretical interpretation of law to its practical application. He explains in his preface that this study had its origin in chance. As he was organizing his notes to write a study of

---

[3] Goodenough, *The Jurisprudence of the Jewish Courts in Egypt: Legal Administration by the Jews under the Early Roman Empire as Described by Philo Judaeus* (New Haven: Yale University Press, 1929).

Erwin Ramsdell Goodenough

shment, enforceable only through lynching of nonprominent Jews
isprudence, pp. 32–33). *Spec.* 2.54–55 illustrates the basis of the
h law applied to apostasy. In *Spec.* 1.56 Philo warns against divina-
, not however with reference to Lev 19:26, 31, which decrees the
:h penalty—which was impossible for Jews to execute in Egypt under
nan rule—but rather with reference to Deut 18:9–14, the account of
zealous driving out of the Canaanite diviners, which would be in
ord with the Roman policy exemplified in Agrippa's driving the
ologers from Rome in A.D. 33 (*Jurisprudence*, pp. 37–39). Philo inter-
ts the laws prescribing correct worship of God (the obverse of prohib-
g the wrong forms) in ways appealing to the Hellenistic point of
w, namely, by interpreting the Jewish cultus in terms of a Hellenistic
stery religion (*Jurisprudence*, pp. 39–41). Philo gives a Stoic interpre-
ion of oaths as becoming natural laws binding on those who make
m. Immoral oaths are not binding, but pious oaths must be kept at all
sts. In his discussion of oaths Philo thinks entirely in Greek terms, yet
has current Jews in mind, as for example when he transvaluates into
reek currency the penalty in shekels as stated in scripture. Philo treats
rjury as false witness, according to the Torah a death offense, hence
possible to punish in Alexandria, so that he has to settle for scourging
the penalty (*Jurisprudence*, pp. 45–46). Concerning the Diaspora law
 gainst blasphemy, Philo sharply distinguishes between those abusing the
cred Name and those speaking against heathen gods (*Jurisprudence*,
p. 47–49).

On usury Philo has to face the economic facts of his society, in
which usury was commonly practiced. His view, akin to that of Plato
nd Aristotle, is that usury is an economic fallacy, since charging exorbi-
ant interest ruins the debtor and leads to total loss by the lender of both
is loan and his interest (*Jurisprudence*, pp. 50–51).

Philo regards prisoners of war and persons born into household slav-
ry to be of an entirely different nature from that of freeborn people.
He distinguishes between true slaves and Jews forced by poverty into
bonded servitude. Although he accepts slavery in principle as a necessity,
he nevertheless urges compassion toward slaves (*Jurisprudence*, pp. 51–
52). He reinterprets Deut 23:16, the law forbidding the return of an
escaped slave to the former owner by the one who gives the slave asy-
lum. Philo teaches that the hearth to which the slave flees is compared to
a sacred altar—an idea completely Greek in origin. The slave is either to
be reconciled to his master or sold to another, and the proceeds are to be
given to the original master. Goodenough remarks that this is a striking
example of assimilation of Hellenistic thought and practice to Jewish life
and thought (*Jurisprudence*, pp. 51–55).

Philo's discussion of the fifth commandment is done almost entirely
from a Greco-Roman viewpoint. The idea that parents are gods to their

the *nomos* of Philo, he found several notes indicating
to have an expert knowledge of practical law. Fur
material led to the present work.

Goodenough argues that in his treatise *The Specia*
as a mystic or theologian trying to allegorize the Jewish
attempting to show that a true understanding of the N
it to be the supreme code for practical administratio
starts not from abstract theory but from the practical la
ment. Philo's basic argument is that the Mosaic code pr
the general principles but also in large degree the speci
Greco-Roman system as practiced in Alexandria. To a
Philo departs from the Torah in a variety of ways, until,
says, "the resulting system is made into one which Jews
in their Egyptian environment under Roman rule"
p. 216).

Philo was a practical political adminstrator. In his tr
cial Laws 3.1–3),[4] he bewails the necessity of spending
matters so that he is deprived of opportunities for philoso
plation. Goodenough suggests that it may be that the v
which Philo there expounds correspond to the laws of the
Philo discusses individual Jewish laws in relationship to t
and his reinterpretation of Jewish law to make it confo
Roman, and Alexandrian law was a necessity. Jews of Al
dently had generous political rights, including both civil
jurisdiction over their own citizens (*Jurisprudence*, pp.
Romans allowed considerable Jewish legal autonomy in m
but Roman law superseded the Torah in major matters (*Ju*
pp. 18–20). A similar situation prevailed in the relation
Greek law in Alexandria (*Jurisprudence*, p. 21). If in exa
Philo's statement in *Spec.* we find distinctively Jewish law (
regarding diet or cultus) carefully interpreted, but common
cantly changed, the latter may be regarded as that used in Je
of Philo's day. Philo in adapting Jewish law to pagan law will
he is only bringing out Moses' intent, not admitting even to h
he is rejecting what the Torah expressly stipulates.

To deny the validity of Philo's interpretation of the la
grounds that Jews were not permitted to exact the death pe
overlook the fact that Rome condoned the lynching of Jews
Otherwise Jewish courts could not exact the death penalty wi
approval of the Roman authorities.

In *Spec.* 1–2, Philo interprets the first two commandme
refutation of various kinds of false-god worship. Here he calls f

---

[4] Hereafter abbreviated as *Spec.*

own children comes from Stoic conceptions. Philo's statement of the rights of parents to discipline their children with increasing severity, even to putting a recalcitrant child to death, is based entirely on Roman custom. To exercise this degree of severity was contrary to the practice and teaching of the rabbis. However, his insistence on agreement between parents before they could resort to extremities in punishment reflects not Roman but Egyptian law (*Jurisprudence*, pp. 71–76).

In his treatment of laws on adultery Philo follows Jewish practice as far as possible, but as a jurist following his code rather than as an exegete expounding scripture. Fines are usually made discretionary. The Egyptian legal equality of women is recognized, and wherever the Torah calls for capital punishment Philo modifies its application under the influences of Roman, Greek, or Egyptian legal practices (*Jurisprudence*, pp. 88–100).

Commenting on the sixth commandment, Philo always understands "kill" as homicide and declares that it always deserves the death penalty because (1) it is a breach of the law of nature and (2) it is *hierosylia*, the most serious kind of sacrilege under Greek law, and for the reason that an attack upon the body of a man is a desecration both of the temple and of an image of God. He distinguishes four classes of murders, which are exactly the categories of murder in Roman law: (1) intentional, (2) unintentional, (3) murderous assault which failed in its objective, and (4) instigation of murder to be performed by someone else. Philo can connect the first three types with the Torah, but not the fourth. Although he justifies the principle that murder is always a capital offense, Philo treats unpremeditated killing with weapons as only half as serious as premeditated killing. Philo also shows dependence on Roman law in the case of murder by poisoning. The Torah does not specifically mention poisoning, but Philo, like Josephus, declares that the use of injurious as well as deadly drugs falls into the class of murder—contrary to Greek, Egyptian, and Roman law, all of which treat poisoning as a special crime parallel to murder. Contrary to Roman practice, Philo recommends that murder by drugs be punished immediately by lynching, and Goodenough concludes that this was the only action Jews could have taken in such cases. It fulfills the Roman penalty but would not require surrendering the offender to the Roman authorities for execution (*Jurisprudence*, pp. 100–108).

Ptolemaic law rendered other types of penalties for stealing than those for open robbery, whereas in Roman law robbery was treated as a special form of stealing. Philo interprets the Torah law against stealing as a principle envisioning an unbroken succession of crimes up to the disruption of the state itself, but in private cases he requires only the Mosaic and Ptolemaic penalty of double indemnity. This mingling of codes reflects the legal situation in Egypt under Roman rule in Philo's day. Roman law prevailed when the public peace was threatened, but the Romans permitted the application of local law in lesser cases involving non-Roman private citizens. Philo's defense of the penalty for theft is threefold: (1) the thief is guilty of inordinate greed, a vice despised by most of the philosophical schools; (2) theft is a breach of property rights, a distinctly Roman legal notion; and (3) the inherent secrecy of theft, a principle of Greek law (*Jurisprudence*, pp. 145–54).

Philo's defense of the commandment against false witness would appeal to his Greco-Roman neighbors. False witness is a willful perversion of justice, an idea agreeable to the Greeks. Since a judge renders his decision on the basis of testimony given, a false witness could cause him to render an erroneous judgment, thus causing him to break his oath of office. Consequently, the perjurer is guilty of a sacrilegious act which is actionable by the state. In Ptolemaic Egypt this would correspond to breaking an oath in the name of Ptolemy the king, the crime of *lèse majesté*. This always had a religious character because of the king's divinity. This Hellenistic conception was accepted by the Romans to apply to oaths taken in the name of the emperor (*Jurisprudence*, pp. 174–86).

Philo discusses the character and duties of the ideal judge entirely on the premises of the Hellenistic philosophy of kingship. As Goodenough writes elsewhere, "The true ruler is *nomos empsychos*, an incarnation of the Divine law, or of the Law of Nature, which is the Divine Logos in the Universe. . . . Into him flows the divine Nomos-Logos, and out of him flows in turn a great stream of this same power, which is an effulgence of ideal justice and God's Logos."[5] This conception of the judge probably was current in the Jewish courts of Alexandria. Philo also harmonizes Greek rules of procedure and evidence with Jewish law. The judge is not to listen to sophistry, neither is he to accept hearsay evidence. The first is merely good advice, but the second is supported by both Greek law and the Torah. By the same double authority he supports the prohibition of a judge's accepting gifts and proposes the death penalty for those who do. The Torah provides no such penalty, but it is supported by Greek practice (*Jurisprudence*, pp. 191–200).

Philo's insistence upon the impartiality of the judge and his representation of justice as a divine gift could just as easily derive from a Greek or an Egyptian source as from a Jewish biblical source. In commenting on the Jewish law that the judge is not to give special mercy to the poor, Philo states that this law refers only to criminals. He has in mind the concept of the justice-dispensing ruler, one of whose virtues is granting mercy especially to the lowly and weak, an idea that clearly derives from a Hellenistic background (*Jurisprudence*, pp. 200–206).

Philo completes his discourse *The Special Laws* by discussing the

---

[5] Goodenough, "Political Philosophy of Hellenistic Kingship," 53–54.

law against coveting. For him this commandment is the basis of the entire Jewish dietary law, the purpose of which is to promote moderation. He concludes that the whole intent of the Decalogue is to inculcate virtue. Goodenough observes that, in this discussion and in *On Rewards and Punishments*, the final treatise of the great *Exposition of the Law*, Philo's viewpoint changes from that of the lawyer to that of the ethical philosopher (*Jurisprudence*, pp. 206–12). The last treatise ends with a vision of the fulfillment of Israel's messianic hopes, and, as Goodenough remarks, "the Jewish people, by reason of their having become law-abiding, will be brought into the bliss that has so long been awaiting them" (*Jurisprudence*, p. 213).

Goodenough attempted several beginnings at investigating Philo's political thought, but the publication of a comprehensive Philo bibliography in cooperation with Howard L. Goodhart gave him the occasion to develop his study at length in *The Politics of Philo*.[6]

Chapter 1, "Politics Direct." One political incident is known from the life of Philo. At the accession of Caligula (Gaius Julius Caesar Germanicus) the Alexandrian mob, knowing that Gaius desired divine honors, insisted that Jews erect cult statues of him in their synagogues. When the Jews resisted such impiety the mob instigated a pogrom against them. Philo gives an account of this crisis in two treatises, *Against Flaccus* and *The Embassy to Gaius*.

The first storm center was the prefect Flaccus, who not only failed to protect the Jews but also encouraged the rioters against them. When Gaius ascended the throne the Jewish senate of Alexandria addressed a resolution of congratulation to the new emperor "in which they had gone to limits allowed by their law in recognizing his sovereignty" (*Politics*, p. 9). They asked Flaccus to forward this document to the emperor, which he promised to do, but he suppressed it instead, thus making it appear that the Jews of Alexandria were disloyal subjects. *Against Flaccus* addresses this situation. Since the refusal of the Jews to pay homage to the emperor was at stake, a direct appeal to the emperor had to be made. *The Embassy to Gaius* describes how Philo led a delegation of Jewish political leaders of Alexandria to Rome to present their case directly to the emperor.

Goodenough asks why these two treatises were written. The fragmentary nature of *Against Flaccus* makes difficult the determination of its purpose, but Goodenough is convinced that it was written for Gentiles unfamiliar with Alexandria. It directs its invective against Flaccus, yet it was written after the death of the emperor Gaius during the reign of his successor Claudius, who ultimately vindicated the Alexandrian Jews. By

---

[6] Howard L. Goodhart and Erwin R. Goodenough, *The Politics of Philo Judaeus, Practice and Theory with a Bibliography of Philo* (New Haven: Yale University Press, 1983).

that time it would have been safe for Philo to write such a treatise. Goodenough believes that it was written as political propaganda to show that as long as Flaccus was friendly to Jews he prospered, but when he encouraged persecution against them he met his downfall at the hands of God. "The thesis of the document is perfectly plain: it is a bold warning that any prefect will bring himself to the gutter if he deals unfavorably with God's people" (*Politics*, p. 10). It is reasonable to suppose that the document was written for the benefit of Flaccus's successor, and it reflects the boldness and cleverness of Philo as a most astute politician.

This same attitude of Philo is reflected in *The Embassy*. It reviews the history of the Jewish crisis in Alexandria. It tells how the universal joy at the accession of the young Gaius was short-lived. After eight months he was so gravely ill that his subjects feared for his life. But after his recovery they were dismayed by the manifestation of his true character. He followed a life of debauchery and perpetrated various political murders to strengthen his position in the empire. Moreover, he began to pretend to divine honors. Most of his subjects responded to this mad pretension with flattery and acquiescence, but the Jews in their strict monotheism felt helpless before him. Gaius did away with all previous legal guarantees protecting the Jews in their religion and customs. Gaius declared himself to be the law of the empire.

It was in this situation that the Alexandrian mob instituted the pogrom against the Jews and set up images of Gaius in their synagogues. The Jews then assembled the delegation under Philo to go to Rome to plead their cause directly with the emperor. After their perilous winter voyage, and after an agonizing delay of many months, the delegation was received by Gaius in a half-hearted audience. Without even hearing their petition because of his many distractions, Gaius finally dismissed them merely as fools for refusing to believe him to be a god. Philo promises, but we do not have, a palinode describing the final outcome of the crisis. Since this document was written after the accession of Claudius, Goodenough concludes that its message must have been intended for him. It is an elaborate formulation of the function of the proper ruler and the effect he should have upon his subjects and realm. Very prudently Philo always puts such statements in the mouths of others, never speaking in his own voice. In both documents he makes clear that the success or failure of the official function depends directly upon the ruler's attitude toward the Jews. A severe threat to any group of Jews would spark a worldwide uprising among all Jews.

Chapter 2, "Politics in Code." In the preceding treatises we observe the boldness and courage of Philo and his fellow Jews in openly confronting their political crisis. In his treatise *On Dreams*[7] he urges great

---

[7] Philo *De Somniis* 2.81–82.

caution upon any Jews who might have dealings with Roman governors. The statement appears in an extended allegory upon the life of Joseph, and Goodenough is convinced that the entire allegory is a concealed political statement denouncing the Roman character and oppression. This document is part of Philo's *Allegory of the Sacred Laws*, the greatest of his philosophical writings, yet comprehensible only by one thoroughly conversant with the Old Testament. It would be of interest only to Jews who understood the method and aim of allegory. No Roman who might inadvertently look into it would have any interest in it or find anything suspicious in it. Consequently, it would provide an admirable vehicle for Philo to communicate to educated Jews his disgust with and hostility toward the Romans.

In *On Dreams* Philo discusses the nature of dreams as recorded in Genesis. To begin with, Joseph is contrasted with Isaac. Joseph symbolizes the man engaged in political affairs, whereas Isaac lives only for metaphysical realities. In Joseph's first dream of the sheaves, he and his brothers represent various traits of human character. Joseph represents "empty opinion." This is the man appointed as *epitropos*, the governor of all Egypt. *Epitropos* is the very title that Philo gives to Flaccus. Thus Philo uses Joseph to typify the Roman ruler who is in direct authority over Philo and his circle.

Joseph's mounting the chariot second only to that of the king symbolizes arrogance. His zeal in storing up grain represents one who cares for the body but not the soul. Philo illustrates at length how empty opinion persists in extravagance and display rather than in modesty and appreciation of simple things. The elegant ones that he is describing are those who call themselves the rulers over many peoples. Philo anticipates the coming of the great husbandman who will prune the vine of society by hacking off the arrogant ones at the very roots. Goodenough notes the striking resemblance of this figure to that in the Fourth Gospel and that in Q's account of the Baptist's messianic preaching (Matt 3:7–10 = Luke 3:7–9).

The point of the dream is that while Joseph's sheaf stood upright the brothers' sheaves bowed down to it. Thus the man of "empty opinion" puts himself above all things, above cities, laws, and ancestral customs (Jewish law) and becomes a tyrant. The brothers protest, "Shall you become king and rule over us?" (Gen 37:8). "King" to anyone of Philo's place and time would mean one who claims divine rank. No Jew could recognize such a claim. The attitude of flattery and compliance toward any offical could not be carried by any Jew to the point of acknowledging any Lord but the God of Israel.

Joseph's second dream of the sun, moon, and eleven stars symbolizes for Philo the man of strife and "empty opinion" who thinks the forces of nature were designed to serve him. The symbols that Philo uses for "empty opinion" and "arrogance" represent Roman domination and the spirit of Rome and its rulers as these are contrasted with "truth," Judaism, and "right opinion," the true law. Philo urges Jews not to give up Jewish faith and hope for the temptations of prosperity that might come to them if they but renounced their true law in favor of the "empty opinion" of the Roman system.

The treatise *On the Change of Names* refers to Joseph as one who concerns himself with superfluous additions, since his name means "addition." Throughout his writings Philo uses "arrogance" to represent the Romans. Arrogance may seek to dissuade the wise man from observing the commandments of God and the law in exchange for contractual arrangements. But these merely "produce associations of men without any real common ground between them."[8] Philo is not uniformly hostile toward Roman judges. The episode in Exod 18:13–27 in which Jethro gives advice to Moses provides Philo with a basis for explanation. Jethro represents the Roman officials who recognize Jewish law in Alexandria, reserving the more important matters to themselves, but letting the Jews decide the rest among themselves. Some of these Roman officials became so impressed with Jewish law that they became "God-fearers," exemplified in Acts 10:1–2 by Cornelius the Roman centurion.

A passage in the treatise *On the Decalogue*, which Goodenough believes to have been written for Gentiles, expresses Philo's denouncement of Roman arrogance. It says that Moses could not put pure law in any existing city since each was filled with both social and religious evils. Because of their idolatries through the worship of many gods, the people of these cities are like children born to a harlot. Thus does Philo characterize the arrogant Romans, who have subjugated many peoples in their conquest for empire. Goodenough concludes that none of these passages is specific enough to arouse suspicion so that Philo might safely risk one in a treatise for Gentiles.

Chapter 3, "Politics by Innuendo." In Philo's commentaries on the Pentateuch known as the *Exposition of the Law*, other evidence of his politics appear. These commentaries are addressed to Gentiles seriously interested in learning about Judaism. In this series the work *On Joseph* again uses the patriarch's life as an occasion to speak of rulership. Here, however, Joseph is not a screen for Philo's antipathy toward Roman rule. Rather, Joseph is presented as a model of what a good ruler should be. The description of Joseph's training to exercise his exalted office reflects the ideals of a Hellenistic kingship. The king as legislator is to rule in conformity with divine or natural law. Indeed, he is in himself the embodied law (*nomos empsychos*). Joseph's father early recognized the boy's gifts for rulership. Consequently, his early life as a shepherd

---

[8] Philo *Mut.* 103–4.

became an important part of his training. Like all great men he is met with envy expressed through his brothers. This was aroused by his reports of his dreams, although he told of them in good faith.

Characteristically Philo interprets the literal narrative allegorically. Joseph's name means "the addition of the Lord." Earthly government is inferior to God's great government of the universe; therefore, the earthly ruler dealing with earthly politics is concerned with "additions" to what is real; Joseph's multicolored coat symbolizes adaptability. Once in Egypt his true nature was recognized, and he was given increasingly more governing power, in the exercise of which he was always under divine guidance, like the true Hellenistic king. Joseph's first responsibility to be the superintendent of a household was fitting, for household management is the epitome of government.

A further characteristic of Joseph is his chastity and continence. His resistance to the infatuation of Potiphar's wife demonstrates this. Philo thus shows another virtue of the Hellenistic king, that of continence and self-mastery. Joseph's initial status in Egypt as a slave to Potiphar furnishes Philo with further counsel as a ruler. Willy-nilly the *politicus* must recognize that he is the "slave" of the mob, but he must at the same time be aware of his citizenship in the great cosmopolis and deal with the mob as his wards and children. Like a good physician, who must hurt in order to heal, the governor must sometimes oppose the mob in doing what is best for the state. Goodenough takes this to be Philo's advice to every Roman official in Alexandria. This is the subtlest form of flattery. The Alexandrian mob tended perennially to turn against the Jews. Philo here advises the prefect that if he should take bold action against the mob the Jews would stand by him. This in turn should dispose him to protect the Jews.

While Joseph was a prisoner, he so transformed the jailer by his virtue that Joseph himself was appointed acting jailer and in that role transformed the other prisoners and the environment. This reflects another aspect of ideal Hellenistic kingship, that the ruler be a reforming influence in the lives of his subjects. While Pharaoh retained sovereignty for himself, he delegated actual rulership to Joseph. Goodenough thinks that Joseph thus represents the type of the Roman prefect. By inserting these matters into the Old Testament account Philo actually describes the ideal prefect. Philo invents an episode not included in the Bible. Joseph tours throughout all the provinces of Egypt, and in so doing he both confers benefits on their inhabitants and also elicits their great love for him. This suggests the first years of Flaccus's administration, which Philo describes as entirely exemplary.

When Joseph's brothers return to Egypt in time of famine, Joseph in his position of great power could have taken vengeance upon them for his earlier mistreatment at their hands. However, he restrains himself from this. Restraint is another kingly virtue. When later he feasted his brothers Philo says that he feasted both Egyptians and the Hebrews according to their ancestral customs. The Bible actually says that the Egyptians despised the Hebrews and would not eat with them. Philo is not about to perpetuate the tradition of this prejudice. In the final reconciliation between Joseph and his brothers, Philo makes Joseph speak in terms of the ideal ruler endued with natural kindliness. In the episode of Joseph's receiving the brothers' money in payment for their grain, Philo takes occasion to emphasize that Joseph transmitted the funds directly to the royal treasury and did not use it as an opportunity for personal enrichment, another hint to Roman officials. Philo summarizes Joseph's character as exhibiting beauty, wisdom, and power of speech, precisely the qualities of the ideal monarch. Philo's ultimate purpose in this writing was to show that this kingly ideal had been fully exemplified in an ancient hero of the often maligned and persecuted Jews.

Chapter 4, "Statesman and Philosopher." Goodenough is convinced that Philo spent a considerable part of his life in some kind of successful political administration. He considers this likely in the light of the fact that a number of members of Philo's family were deeply involved in politics. In *The Special Laws* 3.1–6, Philo expresses dismay at the necessity of his abandoning the life of philosophic contemplation for the concerns of politics. This may well express his feelings on the occasion of his leading the embassy to Gaius, but Goodenough believes that Philo engaged in a literary career as an interpreter of the Bible only after he had gone into political affairs, and as a relief from it. After a youthful period as a recluse Philo returned to his people when he felt they needed him, and politics became his main career. Writing about the mystic message of the scriptures became the consolation of his leisure hours. Throughout his life he exhibited a strange ambivalence between praise for the state and denunciation of it, between an Aristotelian view that Nature (God) gives human beings reason, which brings harmony into human life resulting in good laws and the establishment of peace in society, and a Stoic and Skeptic position that human beings are exclusively citizens of the universe such that they scorn the life of their environment.

In advocating that philosophers participate in politics, Philo says that the full development of virtue leads to political virtue and that no one should abandon public life for asceticism. He expresses strong disapproval of those who do so and says that they go against the plain teaching of scripture. But Philo can quite astonishingly go on the other tack and declare that the love of God and the love of the world cannot coexist in the same person. Goodenough finds this ambivalence in Philo to reflect the spirit of the age. However, Philo is to be distinguished from other writers of his age in his honest endeavor to find value in both types of life and to show how they may be reconciled with each other. Those who give their full attention either to practical or divine affairs exclusively are only half perfect in virtue. Only those who are distinguished in both are complete.

For Philo the rise and fall of political empires is not by chance, but a manifestation of the great cyclic movement of the Logos. Individual states are temporary phenomena in the great flux of the Logos. In a practical sense this would mean that the cosmic imperium could be entrusted to Rome only for a period and that the cosmic imperium itself was the prerogative of the Logos. Since the state is the direct product of the Logos, it ought to conform to the Logos. God, though not himself the law, is the pattern and the source of law.

Philo is dualistic in his view of human nature and the two laws to which he believes human beings to be subject. On the one hand, by virtue of their divine mind human beings are citizens of the Cosmopolis and subject to the divine laws of Nature. But as beings of material nature they produce civil law and are subject to its authority. Civic law in actuality does not reflect, as it should, the law of Nature. Philo had only too much experience with the perverting of civil law by tyrants. Democratic legislation was no better, since weak individuals in the multitude were kept from tyranny only by their weakness rather than by their virtue. Goodenough concludes that the conflict in Philo between the statesman and the philosopher is a reflection of a greater warfare, that between the material and the immaterial. Philo shares with Augustine the concept that human beings have dual citizenship, in the worldly city and the heavenly city. Humanity's problem is the reconciliation of these two citizenships.

Chapter 5, "Kingship." Goodenough has already discussed Philo's concept of kingship in other works, and it is unnecessary to retrace that analysis. In brief he finds Philo's idea of kingship closely parallel to that of the Pythagorean image of the king exercising three roles—military leader, supreme judge, and high priest—all roles that Philo assigns to Moses. In pagan thought the king's role as high priest was related to the claims of the divinity or semidivinity of the king's nature, although Goodenough argues that no intelligent pagan would so misunderstand this notion as to identify the king with supreme deity. Philo makes a careful distinction between the divinity of the king's rulership, which is an image of God, and his material nature.

A final detail of Philo's kingly theory that later became important in Christian speculation is not native to Greek political theory but appears to have been introduced from Jewish thought. It is found in Philo's remarks about tyrants. God permits tyrants as punishment for a wicked nation. But when the tyrant has done his work he perishes along with the society that he has afflicted. Goodenough proceeds to show how Philo employed his political theory in addressing his Roman rulers in *Against*

Flaccus and *The Embassy to Gaius*. He subtly threatens the prefect with disaster if the latter fails to respect Jewish "rights." In his better period Flaccus has demonstrated the true qualities of kingly rule. But the theory is most fully represented in the rule of Augustus. On the other side, Gaius's failure to fulfill the kingly ideal caused his degeneration. Even though Philo, like other Hellenistic Jews, had evidently adopted much of the current Hellenistic theories of kingship, why was it the case that he refused to allow the Greek and the Roman in politics to use the word "divine" as freely as he himself used it for the Patriarchs? "Why did Jews like Philo, who described the king in exactly the same terms as the Pythagoreans, refuse, when claimed for an actual Roman emperor, to recognize the divinity they otherwise theoretically admitted?" (*Jurisprudence*, p. 110).

Goodenough finds this to be completely illogical and appeals to the modern psychological theory that when logic breaks down we must look for a motive or emotion that has invaded the problem from the outside. He concludes that at bottom it was Philo's Judaism that was at stake rather than, as is usually supposed, his monotheism. If he had once admitted that the Roman rulers had a greater share of the divine nature than other people—precisely what he claimed of Moses in his kingly role—then the whole reason for the existence of Judaism as a distinct race would have vanished. Goodenough argues similarly that it was not simply antipathy to image making that drove the Jews to refuse to erect in their synagogues the image of the emperor. Again, it was rather a passionate affirmation of Jewish patriotism in the face of the hated Roman rule. This can be shown from recent archaeological discoveries of Jewish synagogue art not more than a century later than Philo's time. Goodenough points out that it is from this Hellenistic Jewish heritage that the later development of the Christian theory of kingship originated. Every point of the ancient theories of the king was accepted except the claim of the king's personal divinity.

One further aspect of Philo's idea of kingship remains to be examined. Over against the claims of the Roman rulers Philo gives glimpses of a higher messianic king. Goodenough, contrary to a number of earlier scholars, takes these references seriously. From scattered statements the nature of the great hope can be discerned. The great age will begin when the scattered and enslaved Jews will undergo a universal transformation of character of such an astonishing sort that their present rulers will set them free, being ashamed to govern a people of such obvious superiority to themselves. This will come about when enough Jews in political power and responsibility have become transformed through the mystery. Then the prayers of the patriarchs will be answered, and Jews will enjoy the peace and prosperity of a happy age such as their ancestors have never known. The point of this is that these divine mercies would become available because of the presence of mystic leaders in practical politics. This may well have been Philo's sense of call, difficult as it must have been living as a mystic in Roman Alexandria. "But only as he, Philo, faced this calling with the courage of his embassy to Gaius, could the rest of the Jews hope for the deliverance of the great Age to come" (*Jurisprudence*, p. 118).

4

PHILO AND THE GOSPEL OF MYSTICISM

Philo has customarily been treated as a philosopher, but Goodenough proposes that Philo used philosophy primarily as a means to interpret the meaning of the Jewish religion. Although *Introduction to Philo Judaeus*[1] was nearly the last work that Goodenough devoted to Philo, it is appropriate to look at it first because of its comprehensive overview of Goodenough's interpretation of Philo's life and work. It is a summing-up of the insights and conclusions stated in his earlier works on Philo.

In the preface Goodenough argues that, if the hellenization of early Christianity is to be understood, more than simply the parallels between Christian and pagan thought forms must be studied. A bridge must be found between the two realms adequate to explain the rapid hellenization of Christianity. Goodenough believes that such a bridge is to be found in Hellenistic Judaism as exemplified in Philo. Once again appears the goal of all of Goodenough's research, to compose the history of Christianity's earliest beginnings in the light of its cultural environment.

Goodenough treats method in the first chapter. Philo must have lived from about 25 B.C. to A.D. 45 or 50. If he is typical of Jews in the Roman world, a still disputed point, he gives an invaluable picture of the Judaism on which Christianity was built. Direct knowledge of Philo's public life is restricted to one episode that Philo reports in *Embassy to Gaius*. This tells of Philo's leading a delegation of Jewish leaders of Alexandria to Rome to appeal to the Emperor Gaius (Caligula) for relief from the pogrom unleashed against the Jews of Alexandria for their refusal to give divine honors to the emperor.

In several passages Philo gives autobiographical clues. He speaks of the near ecstasy he had experienced in philosophical and mystical contemplation. Although he would long to continue in that realm, he found himself pulled back into the world of political cares. Yet on occasion he found opportunity to return to the world of scripture and the investigation of its meanings. His difficulty lay not in the narrowness but in the

[1] New Haven: Yale University Press, 1940; 2d ed., Basil Blackwell, 1962. All page references are to the 1962 edition.

diversity of his interests. He seemed to be acquainted with every detail of the vibrant public life of Alexandria. If only later in life did Philo emerge to share actively in political affairs, it was because his heart was primarily in philosophical and religious study.

Philo's extensive writings consist primarily of scriptural commentaries resembling midrash, but their explanations and objectives are very different from those of the rabbis. Philo was enamored of the ideas of Greek civilization, but not indiscriminately so. He was drawn to the more mystical ideas of Platonism and Pythagoreanism but rejected Stoic materialism and Epicurean humanism. He scorned the idolatry of the pagan cults, yet he was deeply moved by the ideas behind the mystery religions. The language of the mysteries influenced the expression of his own religious ideas. This brings us to the heart of the problem of interpreting Philo. Was he primarily Greek or primarily Jewish?

Goodenough begins by reviewing the most important studies on Philo of the 1930s and 1940s. The first is by Isaak Heinemann.[2] Heinemann asks what is the exact nature of the mixture of the pagan and Jewish elements in Philo? He investigates the legal interpretations rather than the more metaphysical writings. He concludes that the superiority of Judaism for Philo was its possession of the Torah, which through allegorization could provide the true sources and objectives of all Greek science and philosophy. Goodenough questions whether Heinemann adequately presents Jewish halakah.

Goodenough next presents his own viewpoint as expressed in *By Light, Light* (1935). He concentrates on Philo's more allegorical writings, believing that in these Philo wrote more "from the heart" than in his other writings (*Introduction*, 13). Goodenough believes that he is carrying on the best of Philonic scholarship of the preceding thirty years. He says:

> We disagree sharply among ourselves about details, but agree that the basic departure of Philo from normative Judaism lies in the fact that he took to his heart the pagan idea of salvation; that is, that the spirit be released from the flesh in order to return to its spiritual source in God. This, rather than his adoption of the formal philosophy of classical Greek schools . . . seems to us the critical step of Philo. (*Introduction*, 14)

The third study on Philo, that by Walther Völker, sharply attacks Goodenough's viewpoint.[3] Writing from an extremely conservative Protestant position, Völker denies any true mysticism apart from *en Christo* and the sacrament. He denies a priori that Philo as a Jew could have

[2] I. Heinemann, *Philons griechische und jüdische Bildung* (Breslau: Marcus, 1932).

[3] W. Völker, *Fortschritt und Vollendung bei Philon von Alexandrien: Eine Studie zur Geschichte der Frommigkeit* (Leipzig: Hinrichs, 1938).

been influenced by the mystery ideas of his time. He denies that Philo has a "system" that can be elaborated. He states that Philo's attitude was simply that of a pious Jew, "a simple Jew who liked to talk in philosophical language to impress his education upon Greek readers" (cited by Goodenough, *Introduction*, 15). Goodenough finds Völker's book to be the most extreme example of oversimplification of Philo, further flawed by its a priori assumption that nothing in pagan religiosity could appeal to a Jew.

In 1947 Harry Wolfson published a two-volume study of Philo in which he undertakes to show that Philo was one of the most influential philosophers in the West.[4] His study was intended to be a part of a major work showing the development of all of the philosophy of the Middle Ages in Christian, Islamic, and Jewish circles. For Wolfson medieval philosophy had a distinctive source of knowledge foreign to both Greek and modern thinkers—namely, "revelation"—but which Wolfson calls the "preamble of faith." Whereas Greek and modern thinkers try by observation, hypothesis, and intuition to discover the truth about human nature, about the environment, and even about the deity itself, medieval thinkers had to square all such data of "reason" with the data of inspired scripture. Philosophy itself had to be tested by what Wolfson terms a "set of inflexible principles of divinely revealed origin" (cited by Goodenough, *Introduction*, 17). Wolfson declares that these very principles were worked out by Philo himself and that this explains why Philo became the "most dominant force in the history of philosophy down to the seventeenth century" (cited by Goodenough, *Introduction*, 17).

Goodenough confesses that "even as ardent a Philonist as myself must blink at so great a claim for our hero" (*Introduction*, 17). He readily concedes that the Philonic school of hellenized Judaism had a most important formative influence on the making of Christianity. Also he recognizes that medieval philosophy is distinctive in its requirement that reason must be held within the limits of revealed religion. But Wolfson's claim that the single philosophy of Philo dominated the whole of medieval philosophical thinking seems excessive. Goodenough criticizes Wolfson's persistent effort to reconcile all of Philo's seemingly inconsistent statements and his refusal to make room for Philo's mysticism. Moreover, Wolfson does not allow for Philo's way of thinking; hence, like George Foot Moore, Wolfson sees Philo as unique both to Hellenism and to Judaism. He sees only "native " Jewish attitudes in Philo, and the Greek elements are seen only as "veneer" on this Judaism. Wolfson thinks that the more mystical

---

[4] H. Wolfson, *Philo* (2 vols.; Cambridge, MA: Harvard University Pres, 1947). Wolfson is mentioned only in the 1962 edition of Goodenough's *Introduction*. Goodenough's critique of Wolfson stated in *Introduction* appeared in expanded form as "Wolfson's Philo," *Journal of Biblical Literature* 67 (1948) 87–109.

elements in Roman philosophy from Plutarch onward have little relevance for understanding Philo. Rather, he believes that Philo worked exclusively from the classical tradition of Greek philosophy.

> This classical, rationalistic philosophy, Wolfson feels, was what Philo had to adjust to Jewish revelation, and it was the philosophy rather than the revelation that gave way. As a result, Philo seems to Wolfson to have produced a body of thought which, like all subsequent philosophy until Spinoza, really offered a system of scriptural passages rather than a rational approach to life itself. (*Introduction*, 18)

Although Goodenough disagrees with both Wolfson's method and his conclusions, he states that no one henceforth can study any aspect of Philo's philosophical thinking without reference to Wolfson's work. Goodenough thinks that the systematically organized mind that Wolfson attributes to Philo is rather that of Wolfson himself. "Later Christians had little interest in the saving power of the Jewish Patriarchs and their wives, or in Moses as the unique mystagogue; but they were the centre of Philo's thinking" (*Introduction*, 19). Goodenough admits that he may have overemphasized Philo's mystical side, but Wolfson overemphasizes Philo's philosophical consistency and underestimates the influence of Greek religious concepts upon Philo's religious attitude.

Goodenough states his own methodology for understanding Philo. First, it is necessary to read all the works of Philo in their entirety, in both the Greek and the Armenian versions. So he said in the 1940 edition of *Introduction*. "To do any special study of Philo without such a beginning is extremely dangerous" (p. 19). Such a comprehensive reading of Philo permits us to read him "with the grain," allowing Philo to speak in his own way without intruding our own questions or presuppositions. In the 1962 revision Goodenough tempers his earlier recommendation. "To do this in the Greek and Armenian, considering the mass and difficulty of his Greek and our general ignorance of Armenian will for most of us be impossible" (*Introduction*, 19). He directs the reader to appropriate editions of Philo. It is significant that his original advice represents the carefulness of the scholarship to which he himself aspired and which he sought to inspire in his students.

After we have heard Philo patiently and at length, we may begin to pose our own questions. In spite of its possible disadvantages we must assemble passages on particular points, since Philo himself gives us no systematic or exhaustive discussion of any point. The most difficult stage of Philo study is evaluating passages that are frequently flatly contradictory. We must first examine each passage in context, determining as far as possible the purpose of each writing—whether propaganda, scriptural commentary, or some other purpose—and determining if possible the audience being addressed, whether Jewish or Gentile.

After they have been studied in context, passages must be examined for the ancestry of their language. "Only by a thorough acquaintance with the language and ideals of both Jews and Greeks in Philo's day will we be able to know what language he is using, and to what extent he changed its meaning for his purpose" (*Introduction*, 21). We must read him as far as possible as his contemporaries understood him. Every interpretation can be only a paraphrase, however: "Unless human nature is constant, however different may be our conditioning in different ages, we can never understand any figure out of the past" (*Introduction*, 23). We must put aside our own presuppositions as far as possible and let Philo speak to us. Goodenough finds Philo to be a mystic and says that in seeking a definition of experiences called mystic "all infuse the human with the divine, and make participation the real meaning of imitation" (*Introduction*, 26).

To his presuppositions already stated, Goodenough adds two more. First, Christianity cannot be explained apart from the preparation within the form of Judaism that Philo reveals. Second, Philo's position in Judaism was not unique. Rather, he appears as a man with a long tradition behind him. Goodenough concludes his chapter on method with statements that are highly personal. He says, "I cannot understand the emotional intolerance which so often invades and nullifies scholarship. Books written by charlatans or by fond amateurs we may ignore, or even sharply rebuke. But there is no reason to ignore the product of a serious scholar, however much we may disagree with him" (*Introduction*, 27–28). Goodenough was sensitive to an alienation that he felt between himself and certain other theological scholars among his colleagues. He attributed much of it to the resistance of orthodoxy in religion to his own unorthodoxies, but in his sensitivity there were strong personal elements involved as well as ideological differences. He protested the tendency that he perceived in certain circles to deny the possibility of objective history. He does not deny the subjective element at work in a historian, but he is unwilling to believe that scholarly research in history is futile.

> Always we hope that by recognizing our own limitations we may gradually come to approximate the truth. . . . To me, no religion is more than intellectually comprehensible which does not include the mystic longing for inner completion by participation. This is bound to affect my understanding of Philo. Unquestionably I shall respond as others do not to passages where he expressed a mystic longing. Such disagreements we must expect; and I can see no reason why cheeks should flush when we discuss interpretations of Philo with which we do not wholly agree. In this field as in all fields the goal of scholarship should not be knowledge but wisdom, a wisdom which finds itself from learning from one another. (*Introduction*, 29)

It is not unfair to Goodenough to say that for him scholarship was a religious act. He was truly a humanist for whom the goal of scholarship was to cultivate in men and women that which is most distinctively human: the inclination toward truth, toward beauty, and toward community.

Goodenough devotes the second chapter of *Introduction* to Philo's writings. He says that it is important to distinguish between the different sorts of writings, and he takes them up in the order recommended for the beginner. He classifies Philo's writings into three groups. The first group is an apology for the Jews but is addressed to friendly rather than hostile pagans who desire to know who the great Moses was and wish to know more about the Jewish tradition. In this group falls the *Exposition of the Law*. Goodenough expresses pride that his suggestion that the *Exposition* was designed for Gentiles had won out over widely held contrary opinion among scholars.[5] He writes, "Unlike many of my publications, this one has been received with almost unanimous approval" (*Introduction*, 35).

The second group of Philo's writings are those addressed to Jews themselves, to whom Philo refers as "initiates," "those Jews who had learned to look beyond the letter of the Torah, and, through the lens of allegory, to discern as the true objective of Jewish revelation a great new immaterial world of mystic accomplishment" (*Introduction*, 46). These writings constitute Philo's great *Allegory*, consisting of eighteen titles, twenty-one books, that survive from an orginally much longer work. These writings are difficult for modern readers to follow, but Goodenough deems them to be Philo's greatest work and urges readers to persist in them and not merely skim and skip. These writings were designed for those initiated into the main outlines of Philo's thought, who would read them as books of devotion.

Of Philo's third great series, *Questions and Answers*, only a remant survives. This is a commentary giving both the literal meaning and the intellectual or mystical meaning of each verse of text. Beyond these writings only a scant few of Philo's works remain. Goodenough remarks that anyone who has come to this point has accomplished what few have done, reading Philo through. The versatility and magnitude of the man will have been revealed, which should guard against any easy formula for identifying "the essence of Philo's position." The key to understanding Philo is the man himself rather than any philosophical or religious position that he reflects.

The third chapter of *Introduction* considers Philo as a political thinker. It is a concise restatement of the points that Goodenough presents in *The Politics of Philo Judaeus*. The fourth chapter deals with Philo the Jew. Philo's relationship to Judaism is hard to define since he

---

[5] See Goodenough, "Philo's Exposition of the Law and his de Vita Mosis," *Harvard Theological Review* 26 (1933) 109–26.

claimed in the name of Judaism everything he had taken from the Gentiles. His Hellenism probably came to him in a form already assimilated into Judaism. In the observance of Jewish traditions Philo was a completely loyal Jew. Although through allegory he might present the inner meaning of the law, he insisted on the literal practice of the law by Jews. What distinguished the Jew of Philo's world was not an absolute monotheism, but rather seeing other supernatural entities as only servants of God and refusing them any rites or cultus. It was insistence on the exclusive worship of the God of Israel that made Judaism distinctive.

Philo was bitter in his condemnation of the forms of worship used by the Gentiles for their deities, yet Greek philosophical theology had great appeal for him. Nevertheless, as Goodenough remarks, "Far as Philo went in accepting the abstract Pure Being of the Greek philosophical deity, he never lost the personal and merciful God of the Jews" (*Introduction*, 85). Goodenough believes that Philo's entire literary labor was prompted by his Jewish loyalty. It is less easy to understand his relationship to any particular Jewish group such as Sadducees or Pharisees.

Goodenough insists on the correctness of presenting the mystic side of Philo in terms of Greek or Hellenistic conceptions. In representing the patriarchs as mystic saviors of the Jewish people through their having gone from matter to the immaterial—thus opening the way for which Hellenistic religious and mystic philosophy were vainly looking—Philo offers a kind of salvation quite foreign to any other form of Judaism previously known.

Chapter five presents Philo's metaphysics. As an Alexandrian Jew, Philo was well acquainted with the questions raised by Greek philosophers to which Judaism had no replies. Goodenough declares that Philo was not an original philosopher at all. "His task was to show that the best of Greek philosophic teaching was derived from, and got its highest expression in, the Torah, and his whole objective would have been lost had he been inventing anything especially new" (*Introduction*, 95). Concerning the nature of reality, the basic distinction for Philo is the complete disparity between matter and the immaterial realm, which alone has reality. As a consequence of his metaphysics Philo found it necessary to construct an elaborate scheme whereby God, who was ontologically distinct from the world, could nevertheless be connected with the world.

The Logos and the Powers whereby God deals with the world constitute the most important formulation of this idea of mediation. Logos, a term difficult to define, is Philo's favorite term to designate the Light Stream which emanates from God. Of this Goodenough says: "The universe, while thus intimately under the providence of God . . . had meaning at all only with reference to something essentially beyond and foreign to what was inherent or possible for matter. . . . Such a view of the universe seems to me to be not at all a thing to dismiss lightly. It is a serious and sensible philosophy of nature" (*Introduction*, 109). Goodenough mentions that scientists of his time seemed to be approaching such a conclusion. Yet, whatever scientists might conclude, he believes that some such philosophy is needed so that science may somehow be squared with human experience and hope, hope "that the universe is not indifferent to human values" (*Introduction*, 109). Surely the religious yearnings of Goodenough's youth still speak out here, however changed their vocabulary.

In the sixth chapter Goodenough takes up Philo's thought about humanity and ethics. In the universe that Philo describes human beings have a unique place. Human personality is a mixture of mind, the higher part, and a number of subordinate bodily parts. Like Aristotle, Philo distinguishes between the higher and lower mind. For Philo the human personality is not in the higher mind but in the mixture of bodily parts, soul, and mind. He asks, In this mixture where is the self? In this mixture the soul, or higher mind, has become united with the body. Clearly the personality which survives death cannot be the earthly personality. At death our immaterial part will be joined with the immaterial realm and thus experience a new birth. Through mystic experience Philo hoped to undergo this rebirth while still in the body. Goodenough remarks that some philosophy of soul or mind similar to Philo's must underlie the "new creature" of early Christian experience.

For Philo, as with Plato, the personality might be compared to a city. When the mind is swamped by the lower impulses anarchy results. Only the higher mind is capable of creating order within the self, exercising rulership and bringing into balance the conflicting laws of our individual members. The Logos or Spirit abides in the human being as the higher mind. This suggests to Goodenough Paul's contrast between the "mind of the flesh" and the "mind of the Spirit." In addition, Paul's "redemption of the body" may be compared to Philo's idea of regeneration. The inner adjustment that Philo seeks he may call peace, harmony, justice, salvation, or virtue. When God governs one's inner life then just acts may be expected to follow. Virtue in one's life should be like the tree of Eden that bears good fruit. This image is close to Paul's "fruits of the Spirit."

Philo expresses his distinctive ethic with respect to various groups in society. He accepts slavery without protest but notes the special conditions of the Jewish slave as limited by the Jewish law. Toward Gentile slaves he shows the attitude of the typical slave owner. Slaves should not be abused, and in the light of the Jewish law a master who kills a slave should himself be executed. Philo is simply a man of his own times, and he does not present the idea of the general human fellowship in the Logos that some of his contemporaries were teaching. Although Philo places great emphasis upon the sanctity of the family, he shows a low opinion of women, who are to be much circumscribed in their activities. Sexual relations are permitted only for procreation. Concerning children Philo does not relax the Old Testament idea of the complete power of parents over children, which of course found its counterpart in Roman law.

Philo exhibits a strong sense of justice in society, but on this Good-enough comments: "He was not an ethical utopian who expected more than was reasonably possible from human nature. His idealism, like the idealism of the pagan world, was turning increasingly inward as society became less and less hopeful" (*Introduction*, 129–30). Goodenough finds Philo's basic desire for inner adjustment, inner harmony, and inner victory to be peculiarly the product of Hellenistic Judaism. Likewise, as Christians became hellenized in thinking, the Christian ethic focused increasingly on humanity's search for salvation, expressed of course in kindly deeds but also, as is the case with Philo, exhibited much less in passion for social justice.

Goodenough discusses Philo the mystic in the final chapter. For Philo the real was the immaterial. Life took on reality only to the degree that it became filled with the immaterial. How are we to come ever closer into relation with this reality? All of Philo's philosophical discourse is subordinated to this. What concerns Philo the most is not the immaterial as the true reality but rather the religious experience of that reality. For Philo the only answer is correct education. While the uneducable masses were unable to achieve this goal, an intelligent minority through rigorous training in the sciences of the day might ultimately achieve that higher flash of perception which would reveal the world of forms. Through allegorical interpretation of Hebrew scripture Philo shows how this ideal was realized by some of the greatest patriarchs of Israel's past.

Hellenistic science failed to produce a spiritual leader for which there was great longing in the Hellenistic period. Consequently, the mystery religions provided the way for many to the achievement of communion with ultimate reality. The cult myth made the abstract idea come alive through personalizing it. The coming of Dionysus or Osiris became the coming of the Logos or Sophia in its immaterial power. The Greco-Roman world became increasingly fascinated by this mode of religious thought and practice. Philo, impressed as he was with Greek ideas, could not resist the force of this conception of mystery. Through allegorization of the Hebrew scriptures Philo shows Judaism to be the true mystery.

It has seemed appropriate to begin this chapter with Goodenough's summing up of his investigations and conclusions concerning Philo before coming to *By Light, Light*, his major contribution to Philo studies.[6] This study had been germinating for ten or more years. Many

---

[6] Goodenough, *By Light, Light: The Mystic Gospel of Hellenistic Judaism* (New Haven: Yale University Press, 1935).

years later he explained that his doctoral study on Justin Martyr convinced him first that Justin's Old Testament allegory was not of Christian origin, and second that, although Justin's allegory shows strong parallels to Philo, Philo did not necessarily have to be Justin's source. Goodenough suggested that the Hellenization of Christianity occurred as rapidly as it did because it was early espoused by Jews who were familiar with a hellenized form of Judaism to which Christianity became readily adapted. Goodenough says, "To investigate the possibilities of this hypothesis has been the concern of all my subsequent investigations."[7]

During his studies on Justin Martyr, Goodenough's attention was drawn by a fellow student to mosaics depicting Old Testament scenes in the church of Santa Maria Maggiore in Rome. When Goodenough had an opportunity to view these mosaics, he was struck by their resemblance to allegories in Justin. He asked himself whether this art might not have been borrowed by second-century Christians from an earlier tradition of Hellenistic Jewish art. But always the same objection was raised against this suggestion: since Jewish law prohibited image making, the possibility of a Jewish art was unthinkable. Goodenough turned to the investigation of Philo's doctrine of law. Philo's terminology for the patriarchs as "incarnate laws" led Goodenough into studies that he published in his "Political Theory of Hellenistic Kingship," which develops the doctrine of the king as incarnate law. Goodenough intended to continue his investigation of this aspect of Philo's thought, but he was not able to pursue this until he had written his *Jurisprudence of the Jewish Courts in Egypt.*

His studies in Philo and elsewhere gave Goodenough new insights into the imagery of the mosaics of Santa Maria Maggiore and some newly discovered paintings in the catacomb of the Viale Manzoni in Rome. He was ready to pursue studies of Christian art with a view to the possibility that it showed evidence of influence from an earlier Hellenistic Jewish art. At that moment the great breakthrough came. He was informed by his colleague, Professor M. I. Rostovtzeff of Yale, of the amazing discovery of the paintings on the walls of the synagogue at Dura. When soon thereafter he was able to view photographs of these paintings, he became immediately convinced that there was a common ancestor to the mosaics in Rome and the Dura paintings, namely, a Hellenistic Jewish religious art. But other scholars explained the Dura paintings in every possible way to defend the dogma that Jews always and everywhere observed the law against image making; hence the Dura paintings had to be explained as some strange exception or aberration.[8] Goodenough writes:

[7] Goodenough, *Symbols*, 1. 6.
[8] Ibid., 1. 23–29.

> It soon became clear that if I were to convince others of the mystic character of these pictures, and of the Judaism they seemed to me to represent, I could do so only by following a very long road. Obviously I must first publish what literary sources seemed to me to tell of the character of hellenized Judaism. So I began at once to write *By Light, Light*, which I put forward as the first installment of a series of studies, the next of which would consider the Dura art. By 1934 *By Light, Light* had gone to press, and late that year I began seriously to study the problem of the art.[9]

Far more than the study of the Dura art lay ahead for Goodenough. Nineteen years were to pass before, in 1953, he published the first volume of *Jewish Symbols*, the twelfth and last volume of which would appear in 1965, the year of his death. We turn now to the first volume of Goodenough's great scholarly plan.

By Light, Light

The introduction states that in Hellenism there was much borrowing of the mythology of the mystery religions. The rationalism of the Greek mind caused myths to become symbols of metaphysical truth, the basis for an emotional experience of philosophical concepts. Philosophical rationalism was never the solution of life for most Greeks. Out of the heart of Greek civilization arose the inclination toward mythological presentation of the divine mystery through initiations and sacraments as the gateway to a larger life. The most influential forms of mystic thought were those of the neo-Pythagoreans or Platonists. Goodenough's thesis is that not only early Christianity but also Hellenistic Judaism became strongly influenced by mystic thought. Philo gives us the best examples of the adaptation of mysticism to Jewish thought. Philo definitely does not adopt the literal myths of pagan cults. Rather, by allegory he transforms the Old Testament God into the Absolute joined with phenomena by his light stream. Moses and the patriarchs become embodiments of the divine law or Logos. Moses becomes the hierophant leading the questing Jew up the mystic ladder and along the royal road of the light stream to the vision of the Absolute.

Goodenough devotes the first chapter to the God of the mystery. For Philo, as for other Hellenistic thinkers, the sun with its life-giving rays provides the image to show how God the Absolute could be brought into relation with the material world. Two main types of formulation of the light stream arose: first the Persian type of *pleroma*, "fullness." In this form the king is the sun, and his satraps are his rays as lesser manifestations of the royal power. These lesser powers guide the neophyte toward the vision of the supreme God. The second formulation is the female

---

[9] Ibid., 1. 29–30.

principle type where the mysticism of sex is fundamental. This can be observed in the myth of Isis and Osiris, which reflects the notion of mystic ascent by a sexual mystic union with the female principle of nature. The same idea is embodied in various mystery religions, whether of Demeter and Persephone or the *magna mater*. Around the myth developed the *thiasos* or "local congregation" through which individuals could participate in initiation into the cult and its mysteries.

The myth of the cults expressed the idea that the universe is explicable in terms of a supreme deity who, through intercourse with the female principle, engenders the savior god, for example, Dionysus. A more philosophical formulation like that of Orphism represents human nature as a dualism of flesh and spirit. Jointed with this is the conception of the uncleanness of matter and an accompanying sense of sin, thus arousing the need for regeneration and purification. In the classic age this was expressed as the search for a divine savior. In the mysteries involving the female principle just such a savior arose as the son of the supreme god and of the female principle. In the mystery cults it was promised to worshippers that they could rise into the very being of the savior and experience salvation and immortality.

The appeal of the Greek mystery was not in the myth itself but in the philosophy and promise of immortality that it offered. With the female principle goes the notion of bisexuality, in which the female herself possesses the power of impregnation. The myths showed great variety. None was ever made into a creed, for the myth had significance only as it threw light on the objective of escape from the body into immaterial immortal life. Goodenough believes that this tradition served as the mystic background for Philo and his group.

What Philonic Judaism was trying to do was not to find a Jewish mother goddess but to find within Judaism a symbolic basis upon which to express and achieve the Greek mystic goal. The possibility for this lay in the independence of the mystic goal from its mythological formulation. Although the body is helpless, by the soul one can ascend first to God revealed in his work and finally through reason to the apprehension of God himself. Philo accepts the stream from God and finds the female principle in Jewish wisdom, which in Greek had become Sophia. Philo identifies Sophia with the Logos, and identifies the light stream as pleroma with the ark of the covenant, which as the abode of God's presence was the heart of all that was sacred in Jewish religion. Through the symbolism of the ark, Philo finds all of the powers of God to be revealed, as similarly he finds them in the cities of refuge. However Philo represents the powers of God, his chief concern is that they afford a means of escape from material bondage and a way of access to God.

Philo's repeated reference to God's dual powers, sovereignty and goodness, might seem to endanger his monotheism. Yet he meets this danger by suggesting that although God might to the human mind appear as threefold, the two powers accompanied by the Logos, these are only several aspects of a nature that is essentially one. For Philo this was not theological hair splitting but the very heart of the "mystery" through which Philo hoped to find salvation. Goodenough compares this with early Christian modalism, which was ultimately rejected as heresy, since not only the divinity but the individuality of Jesus had to be affirmed.

This representation of God and his powers is found in the Hellenistic concept of kingship, a topic that Goodenough had already investigated at length. In Hellenistic thought "the king was deity and deity king." The king is the embodied law. As such he both executes justice and promotes beneficence. Likewise, just as the great king of Persia, remote in his palace, rules his empires through his vice-regents, so God through his Logos together with his two powers rules the universe. These powers correspond to the two chief functions of the king, to be the author both of benevolence and of justice.

Another source of Philo's concept of a hierarchy of God's powers is the light mysticism of the mystery religions. He asserts that knowledge of God cannot come to human beings directly but only from God's primary and guardian powers. Goodenough believed that Philo did not introduce *de novo* the idea of God's appearing as a light stream manifesting himself in lower powers. Among his fellow Jews this would have branded him as a heretic. This, rather, must represent the culmination of a process working in Hellenistic Jewish thought over a period of time. Concerning whether Philo was more a mystic than a philosopher, Goodenough reminds us that Philo's primary interest was in the nature of God, the possibility of divine relationship with human beings, and comprehension of God by human beings. Whatever mystical urge moved Philo, he combined this with a profound mind intent upon thinking through the intellectual problems arising from his mysticism. Although he was primarily concerned with the hope of salvation, he was no less concerned with presenting it in terms of the best philosophical thought of his day.

The second chapter takes up the subject of the higher law. Different as Philo's thought might appear to be from traditional Judaism with its concentration upon doing the law, the law nevertheless is important to Philo's thought. For him the individual laws were primarily manifestations of a higher law. The higher law was that which gave form to matter in creation. The Law or the Logos was that which came from God into matter to make it a cosmos. Philo finds this demonstrated in Genesis 1 and 2. When Philo discusses nature and creation, "nature" (*physis*) often becomes interchangeable with "God" (*theos*). For Philo natural law means the rule of God in nature in a synonymous sense.

The universe, like a well-ordered city, reflects the law of its ruler. Philo repudiates the Stoic notion that there is a law inherent in nature to which God himself must conform. Only when Philo deals with the problem of evil does he distinguish a law of the material nature which seems to be at enmity with God's law. In this Philo resembles St. Paul. Goodenough illustrates liberally from Stoic sources that *logos, orthos logos,* and *nomos* had by Philo's time become quite interchangeable in Stoicism, as they are in Philo's thought. The identification of the law and the Logos is complete in Philo, yet it must always be remembered that Philo's is not the Stoic Logos concomitant with matter but rather the light stream coming into matter. For Philo the law is but one of the steps toward higher reality. To go beyond the law would not mean to reject it but rather would mean to move closer to its source.

Philo uses several cognate figures to develop the conception of the law of God. First is his conception of justice, *dikē.* To Philo as to all Greek traditions, the legal was always the just. For Philo God is only the means of salvation, the cause of good things only and not of evil things. Hence, the role of *dikē* is to serve as God's minister of justice in enforcing punishment upon malefactors. Goodenough notes a weakness in Philo's theodicy. Although *dikē* sometimes seems to relieve God of direct action in punishment, at other times in complete subordination to God *dikē* is said to be inflicted by divine will. Philo's theodicy appears to be devoted to defending not the justice but the goodness of God. God himself is not to be thought of as having justice as part of his nature since he in fact is the source of justice. In the perfect mystic vision God has no quality in himself, for he is unmixed and unmingled. *Dikaiosynē* is the quality of conforming to God's law or nature. It is the highest state of a created being and is truly salvation. Philo speaks of God's law also as a regulative force in the universe in mathematical terms of the Pythagorean *isotēs* or equality. For him this becomes one of the chief principles of the cosmos. It is the creative and controlling feature of the universe, the cosmic law used by Moses as the basis of all his laws. Philo treats equality as synonymous with justice.

Another figure for the law employed by Philo is the oath of God. Philo understands God's giving his oath to Abraham as the gift of natural or divine law. Elsewhere only in the New Testament Epistle to the Hebrews is the divine law compared with God's oath. Philo illustrates many ways in which natural law, which is a creation of God, governs every aspect of nature and human nature, including human sexuality.

The third chapter is devoted to the Torah. Much as Philo's treatment of laws shows his Greek background, his stress upon the law as the way to salvation demonstrates his essential Jewishness. For Philo, the Jew, the law was more than statutes; it was divine revelation and instruction—in short, it was *torah.* Yet sometimes the Jewish sense of *torah* is absent, and *nomoi* become for Philo *logia* in the Greek sense. Like other Jews of his time, Philo reserved the term *nomos* for the Pentateuch. The Judaism that Philo brought to Gentiles makes no reference to other Old Testament books apart from the Pentateuch. Philo apparently regarded the rest of the Old Testament as inspired but not as Torah. He deemed the inspiration of other biblical writers to be inferior to that of Moses, although the psalmists and prophets he regarded as disciples of Moses. Philo's Judaism was Moses-centered in a way that is in striking contrast to other Jewish, not to say Christian, writing of his time.

Philo knows nothing of a Jewish oral tradition, thus indicating, as Goodenough thinks, possible influence by the Sadducees. Like them also he repudiates determinism, although he retains the doctrine of providence. His lack of an angelology may show further Sadducean influence. The Pentateuch as Torah taught Philo his Judaism. He revered it as a revelation of the existence and nature of God, and of God's higher law. He loved the individual laws because they taught gentleness and humanity. For him, doing the law meant inevitably receiving God's blessing. Contrariwise, disobeying the laws most surely subjected one to the penalty of God's curse. Although Philo, through many an allegory, dwelt upon the inner meaning of the laws, he nevertheless was fully sympathetic with a Deuteronomic conception that law was to be literally performed. Consequently, Philo is critical of the Alexandrian Jews who called themselves allegorists and who emphasize altogether the inner meaning of the law to the neglect of its outward requirements. For Philo the literal law is the body and its inner meaning is the soul. Yet, for all his loyalty to the literal law, his regularity was that of a symbolist. Philo was not a normative Jew for whom obedience to the law was the primary virtue. He was primarily Greek in his ethical motivation, and ultimately for him the written law was inferior to the unwritten.

Philo speaks of the written human law as a copy of the true divine law. Goodenough calls this good Platonism. Not only did Moses possess the divine law, he was in fact the incarnation of it. The written code was no more than the imitation of the true laws incarnate in the patriarchs. Those who act according to their inner light use the law only as a check. For Philo even the written laws of the Jews are of no help to one aspiring to the mystical ascent to God. The whole objective of Philo's life was to get beyond all material images that he might come at last to the Logos or God himself as the ultimate spiritual origin of all things. The Torah was a source of instruction for beginners, the majority of whom never pass beyond this initial stage. For others, however, the Torah gave an exposition of the nature of God and of the mystic way to him. For Philo the Torah was the *hieros logos* of the mystery. Goodenough is convinced that Philo did not invent this interpretation but rather gave classic expression to a mode of understanding Judaism that had become increasingly well known by Philo's time.

For Philo there are two ways to God: first, the way of unwritten law and Logos or Sophia; second, there is the way of the written law. Philo does not disdain the second way, although it is inferior to the first, for the lower may become the introduction to the higher. These two are the "Greater Mystery of Moses" and the "Lesser Mystery of Aaron." No one in the lower mystery can approach God save with the aid of something that goes out from him. He cannot have apprehension of pure Being.

The mystery of Aaron gets its symbolism from the Jerusalem cultus. The mystery of Moses focuses only on the Holy of Holies and the ark, which was closed to the Aaronic priesthood. This symbolism was based on parts of the tabernacle rather than the Jerusalem temple and upon the functions of the high priest which were outwardly visible. Every part of the tabernacle symbolizes a different stage of the spiritual progress of the proselyte. In his treatise *De vita Mosis*, his "primer for proselytes" (Goodenough), Philo explains the symbolism three times. Both Clement of Alexandria and Josephus interpret the tabernacle or temple symbolism in similar ways. From this Goodenough concludes that all three drew from a common Hellenistic Jewish mystic and philosophic interpretation of the Jewish cultus.

Philo explains the significance of the priesthood which ministers in the cosmic temple by detailing the symbolism of the priestly robes, which imitate the details of the cosmos. The double nature of the breast-plate is symbolic of the double nature of the Logos: first a source, second a stream. Goodenough believes that for Philo there was but one Logos, yet the Logos combined with matter makes the dyad which is the material world.

Philo describes the high priest in terms of the Logos, comparing human reason with the high priest. Although the high priest always dwells among the holy doctrines, he cannot enter to consort with them more than once a year. The goal of the higher mystery is the unmediated vision of the Logos as One, but ordinary human beings cannot achieve this goal in a single leap; hence the importance of the symbolism of the temple to afford the vision of the Logos clothed in matter. Urim and Thummim symbolize the Logos in the material world. The royal tiara symbolizes that the priestly office is superior to kingship. The priestly robes symbolize that goodness and merciful power are aspects of the Logos that hold the created world together.

This symbolism of priesthood and temple indicates that the earthly cult enables those not worthy of mystical union with God to be transformed into the cosmic being by means of Logos and matter. Goodenough is uncertain whether at this point Philo has in mind a mystic gnosis without rites or a mystery proper in the sense of an organization with a formal initiation. If it is the former, then those without spiritual experience receive only the lower teaching, which is reminiscent of the contrast between "adults" and "babes" in Paul and the Epistle to the Hebrews. The less elaborate form of this symbolism in *The Special Laws* suggests that it was intended for somewhat more advanced Gentiles who had progressed beyond elementary understanding. The fact that varying forms of the same symbolism appear in Josephus and Clement suggests that Philo is not the author of the symbolism but shares in an already rich traditon. In *The Special Laws* Philo identifies the high priest with the *theios anthrōpos*, having put off his lower nature altogether. The spirit in which the sacrifice is offered is more important than the animal presented. The priest who makes the offering is made holy and transcends earthly things. The immediate object of the sacrifice is conciliation of the merciful powers of God. Common to the traditions concerning details of the mystery of Aaron was that the Jewish priesthood and temple constitute a cosmic mystery.

Philo also conceives of a higher mystery open to Gentiles which would produce piety by means of philosophic teaching. He tries to bring Gentiles into the higher mystery of Moses without converting them into literal Jews. Goodenough traces the Logos and cosmic mystery to the Hermetic literature and the cult of Isis rather than to Stoicism, as some scholars do. He thinks that it is possible that the mystery of Aaron can be traced to Palestinian Judaism, whereas the mystery of Moses may even have oriental roots.

The fifth chapter interprets the significance of Enos, Enoch, Noah, and Abraham. For Philo the approach to God in the higher mystery was through the lives of the patriarchs, who themselves are *nomoi empsychoi*, embodied laws. But first must come study of the creation as taught by Moses. Philo demonstrates this to be conceived of in the same way as that of the Platonic and Pythagorean philosophers. Genesis teaches that the material world has been created by God according to the pattern of the immaterial through the agency of the Logos.

Who are the persons who are not worthy to approach the mystic teaching? They are the *castrati*, atheists, polytheists, and "rationalists," those who put ultimate trust in the human mind. Philo does not draw the line of exclusiveness between Jew and Gentile, but only those Jews and Gentiles with an honest desire and with a correct philosophical point of view may be accepted into the mystery. Philo begins his exposition of the higher mystery by examining the lives of the patriarchs. Goodenough says that Philo is appealing to the popular mind, which prefers to learn virtue through the model of great human lives rather than through applying ethical principles alone. Goodenough declares that this popular desire to locate in the "man of God" an incarnation of virtue finally found its ideal in Jesus of Nazareth. Philo's exposition of the significance of the patriarchs rests on both his Jewish background and his background in philosophy.

Seven great types of achievement are exemplified in the Torah. Enos symbolizes hope. Enoch typifies the next step, repentance for sins and improvement. Noah, the last of the first triad, represents justice, having conquered his lower passions and abandoned the confusion of sinful society. For his reward Noah was spared the calamity of the flood and became the founder of a new race. The ark in which Noah took refuge along with the animals was symbolic for Philo of the body of one who is compelled to make room for untamed passions and vices. The career of Noah illustrates the battle between the flesh, with its appetites, and the soul or mind. Noah's God is the God of the mystery, who expresses himself in the Logos with the two powers. The story of Noah and the flood is a revelation of the royal road to God, the road of Sophia, wisdom.

The next triad of patriarchs, superior to the first, are the fully perfect men—Abraham, Isaac, and Jacob. With the help of the powers these have come to the end of the mystic road and have been given the vision of God. As such they are a "holy priesthood." Because of Abraham's importance to Philo's scheme, Goodenough devotes half a chapter to Abraham. He is the higher type, the "embodied law," because of his attitude of obedience toward God. Philo treats Abraham's migration from Chaldea as his migration from erroneous opinion about the character of God to the recognition of the truth. According to Goodenough this is Philo's rejection of materialistic pantheism. Abraham's sojourn in Paran led to his experiencing revelation from God, bringing to Abraham the knowledge that the true nature of God, the ruler and creator of the universe, is outwardly invisible. Abraham's name is changed, which signifies that he has become the Sophos, the wise man. Philo explains Abraham's marriage to Sarah as symbolic of the marriage of mind, *nous*, to virtue. Philo explains that paradoxically in such marriage, Sophia, the female principle, the "wife," sows seeds of good intentions and virtuous speeches in reason, the "husband." The human mind must put itself into a feminine attitude of passivity in order to receive the masculine activity of Sophia or virtue, *aretē*.

The visit of the three angelic strangers is symbolic of the ruling and creative powers of God connected by the Logos. These appear as three to the beginner, but the more advanced person recognizes this as the vision of the One. With great feeling Philo represents Abraham's sacrifice of Isaac. Isaac, whose name means "laughter," represents the highest happiness toward which the good person aspires. But humans must be ready to sacrifice their own desire for happiness (*eudaimonia*) in complete dedication to make themselves subject to God. God will then give them happiness because of their dedication.

Philo completes his treatise on Abraham by showing how Abraham excelled in the four cardinal virtues of justice, courage, self-control, and wisdom. Because of his spiritual development, Abraham is in a sense on a plane of equality with God. He is more than law-abiding, he is embodied law, *nomos empsychos*, and savior, with power to help others along the path of spiritual development.

The sixth chapter explains the significance of the patriarchs Isaac and Jacob. Philo says that so exalted and perfect in character was Isaac, so completely at one with the power behind the cosmos, that he typified joy. He embodied *eudaimonia* since he is completely and effortlessly at one with God's law. Philo attributes to Isaac a virgin birth, Sarah's virginity being miraculously restored prior to his conception. Thus, God would most accurately be called Isaac's father. Moreover, Isaac was the self-taught, having been from the beginning so filled with Sophia that he had no need to submit to ordinary forms of instruction.

Goodenough finds the Isaac story to be an allegory of the mystical achievement of those who hasten to immortality. The story centers on Isaac's marriage. He could not marry a Canaanite woman, since Canaan means "stupid." Therefore, his servant brings him a wife from the house of Nahor, which means Quiet Light, or Sophia. Thus Isaac, the self-taught, achieves the mystic marriage with the ever virgin, daughter of the God, daughter of the Logos. Goodenough remarks on the confusing nature of this imagery and admits the contradictions in it, judging from this fact that mythologies had no absolute value for Philo. In the end, for Philo, allegories were only figures of speech for the great light-bearing God. Upon examination of possible sources for Philo's imagery, Goodenough reaches the following conclusion: a *pleroma* conception of the light stream of apparent Persian origin and a female principle conception of uncertain origin had both found their way into the Judaism that Philo knew. He treats them both as parallels without adequately fusing them together. Continuing the allegory, Philo tells that following Isaac's marriage the birth of his two sons represents the discrimination by the Light of the good (Jacob) and the bad (Esau), which struggle against each other. Important as the patriarchs are as symbols to Philo, Goodenough believes that Philo still regarded them as important historical figures.

Jacob, though not so exalted as Abraham and Isaac, represents virtue won through ascetic discipline. Jacob comes to believe in one God by direct illumination. His contention with Esau shows his life to be one of endless struggle, and his mastery over Esau symbolizes his victory over the lower parts of the soul. Jacob's dream on his way to Laban is elaborately expounded. There are two grades of the Light of God: first, the archetypical beams of God himself; and second, copies of these beams, the immortal *logoi* commonly known as angels. At Bethel Jacob sees the second type of vision. His thought upon awakening from his dream, "God was in this place," shows that he could not conceive of God beyond space. His marriages with Laban's daughters, first Leah, then Rachel, teach that Jacob must first pursue encyclical studies, then philosophy, in that order. His becoming shepherd for Laban symbolizes the fact that the good king and wise man is a shepherd. In his further dream of the varicolored sheep, the three kinds of sheep born to the ewes of the dream represent three grades of experience of the soul. The white sheep are the souls in the highest mystery. The variegated sheep represent the possibilities of musical concord. The third type, with the ash-colored spots, symbolizes the road to the beautiful and the good. For Philo these represent the three stages of temple worship that are symbolic of the stages in the higher mystery. Jacob represents the type of man who has gone beyond the "heavenly ladder," that is, the lower mystery, to the immediate comprehension of God as this is afforded through the light stream or Logos. Jacob's shrunken thigh, which resulted from his wrestling with the angel, symbolizes the subjugation of his lower nature. After the mystic rises above the body so as to gain spiritual apprehension of God, the final stage of the mystery is to return to the body and so to master earthly life that the body becomes a perfect instrument of the spirit.

Chapter seven explains Moses as presented to Gentile inquirers. Goodenough points out that in following Philo's allegorical interpretations of the patriarchs we are following the method of presenting the mystery to Gentiles that was originally Philo's own. Philo's allegory is in very large part consistent wherever it is found in his writings. Goodenough doubts that Philo developed the allegory of the mystery *de novo*. He believes rather that Philo is referring to an already existing Jewish mystery and can presuppose a sympathetic Jewish audience able to understand and appreciate what he is trying to express.

Moses occupies his proper place in Philo's scheme as the great climax of the mystagogues, chief among the patriarchs who are presented as guides into the mystery for Gentiles. Philo begins by demonstrating that Moses is the ideal king. The Egyptian princess took him into her keeping because from his infancy he showed himself to be of a finer sort than other mortals. Like Isaac, Moses is self-taught, although he mastered completely all the studies to which he was introduced by various teachers. To this instruction he added the rule over his body, as did Plato's *Phaedrus*. In all things, however, Moses did not forget his Jewish loyalties. His role as Jethro's shepherd further exemplified his kingly training, since a king must be a shepherd to his people. According to Philo, Moses' ability to speak is from God and unhampered. Aaron was simply his interpreter.

Moses was given leadership of his people in the Exodus because of his nobility of soul, his magnanimity, and his hatred of evil. Moses eschewed those things that commonly mar the rule of kings. He sought to establish no dynasty, and he refused to make himself personally rich, whereupon God committed to Moses the entire cosmos as a possession fit for an heir. Philo declares that, since Moses was to be a lawgiver, in advance of that event he himself became the incarnate and vocal law. Moses is now fully a king both by choice of the people and by God's approval. Goodenough observes that Moses is largely lost in the story of the adventures of the Israelites. The miracles are either rationalized or omitted. This is accounted for by the fact that the book is designed for Gentile readers who believe in divine providence but might be critical of tales that seemed too fanciful.

Philo's first book on Moses has shown Moses in his kingly role. The second book shows him as the ideal lawgiver, priest, and prophet. As lawgiver, Moses must possess four qualities: social-mindedness, justice, love of good, and hatred of evil. Moses as ideal king was the incarnation of the great law of nature, identical with the Logos. The king was not only the embodiment of law but was also the one who makes the law articulate. For Philo the entire Pentateuch was the law of God given by Moses.

Moses' second role is that of priest, although Philo has to contradict scripture, which says that Moses made Aaron the priest. In the ancient world the priestly and the royal offices were almost universally associated. Since Moses is king he must also be priest. In this Philo follows the Pythagorean formulation of royalty. Even though fit for priesthood, Moses must first be initiated into the mysteries. This occurred when after a period of abstinence Moses ascended the mountain where he received the vision of the immaterial forms, which qualifies him to be the true high priest. For practical purposes he passed on his priestly prerogatives to Aaron and his sons. Philo reverses the sequence of the biblical account of his two sojourns on Mount Sinai and the golden calf episode. Goodenough believes that Philo's purpose for this is to show Gentile readers that mediation through Moses, the true high priest, is vastly superior to that offered by the lesser priesthood of the temple cultus.

The third role that Philo assigns to Moses is that of prophet. His utterances took three forms: first, direct utterances of God; second, oracular responses from God which Moses requests; and, third, the response that Moses himself gives when he is in the state of being possessed by God. Because of this third type, he is preeminently called a prophet. Examples of this type are Moses' foretelling of the salvation of the Israelites and the destruction of the Egyptians at the sea as well as his forecasting of the supply of manna.

Philo's comments upon Moses' death are among his most significant. Moses was summoned by God to leave mortal life and be made immortal, exchanging his dual nature of body and spirit into mind with sunlike brilliance. In this new state Moses prophesied the fate of each tribe. Moses presents his life as a good model for others. His desire was that his powers and honors not go to his own heirs but to someone of God's own choosing. This was Joshua, whom Moses presented to the people.

Moses began his final song while still in the body, summoning to join him as chorus the very elements of the universe. Only then did he begin to change from mortal to immortal life. Goodenough sees in Philo's Moses the model for the whole people of Israel, comparable to the role that Jesus fulfilled for Christians. Goodenough points out that in the allegorical writings, where the mystery is made explicit, Moses is represented as the savior of Judaism *par excellence*.

Chapter eight interprets Moses as Philo presents him in the Jewish mystery. Goodenough finds in Philo's various references to Moses a standardized allegory in which Moses is a special incarnation. From birth he was a stranger to the body and fully aware of the immaterial world and its nature. He lived his entire life on this level as a complete mystic. In Midian, Moses received his divine commission. His protection from attack of the daughters of Raguel-Jothar symbolizes his protection of the mind from malice so that it is able to rule over the lower life. Since it is the Logos that accomplishes this rescue, Goodenough believes that if Philo does not intend here to represent Moses as Logos he shows him at least to be its agent. Moses' marriage to Zipporah represents his mystic marriage with Sophia. This is not something acquired by effort and aspiration, but something given to him by God, that is, a wife already impregnated by God. Earlier in his allegory of Isaac, Philo had already expounded the significance of mystic marriage, which Moses now experiences.

Moses as shepherd symbolizes the divine power of salvation, God's care for those who come to him. In writing about the burning bush, Philo states that Moses there learned of the three powers of God: teaching, perfection, and discipline. Moses' rod symbolizes discipline, which, when thrown away, becomes the serpent pleasure. One must not flee from it but grasp it, turning it once again into discipline. Concerning Moses' supposed inability to speak, Philo explains that because Moses has been stamped by Sophia he is the source of speech but not himself "utterance." This he delegates to Aaron. Pharoah and Egypt represent all that is bad in human nature and the body. Israel represents the mind, which must be led out before it can perceive the heavenly vision. For Philo the Passover is the symbol of abandoning the life of passions and is the beginning of the journey to the savior God. The people united in the act of the great migration are changed from a multitude into an "ecclesia," a church. The Exodus is an allegory of Moses who can lead the soul from its lower aspects to the vision of God. Moses is the hierophant and savior of the mystery.

The Israelites are to understand three stages of the mystery: (1) the cosmic stage; (2) the immaterial stage represented in the Logos; and (3) "Being," *to ōn*. The last stage is inaccessible to humanity, but Moses can lead one into the first two. The herd of animals that the Israelites unwisely took with them represents "opinions" which impede their journey. The death of the Egyptian pursuers represents the destruction of the body and lower mind. The years of wandering are typical of the struggle of the one who has renounced the lower life but is still hampered by "somatic survivals." This reminds Goodenough of the continued struggle reported by Paul. During the struggle, however, there may be "showers of refreshing" represented by the manna, which symbolizes wisdom from the Logos. The bitterness of the waters of Marah represents Israel's apprehension for the future. This is alleviated by Moses, who is both creator, *demiourgos*, and savior when he throws in the purifying wood, which is from the tree of life, that is, immortality. The rock that Moses strikes to draw water symbolizes the Logos or Sophia. Moses' holding up his hands, bringing victory to the Israelites over Amalek, shows how the soul triumphs over mortal things only as the mind is elevated above them. Moses, who "sits alone" outside the camp, is the Sophos, the Logos without speech, who is constant and one, the monad. He stands in contrast to the high priest, who represents the Logos in speech. This logos is not one but two; hence, the high priest can have recourse to the sacred doctrines only once a year, whereas Moses, the type of perfect mystic, comes to the highest doctrines of the mystery, living on that level constantly.

Moses' supreme desire was to see God, which caused him to leave the people at the foot of Sinai as he pressed on through the darkness. Ultimately Moses has to conclude that to see God directly is impossible, and that humans must be satisfied with seeing God only through his powers that range the universe, just as Moses saw only the "back parts" of God while he was in the cleft of the rock. Moses was an "incorporeal listener to the divine music of the cosmos" (*By Light*, p. 213) and lived thus for forty days without food, showing his renunciation of the body. Philo in various writings expounds upon the significance of Moses' sojourn on Mount Sinai. Throughout all these experiences Moses became the supreme hierophant of Israel.

In preparation for the building of the tabernacle, the apparatus of the lower mystery, the already exalted Moses requires an intermediary. To this end Moses produces the archetypes of the tabernacle while Bezalel makes from them the material copies. The allegory says little of Moses as author of specific laws, which shows that the mystery there presented has moved beyond the specific commands to the realm which in Philo's view was that of true Judaism.

While Moses was being initiated, the multitude at the foot of the mountain had little immediate experience of the great revelation at Sinai. Moses as Sophos was able to take God as his teacher, but Israel, the less perfect, must take Moses. Yet so perverse were they, being still tied to the body and its passions, that they were unable even to see the revelation

mediated by Moses. They projected their lingering passions into the forma-
tion of a golden calf, and this had to be destroyed, which symbolized the
destruction of the passions.

The choice of the seventy elders figures as part of the installation of
the mystery. Just as fire is not diminished though it light ten thousand
torches, so Moses' spirit is shared among the elders. This is the sharing of
Sophia, the Logos, the light stream. This reminds Goodenough of the
Christian doctrine of the apostolic succession through the laying on of
hands.

As Israel continues its journey, the going out and the return of the
spies from Canaan symbolize Israel's readiness for a glimpse of the
higher mystery. The refusal of the Edomites to let Israel pass through
their land points up the fact that in contrast to Edom, who are people of
the material world, Israel is following on the royal road of Sophia to
God. Here as in subsequent episodes Moses functions always as savior
and hierophant and as the Logos mediating between God and the
people. Philo ends Israel's story without taking Israel into Canaan. The
final episode concerns the song of Israel at the well as described in Num
21:16–18. Philo interprets this as the well or stream of Sophia, and the
song as a portion of Israel's initiation into Sophia under the leadership of
Moses, their hierophant. This is the third and final stage of Israel's
migration, following the first (leaving Egypt) and the second (destruction
of the passions at the Red Sea).

In Philo's description of the death of Moses, Goodenough finds the
basis for believing that for Philo Moses was a god. Even though Philo
often represents Moses only as "the perfect man" and no more, it appears
that he is not fully consistent in his monotheism. Under stress of emotion
he makes statements about the divinity of Moses. He declares that Moses
did not die in the ordinary sense but was translated by the word of the
Logos. The human element was such a little part of Moses that the loss
of it made no change. Goodenough says that we cannot ignore Philo's
inconsistencies. Thus, his frequent statements about Moses' divinity allow
us to assume that this really represents one of his attitudes toward Moses.
Moses is a substitute for God when he acts in relation to Pharaoh. When
God on Sinai said to Moses, "Stand thou here with me," God gave Moses
a share in his own nature. Although Moses is not God, he is yet divine
man, *theios anthrōpos.* In him the gulf between humanity and God is
bridged. This appears in his exercise of saving power, first in giving the
law. Yet Philo declares that the saving power of Moses and the patriarchs extends beyond the giving of the law to influencing people in later
generations. This appears in those few who are initiated in the higher
mystery, the true essence of Judaism, those who have been stamped by
the image of the Sophos. Moses and Abraham function as intercessors
and saviors of human beings. God is merciful to all people when even a

remaining spark of virtue in one person rekindles it in others. Moses' communicating the spirit to the seventy elders illustrates this. Moses, the savior-sage, causes God to be compassionate to all people. In Moses the entire race has been accepted by God. Philo addresses prayers to Moses not as to one dead but as to one with present and active power. Goodenough finds in Philo's mode of thinking at least a partial origin of the later Christian mode of thinking about Christ.

In chapter nine Goodenough recapitulates the mystery that he has detailed in the previous chapters. Before doing this he makes certain observations concerning the sources of Philo's thought. Philo is an eclectic neo-Pythagorean Platonist who fuses to the ideas of Plato mystic notions from the Orphics, from Persia, and from Isis. Philo is not an innovator, and Goodenough believes that this whole scheme of mystic philosophy was in an advanced stage of assimilation when Philo adopted it. In the development of his own scheme of the higher and lower mysteries, Philo may well have been influenced by an already independently developed Hellenistic-Jewish mystery. Philo's contribution was to give the fullest expression and classic form to the mystery.

Goodenough raises the question of whether the rich allegorical imagery in Philo could have produced an iconography. Philo's acquaintance and sympathy with art could leave room for such an iconography, although he makes no mention of it. That Philo's attitude toward art stands in marked contrast to the general attitude of Jews of the time is shown by Josephus. The astonishing discovery of the Dura synagogue with the rich imagery of its frescoes intensifies the question of a possible Philonic iconography. Goodenough also reads in Philo's writings possible references to an actual mystic rite with which Philo could have been familiar, including a common meal. It seems highly probable that there was a literal Jewish mystery, with cult and iconography, which could account for the pictures at Dura. It may not be possible to estimate the significance of Philo's writings as witness to Hellenistic Judaism in general, but Goodenough is persuaded that Philo is a primary source of information for a Hellenistic Jewish mystery and exceeds any other source for such knowledge.

Chapter ten is devoted to consideration of evidence of the mystery in non-Philonic writings. Certain Pseudo-Philonic writings reveal knowledge of light mysticism, vision of the Logos, and the symbolism of white garments, which clothed not only Samuel and Osiris but also suggest Jesus at the Last Supper. These writings also speak of the glorification of Moses and the symbolism of God as Light. 4 Maccabees shows a Philonic understanding of the Law. The Wisdom of Solomon knows of the mystery of Aaron and represents Solomon as hierophant. Wisdom also speaks of Solomon's mystic marriage with Sophia, and Sophia is closely identified with the giving of a higher law. Wisdom likewise contains allegory of the patriarchs, details of which Goodenough finds suggestive of Philo. Wisdom appears to show mystic Judaism at a stage earlier than Philo's, yet in the same line of development.

Eusebius contains fragments reflecting still earlier stages of the Jewish mystery, mainly from writings of Aristobulos and Alexander Polyhistor. Thus, two centuries before Philo certain Jews had begun to transform their doctrine of wisdom into the mystic doctrine of Sophia as the light stream. The sibylline books also throw light upon the mystery in an early syncretistic stage. Further evidence appears in the Pseudo-Justinian *Oratio ad Graeces.*[10] Goodenough concludes that this fragment is not Christian in origin but rather comes out of a Philonic type of Judaism. It is a defense of turning from Greek religion to the religion of the Logos, denouncing the immoralities of the Greek divinities. The fifth chapter is particularly revealing of mystic Judaism, for it celebrates the salvation that comes through the Logos, which is a "city of refuge" from the bodily passions, the tyranny of the lower nature. The Logos quenches this destructive fire within the soul. Goodenough concludes that each of these non-Philonic documents is an independent witness to a thriving Jewish mystery.

There is enough material to prove the existence of mystic Judaism, enough even to trace its history. Although Jews sincerely endeavored to maintain their religion free from alien influence, the task was difficult. The new legalism of postexilic Judaism and the centering of worship in the temple at least kept Judaism exclusive in Palestine. But outside Palestine this was well-nigh impossible. Some Jews simply apostatized. Many more evidently adopted the way of syncretism, embracing concepts and values from pagans, then adapting them to Judaism. Syncretism was the middle ground.

Chapter eleven treats the mystic liturgy. Evidence for this is found in a largely neglected study by W. Bousset of fragments of Jewish liturgical material interpolated into the *Apostolic Constitutions.*[11] Because of the inaccessibility of this material, Goodenough prints sixteen fragments of it in his own translation, pointing out the unmistakable characteristics of mystic Judaism. Goodenough considers fragment VII to be the best guide to the theology and philosophy of the fragments. In terms already familiar in Philo, this hymn praises God as unbegotten and eternal, the bestower of everything that is good. One portion shows how such a prayer could have been readily adopted into a Christian liturgy and demonstrates striking parallelism to Philo's thought:

---

[10] For a fuller treatment of this fragment see Goodenough, "The Pseudo-Justinian 'Oratio ad Graeces,'" *Harvard Theological Review* 18 (1925) 187–200.

[11] Bousset, "Eine jüdische Gebetssammlung im siebenten Buch der apostolischen Konstitutionen," *Nachrichten von der königliche Gesellschaft der Wissenschaften zu Göttingen,* philologische-historische Klasse (Göttingen: Dieterich, 1915 [1916] 435–85.

> Thou art Gnosis . . . who didst bring all things out of not-being
> into being by Thy only Son, but didst beget Him before all ages
> by Thy will, Thy power, and Thy goodness, without any agency,
> the only Son, God the Logos, the living Sophia, the first-born of
> every creature, the angel of Thy great counsel, and Thy High-
> Priest, but the King and Lord of every intellectual and sensible
> nature, who was before all things, by whom were all things. (*By
> Light*, p. 320)

In three places the name of Christ appears, and these seem to be insertions, since the context makes perfect sense if they are removed. At one point God is characterized at length as the creator of the natural order, God "who didst encompass the world, which was made by Thee through *Christ* with rivers, and water it with currents" (*By Light*, p. 321). The prayer celebrates God's creation of humanity. In that context we read, "For Thou, O God Almighty, didst by *Christ* plant a paradise in Eden" (*By Light*, p. 322). In a listing of God's dealings with the patriarchs, these words occur: "Thou art He who didst deliver Abraham from the impiety of his forefathers, and didst appoint him to be the heir of the world, and didst discover to him by *Christ*, who didst aforehand ordain Melchizedek an high-priest for Thy worship" (*By Light*, p. 323). Goodenough concludes that the prayer has been adapted Christian usage simply by the insertion of "Christ" for "Logos" (*By Light*, p. 324).

Another striking feature of the liturgical fragments is the repeated listing of Hebrew patriarchs, who are celebrated for their piety. This recalls Philo's expositions of the patriarchs as fulfilling various roles within God's scheme. In one of the most notable lists the patriarch-heroes Abel, Seth, Enos, Enoch, Noah, Job, Abraham and the succeeding patriarchs, and Moses are all celebrated as priests. Such a list could come only from the Jewish mystery, since only in that milieu were the patriarchs regarded as priests. Goodenough concludes that there must have been an actual Jewish sect whose prayers were expressed in the language of the mystery.

In an epilogue Goodenough traces evidence of the mystery in the Kabbalah. In spite of important differences, there are striking similarities between the allegory of the Hellenistic Jewish mystery and of the Kabbalah. Goodenough says, "Both the Kabbalah and Philo have fundamentally the identical conception that the Absolute and Unrelated God is related to the lower world or worlds through a series of emanations which are as a whole to be conceived by the figure of a single stream of Light from the Source" (*By Light*, p. 360). From similarities between the Kabbalah and Hellenistic mystic Judaism Goodenough concludes that either the Kabbalah preserves traces of the earlier mystic Judaism or it demonstrates that mysticism persisted in Judaism. Consequently, there is no better reason for denying the existence of a widely popular Hellenistic mystic Judaism than to deny the existence of the Kabbalah itself.

Readers of *By Light, Light* became perplexed concerning whether Goodenough used the terms "initiation" and "mystery" in a figurative or a literal sense. He tried to answer them in an article.[12] He says that for centuries before Philo the Greeks treated philosophy as a mystery without ritual. The Pythagoreans under Orphic influence organized themselves as mystic *thiasoi*, or religious guilds, with an inner group of *mathēmatikoi* to whom alone the saving truths were revealed. Later on Plato interpreted the teachings of Heraclitus as mystic doctrines understandable only to initiates.

Plato's writings show that under the influence of Pythagoreanism philosophy came to be understood as a means of purification and salvation in the same way that popular mystic rites were viewed. In his Seventh Letter Plato declares that he did not intend to put his philosophy in a book; consequently, the dialogues must have been seen as primarily propaedeutic, whereas the essence of his philosophy was retained in his secret discourses. In the *Phaedo*, in a discussion of the mysteries Socrates declares that true purification is in fact not obtainable through the mystic rites but rather through true philosophy.[13] Plato in the *Phaedrus* represents philosophy in the same way.[14] Goodenough says that mystic Judaism, like Platonism, was a true mystery, because only through it could one obtain salvation from the flesh.

There was also a sacramental side to Philo's mystery. From Plato onward there developed the Hellenistic concept of a sacrament. This is best illustrated in Plutarch, who combines a Platonic type of mystery with the popular mystic rites. In this sacramentalism the true meaning of the ritual act was that it afforded the means of revelation of truth. "From that time on men wanted both a ritual act and a mystic philosophy. The act, for the more perceptive members of the group, was a visible sign of an invisible grace; the real mystic experience was essentially not in the visible sign but in the invisible apprehension" ("Literal Mystery," p. 236).

Goodenough's reply to his inquirers, therefore, is that for Philo Judaism could be understood as a literal mystery, but only in the sense of sacrament which unites within itself the outward sign with the invisible grace. For Philo all the Jewish festivals ministered to the soul by philosophy. The true celebration of the festival is through using it as a sacrament. He contrasts the Jewish celebration with the pagan festivals, which seem devoted entirely to fleshly rioting. Philo shows that the mystic Jew

---

[12] Goodenough, "Literal Mystery in Hellenistic Judaism," in *Quantulacumque: Studies Presented to Kirsopp Lake by Pupils, Colleagues and Friends* (eds. R. P. Casey, S. Lake, and A. K. Lake; London: Christophers, 1973) 227–41.
[13] Plato, *Phaedo* 69a–d.
[14] Plato, *Phaedrus* 247c–e.

saw the revelation of saving truth in the Torah. For him it was the true mystery in the Platonic sense.

In 1948 Goodenough wrote on Philo's ideas on immortality.[15] For Philo the soul and body each have a separate nature and destiny. Many souls are engulfed in the stream of matter. "But a few of them by careful study of philosophy practice death with respect to the body that thereby they may get a share of incorporeal and immortal life, in the presence of the One who is himself without beginning or end" ("Immortality," p. 93). God's breathing into the human at creation was not the giving of life, but rather it was God's breathing his spirit into the human's lower mind, a concept familiar from Aristotle. By the soul as prisoner in the body Philo means the higher mind. Abraham's migration represents the release of the soul from bondage to the body. The "sages" like Moses are not "emigrants" from heaven to the material world like ordinary human beings. Rather, they are "tourists" who will presently return home.

It is difficult to determine whether Philo anticipates personal immortality or simply anticipates the reabsorption of the soul into the divine. Eternal life is a flight toward Being. Philo presents a paradox. Whereas the goal of humanity is to become absorbed into the heavenly world and lose identity, the patriarchs nevertheless retain their identity and become intercessors for human beings. Moses is a special case. At Sinai Moses appeared in God's presence without a body. At his incarnation Moses was not a "mixture" like other human beings, so at death he lost nothing. This is a completely docetic view. In contrast, in ordinary human beings at death the mixture is dissolved, and only the higher part of the self achieves immortality. As much as Philo conforms to Platonic tradition, he departs from it in important ways. The Torah and the patriarchs are his ultimate goals. Yet in his indifference to personal destiny he is completely Greek. This little article is Goodenough's latest published study of Philo. He was already deeply engrossed in his studies of Jewish symbols in the Greco-Roman world, the first volume of which would not be published for seven more years. It is to that work that we must now turn.

[15] Goodenough, "Philo on Immortality," *Harvard Theological Review* 39 (1946) 85–108.

5

JEWISH SYMBOLS IN THE GRECO-ROMAN WORLD
Part One

The question that underlies this work came to Goodenough at the time of his research on Justin Martyr. The question is how to account for the rapid hellenization of Christianity following its obscure origin in Palestine. For Goodenough the answer lies in the prior hellenization of Judaism as demonstrated in Philo's works. When Hellenistic Jews became Christian, the same kind of allegorization that Philo practices became a part of their Christianity. But if Philo is typical of widespread Hellenistic Judaism, why is there no documentary evidence of it after Philo's time? The answer is that evidence of post-Christian Judaism comes almost entirely from rabbinic sources, which are silent about Hellenistic Judaism. Only Christian sources tell of hellenized Judaism. Moreover, early Christians referred to Hellenistic Jewish writings only if they were pre-Christian in origin or no later than the first or second Christian century. If hellenized Jewish writings continued into later centuries, neither Christians nor rabbinic Jews would have had any interest in preserving them.

Goodenough disagrees with historians of Judaism who argue from literary silence that in later Christian centuries Hellenistic Judaism had disappeared and rabbinic Judaism had come to dominate the entire Jewish world. By the third century Greek was the predominant language even of Jews of Palestine, and the invasion of Jewish art by Hellenistic ornamentation was as prominent in Palestine as in Rome or Dura. Although from the third to the sixth century a great popular movement toward rabbinic Judaism flourished in Babylonia, this rabbinism was not necessarily typical either of Palestine or of Judaism elsewhere in the Roman Empire. Goodenough distinguishes between rabbinic and mystic (including apocalyptic) Judaism. The aim of the Babylonian rabbis was through proper education to establish good habits of life. Law was not an end in itself but rather marked the way to the good life in relation to God and fellow human beings. This is the religion of the "horizontal path." The contrasting religion of the "vertical path" in apocalyptic Judaism tells of the hero who mounts to the throne of God and returns to tell people of another world. The vertical path is found also within mysticism. Perennial tension seems to prevail between these two forms. Rabbinic or halakic Judaism ultimately prevailed over the mystic form, but did not totally subjugate it.

One of the major clues to Hellenistic Judaism is in Jewish art of the period, which, because of the prohibition against image making, could have no place in rabbinic Judaism. Goodenough tells how seeds sown thirty years earlier bore fruit in his publication of *Jewish Symbols*. In the 1920s a fellow student at Oxford told him of mosaics in Santa Maria Maggiore in Rome that were thought to have been inspired by Justin's Old Testament allegories. When Goodenough himself viewed the mosaics, he agreed that they resembled Justin's allegories, but he felt that the second-century writings of Justin could hardly have been known to the fifth-century artist of the mosaics in Rome. It seemed more reasonable to suppose that this art had originated in Hellenistic Judaism and had been received by early Christians as a part of their heritage from Judaism along with Old Testament allegories in literary form.

Further study of the Santa Maria Maggiore mosaics together with study of catacomb paintings convinced him that the New Testament scenes were largely adaptations of Old Testament scenes. That early Christian art had been adapted from pagan art had long been recognized, so it seemed entirely reasonable that adaptations from Hellenistic Jewish art could readily have taken place. Several of the catacomb scenes show a central figure in a white garment. The figure always carries a rod whether the figure represents Jesus or Moses. Goodenough concludes that the original was the figure of Moses, for whom the rod became an essential symbol. Had the original figure in white been Jesus it is unlikely that Christians would represent Moses in a similar way. But to represent Jesus after the manner of Moses would not be strange. In catacomb art also the white robe of Moses became the uniform of the Christian saint.

From his study of the pictures in Rome, Goodenough became convinced that he had seen Christian pictures adapted with very little change from Hellenistic Jewish predecessors. However, when he was told at Oxford that Christian art could have no foundation in Jewish scripture because of the Jewish prohibition against all image making, he put aside his investigation of Jewish art and turned to a closer study of Philo. Several years later at Yale a colleague dismissed his theory of Jewish art because the Jewish prohibition against image making would make such art an impossibility.

In the 1930s he began to study the patriarchs of the Old Testament, whom Philo represents as "incarnate laws." Philo speaks of the patriarchs who advanced to the spiritual stage where they assumed the garment of light and became the "saviors" of Judaism, the figures through whom the divine light of the Logos revealed itself. This convinced Goodenough that the Old Testament figure clothed in the robe of light was not merely an interesting detail in Philo's thinking, but was the very core of his religious life. Goodenough turned again to the mosaics and the catacomb pictures with new insight. Late in 1932 he presented some of the material and his theory to M. I. Rostovtzeff of Yale, who informed him of the very recent discoveries of the murals of the synagogue at Dura. His first glance at the photographs of the Dura murals persuaded Goodenough that he was viewing examples of Jewish art almost exactly as he had described it. Moses dominated most of the scenes, and he was clothed in the garment of light exactly as he had been portrayed in the mosaics of Santa Maria Maggiore. Goodenough saw at once that if he was to convince others of the mystic character of these pictures, and of the Judaism that they seemed to represent, he must carry on a very long program of research. Thereupon he began to write *By Light, Light* to show what literary sources had to tell about Hellenistic Judaism. This was published in 1935, and the first phase of his research was completed.

I

In 1934 Goodenough began in earnest to study Hellenistic Jewish art. First he had to develop a technique to determine what the artists intended to say. A great amount of Jewish art of the Hellenistic period was elaborately Dionysiac. Wine symbols were the most prominent of any one kind: the vine, bunches of grapes, and the cup. Together with these were a great number of other figures: lions, eagles, masks, the tree, the crown of victory, the cock, and astronomical symbols, together with a number of figures of Greek gods. One of the most striking features of this art was the mixing of pagan symbols with Old Testament illustrations. It was of the greatest importance to try to discover a way objectively to interpret the symbols as well as the Old Testament scenes. Goodenough's enthusiasm for the work is expressed in a 1940 letter to Professor Wallace Notestine of Wooster, Ohio.[1]

> I have got about fifty thousand words written on my book, and the quality I think is excellent. With a good summer of work ahead of me I should round out the twelve months with a decent bit of accomplishment. The work that I am doing is fascinating beyond description. I am either crazy or I am doing something completely revolutionary in the study of ancient religions and Christianity. Time will tell which of these is true.

Jewish Symbols, which eventually encompassed thirteen volumes, began to appear in 1952. In the first three volumes—issued together as

---

[1] Unpublished letter of 13 May 1940 (Archives of Yale University; Erwin R. Goodenough Papers, Yale University Library). Used by permission.

the first installment—Goodenough presents extensive evidence to support his hypothesis, but he does not state it until the beginning of the fourth volume (1953). Samuel Sandmel regrets that Goodenough followed this order, for those who looked only at his first three volumes were never impressed by the importance of what he was doing, and few of those who condemned his efforts of the first three volumes ever considered his exposition in volume four.[2]

In chapter two of Part I of the first volume Goodenough presents the literary evidence for the religion of the Jews in the Roman world. First is the picture of Jewish life and worship reconstructed from pagan writers. Second is the testimony of Christians from the first four or five centuries. Third is the evidence from the papyri. Fourth is evidence from Jewish literature under three categories: the rabbinic, the apocalyptic-mystical, and the Hellenistic. He presents a digest of this material but gives mystical Judaism the most extended synopsis.

Part II treats the archaeology of Palestine. In chapter three Goodenough deals with the Jewish tombs of Palestine. Since Jewish art of antiquity had never been adequately presented, he confines his investigation to that Jewish art that is in some sense symbolic. Palestine is the place to begin, since here Jewish art in the widest variety and over the longest period of time is to be found. If symbolic development is to be traced anywhere, it must be here.

The numerous little tokens common in pre-Hellenistic Jewish tombs show the kind of religious syncretism among Jews that is so sternly denounced in the Old Testament prophets. Palestinian tombs fall into four categories: first, Hellenistic tombs from before the Maccabean era; second, tombs from Maccabean times to the fall of Jerusalem; third, tombs from after the fall of Jerusalem; and, finally, the catacombs of Sheikh Ibreiq discovered in the mid-nineteenth century. Typical of the entire series of volumes, Goodenough gives detailed descriptions of the structures or artifacts that he is interpreting, and he gives full credit to previous studies.

Chapter four deals with the contents of Jewish tombs of Palestine. The first category is water basins, a phenomenon of Palestinian tombs usually ignored. What was the possible funerary purpose of water basins? Where the wine or olive press might actually communicate with the tomb, the symbolism of the grape and wine was, prior to the Christian era, an important funerary symbol for the Jews. It may be possible to associate vessels or wells of water at tombs with the Jewish fountain or well of water of later Jewish tradition. Another form of water symbolism appears in little hollows or cups in Jewish tombstones. Goodenough

---

[2] Sandmel, "An Appreciation," in *Religions in Antiquity: Essays in Memory of Erwin Ramsdell Goodenough* (ed. J. Neusner; Leiden: Brill, 1968) 12–13.

believes that this entire symbolism must derive from Hellenistic origins.

Ossuaries are another feature of Jewish burial rites. These are small stone boxes carved out of a single block, designed to be covered, and made to receive the bones of the dead after the flesh had disintegrated. The origin of the ossuaries is unknown, but the Jerusalem Talmud discusses the custom of *ossilegium*, placing bones in boxes of stone or cedar. Various kinds of symbols appear on the ossuaries which develop into a very careful vocabulary of symbolism. Among these are rosettes, rosettes with borders, and the olive as border and wreath to frame the rosette. Other common symbols include the vase or chalice, the symbolism of columns, and the symbolism of flowers or trees.

Next to be described are Jewish sarcophagi. Few of these are found in Palestine. Most are pagan, but some may be of Jewish origin. These are decorated with many plant symbols, pomegranates, lotus flower rosettes, and vines. One is inscribed in both Hebrew and Aramaic with the name of the dead person entombed. The art of the sarcophagi belongs to the same period as that of the ossuaries. The symbol of the menorah or Torah shrine is absent. The symbols consist almost entirely of wreathes, "round objects," rosettes, vines, cups, doors, and columns.

Lamps from Jewish tombs also offer examples of symbolism. Lamps were so generally used that "they may have had a symbolic value which survives in the Christian identification of life with light, the hope for a new 'day,' the flaming candles from the Holy Sepulchre at the Orthodox Easter, and all other figures we use in which immortality is expressed as the emergence from darkness to light" (*Symbols*, 1. 48). Lamps at graves among pagans, Jews, and Christians suggest that all three groups had much in common in their attitude toward the dead.

In the second century after the destruction of the temple and the dispersal of the priesthood, a great change seems to have come over burial customs and Jewish symbolism as well. The arcade, which had formerly been the symbol of the entrance to tombs, now becomes a symbol on lamps, as earlier it had been on ossuaries. Eventually columns and facades became symbols in themselves. The wine symbol is also frequently found on lamps. Even more prevalent in lamps found throughout the Roman world is the symbol of the menorah.

Investigation of other objects commonly found in widely scattered Jewish tombs of the Roman Empire shows them to be of remarkable uniformity in symbolism. These were beads, bracelets, small glass vessels, either intact or in fragments, and also jugs, pots, bowls, saucers, and the like.

Chapter five treats the synagogues of Palestine. Was the ornamentation on the synagogues as on the tombs purely decorative, or did it have religious significance? Goodenough says, "In the end, whether the images and designs on the synagogues were symbolic or merely decorative must be determined by what images the Jews used, and when and how they used them, not by our own predilections" (*Symbols*, 1. 179). The synagogues are of three types. First is the Galilean synagogue. Archaeologists agree that these synagogues arose in the Hellenistic period and derive in their basic form from the ancient assembly house or basilica hall. Second is the broadhouse type, which shows a departure from the design of the Galilean type. The facade with its three doors was no longer placed on the sacred end nearest Jerusalem. It became conventional to put the three doors on the opposite wall, which permitted the worshipers to enter by them, and as they did so to face the building's center of religious interest, the Torah shrine. No longer is there a screen hiding the Torah shrine, but instead there is a niche or apse built into the wall toward Jerusalem into which the shrine was placed. Apparently a curtain took the place of the old screen. Another change was the introduction of mosaics.

The most famous of the broadhouse type of synagogue was not in Palestine but in Dura on the Euphrates. The second most famous was in Tunis. These synagogues are not of the basilica type; they have no columns and, consequently, no balcony for women. Goodenough surmises that the broadhouse synagogue was an early type, particularly popular and persistent in Palestine or Alexandria under Hellenistic or Roman influence.

The third type of synagogue is distinguished by floor mosaics. This type, whose floor plan can be reconstructed, shows another radical change. All but one are oriented toward Jerusalem—but oriented there by the narrow end, not like the broadhouses. In addition, these synagogues have a permanent apse in that wall built to house the Torah shrine. The entrance stands at the opposite end, as in a Christian church. Investigation of these synagogues strengthens Goodenough's opinion that mystic Judaism is expressed in their ornamentation. The use of animals, human figures, and even pagan deities contrasts radically with what the Pharisees considered proper. The return to the old standards, after the rise of rabbinic Judaism, brought about the destruction of this symbolic ornamentation, which flourished only in the interim between the fall of Jerusalem and the development and acceptance of the Talmud.

Are we dealing only with ornament, or are these symbols embraced by an unorthodox mystical Judaism? To Goodenough the latter conclusion is inevitable. Symbols buried in graves suggest eschatological hope. Synagogues with facades adapted from pagan temples came to represent the presence of deity. Synagogue interiors with the screen marking off the sacred place reflect the Jewish mystic feeling for the sacred. The apse and the screen still survive in the Orthodox Christian church. The transition from eschatology to mysticism is always easy, and Jewish symbols provide solid support for both. Everything about the synagogue suggests that Jews attended sabbath worship in hope of life beyond the grave, but at the same time with the intention of gaining a mystic sense of present sharing in that life.

Within this setting the inclusion of pagan symbols seemed appropriate. The synagogue ornaments of Helios, the zodiac, the seasons, the lions, the eagles, the cupids, and the omnipresent vines were not mere decorations. In fact they were symbols of immortality and of mystical achievement in life. Christians made them expressions of Christian hope by excluding mythology and adding Christian symbols. Certainly the Jews must have done the same.

II

Volume two deals with the archaeological evidence from the Diaspora and simply extends the investigations of volume one. Chapter one treats symbols used with Jewish burials in Rome, and the second chapter deals with symbols from Jewish burials in other parts of the Diaspora. Chapter three is devoted to synagogues in Greece, Asia Minor, Syria, and North Africa. Chapter four describes lamps and objects made of glass.

Chapter five presents a new phase of the study, the Judaism of the inscriptions on Jewish tombs and synagogues of the Greco-Roman period. They appear to come from a people so hellenized or Romanized in language that they could not comprehend the Talmud except in translation. There was a gulf between the hellenization of the inscriptions and the Semitism of the rabbis that was not to be bridged before the sixth or seventh century when the change to Hebrew in inscriptions in Italy shows that Jews had once again relearned their traditional language.

In the inscriptions of the Hellenistic period, Hebrew words appear such as "rest," "peace," or "be with the just," retained in Hebrew evidently as charm words with an eschatological orientation. At the same time some inscriptions suggest that faithful observance of the law was often celebrated. There is evidence that proselytes assumed Jewish names when they adopted the Jewish religion. Nothing from the inscriptions indicates a rabbinic type of Judaism, and they are more intelligible if understood in Philonic terms. If the art remains are to be called Hellenistic-Jewish because of the inseparable intermingling in them of Jewish and Hellenistic elements, the inscriptions are best understood against the same background.

Part four of the second volume treats charms and amulets. A charm is primarily a verbal incantation, whereas an amulet is an object designed to be worn on the person, although this distinction is often blurred. Goodenough begins his analysis of charms by questioning a common distinction made between religion and magic. Magic is supposed to employ material means to compel favorable actions by supernatural or divine powers. In contrast, religion supposedly uses only petition to appeal to divine powers. However, even in the "higher" religions there is expectation that religion must "pay off" or its devotees may be in danger of losing their faith. It is impossible to make a valid distinction between the magic of "lower" or "primitive" religions and the expectation in "higher" religions of the efficacy of a sacrament employing material means, be it water, or bread and wine thought to work *ex opere operato*. Magic turns out to be a term of judgment rather than of classification. Another person's sacrament with which I disagree becomes to me mere magic. Every religion that is broadly inclusive of all sorts of people will contain devotees of all levels of religious feeling and expression. What holds religions together is a common set of symbols and rituals. These may be used with a wide range of understanding, all the way from the intention of achieving a mystic union with God to that of warding off the evil eye. Not only so, but such contrasting religious purposes may reside, albeit unconsciously, within the same individual. It is in this light that Goodenough introduces Jewish magic and charms into the discussion of religious symbols of Judaism.

Jewish magic shows three characteristics: great respect for Hebrew phrases, a sense of the power of names, and an overwhelming regard for angels and demons, which extended into an elaborate angelolatry. The sources of information about the Jewish charms are rabbinic, Christian, and pagan. The charms show a range of types. At one extreme only Jewish elements appear; in the middle range both Jewish and pagan symbols are combined; and at the opposite extreme Jewish elements totally disappear and the charms are entirely pagan. There is no evidence to challenge the possibility that the syncretism may be ascribed to Jews themselves. In fact the charms provide a body of literary evidence of the religious "lower classes" of ancient Judaism.

In chapter seven Goodenough treats the evidence of the Jewish use of amulets. He distinguishes between charms, which are verbal ritualistic prescriptions, and amulets, which are things with symbols that operate merely by being worn on the person. Evidence shows that Jewish use of amulets goes far back in history The regalia of the high priest were amulets, and on a humbler level the prayer shawl and the *tefillin* of the ordinary worshiper were also amulets. Even though the rabbis consistently disapproved of figurative representations and amulets, they were widely used by Jews, and even by some rabbis themselves. Some amulets feature Jewish heroes such as Daniel, Jonah, or Solomon. The largest part of this chapter is taken up with syncretistic amulets showing both Jewish and pagan symbolism. Goodenough admits that with these amulets the problem of Jewish versus pagan origin becomes acute and can be dealt with only on a case by case basis. In the interpretation of Jewish and pagan symbols of the amulets the primary symbols are numerous: Hecate, the much-suffering eye, the tetragrammaton, birds, and the anguiped, which is the figure of the human body with a pair of snakes curved outward. Closely associated with the latter is the epithet "*Iao*" for God. Other symbols found on amulets are Helios, Chnoubis and other snakes, Egyptian figures, and finally Greek deities from the pantheon.

Goodenough admits the difficulty of deciding what part of this material can be taken as representing the life and thinking of Jews in the late Roman Empire. He examines at length the consecration of a magical ring which invokes a variety of pagan divinities, as well as the sacred name of the God of the Jews. Because of the fervency of the Jewish elements, he has to conclude that it represents a widespread form of Judaism of the Roman period. He describes it as a Judaism "of a group still intensely loyal to Iao Sabaoth, a group which buried its dead and built its synagogues with a marked sense that it was a peculiar people in the eyes of a God, but which accepted the best of paganism (including its most potent charms) as focusing in, and finding its meaning in, the supreme Iao Sabaoth" (*Symbols*, 2. 295).

III

The third volume is devoted entirely to illustrations of objects analyzed in volumes one and two. The illustrations include black-and-white photographs, line drawings of artifacts, and ground plans of buildings. There are complete indexes of the material. The diversity of sources and the thoroughness of the entire volume attest to the great and patient industry that Goodenough devoted to the entire work.

Not until the fourth volume does Goodenough deal with the question of method for the study of the symbols. The first chapter treats the rabbinic evidence. Modern scholars have persisted in the view that Jewish symbols became mere decoration, since the Jews did not adopt the pagan meanings. This is to assume that the rabbinic prohibition against image making was in authority everywhere. Ultimately, however, scholars have had to recognize the existence of widespread non-Talmudic Judaism, and in this Judaism ornamentation could be adopted, since the pagan interpretation of the symbols had been abandoned. Goodenough contends that these Jews employed the symbols to express Jewish piety and hopes. In the absence of literary evidence, Jewish motives for employing these symbols must be found through analysis of the art itself.

The very time when Jews were ornamenting graves and synagogues was also the time when the antipathy of Jews to images was the most intense. It was the period of the dominance of the Hasidim and the Pharisees (150 B.C. to A.D. 70). Josephus declares that images were completely forbidden. Steeped though he was in Hellenism, even Philo was as opposed to images as any Pharisee. Since the mass of Jews of this period were loyal to the Torah, how can we account for their adoption of pagan art forms in their synagogues, tombs, amulets, and charms? Did pagan ideas actually penetrate Jewish worship, or is the art merely used for decoration? Is it possible that the symbols, thoroughly Judaized in meaning, served as aids to worship?

More than historical study is necessary. The symbols must be examined from the viewpoint of psychology. It is necessary to distinguish between denotive thinking, which endeavors to convey a single definite idea as objectively as possible, and connotive thinking, which is difficult to convey in words. Yet connotive thinking is our most important thinking, and it is this way of thinking that employs symbolism for much of its expression. Religious symbols not only convey meaning but also exercise power, as demonstrated by the Nazi swastika or the Christian cross. Symbols may die yet come alive again. Christians adopted and revived a failed symbol, the cross, which had degenerated into a mere rosette.

The phenomenon of the migration of symbols can be observed in the adaptation and reinterpretation into Catholic Christianity of former pagan symbols which persisted both in Jewish and Christian art: the lion, the winged victory, and the wreath. These were not mere ornaments but live symbols. They were rationalized in a new religious environment, and they provided a lingua franca for most of the religions of that day. Orpheus could become Christ because he was no longer the figure of Greek myth, but represented the mastery of the passions by the spirit. Helios drawing his chariot through the zodiac could be used by Jews because he was no longer an anthropomorphic god but the Neoplatonic divine principle.

If continuity of symbolic values can be demonstrated in a wide variety of religions, "it would establish meanings for the lingua franca which, as they seem to have stability in other religions, would increasingly suggest themselves as the values of the symbols also for Jews" (*Symbols*, 4. 37). The cup, the vine, and the grape are symbols common both to Orphism and to Christianity, and in both religions they symbolize mystic union with the saving god. The meaning of any symbol is not denotive but connotive, yet it is as clearly grasped by the devout worshiper as meaning expressed in words. It is this language which the historian of symbols must understand.

There is no danger, as Carl Jung feared, that symbolism will overwhelm us. The danger lies rather in the chaos of formlessness against which the symbol protects us. The conflict between science and religion is not between connotive, i.e., primitive ways of thinking, and denotive or discursive thinking. If denotive thinking should completely displace connotive thinking we would have ceased to be human. "Religion will take on fresh life as it becomes less bound to the discursive and more free to create metaphorically" (*Symbols*, 4. 39). It is crucial for us to understand the nonliteral, symbolic mentality. The symbols under study are prehistoric in origin, yet have a continuing potency that today is often ignored. The modern abandonment of religion appears to coincide with a widespread sense of meaninglessness in life.

For long ages human beings evidently lived as animals; this was followed by a long period in which humans had subliterate, subdiscursive intelligence. "Upon these two stages most of us have now superimposed rationality in the full sense. All three of these levels are still represented in all of us" (*Symbols*, 4. 40). Related to our present sense of confusion is the fact that our educational system is directed almost entirely to rational treatment of literal facts. At the same time we accept our animal nature, yet we put aside as childish our subliteral thinking. Freud has recalled to us the power of this element of our human make-up. We study symbols to understand how they continue to exercise power over us.

Freud shows the paradoxes of human nature, in which conflicting impulses constantly confront each other. "Religion . . . has offered man psychic therapy because it has recognized these opposites in his nature, and combined them. . . . A proper religious symbol presents this paradox directly to the believer. The agony, distortion, and death of the cross bring one into divine peace" (*Symbols*, 4. 41). Symbols provide a language of paradox. Meaning in religion may well derive from the power of its symbols, or symbolic acts, to effect a resolution of the believer's inner conflicts. The believer faces inner dissolution "if he must lose the old symbols without finding meaning or value in new ones" (*Symbols*, 4. 42). Rational argument will not usually resolve this struggle. Jews and Christians, as they adapted symbols from paganism, rejected their mythological explanations. "In taking over the symbols, while discarding the myths and explanations of the pagans, Jews and Christians admitted, indeed confirmed, a continuity of religious experience which it is most important to be able to identify" (*Symbols*, 4. 42).

The vocabulary of Jewish symbols was extremely limited. Since only selected designs were acceptable to the Jews who employed them, symbolic rather than decorative value must have governed their choice. The frequent crudity of the designs also suggests this. The Jewish vocabulary of symbols was exactly that of early Christian symbols borrowed from paganism. This suggests that pagan emblems came to early Christianity not directly but by way of Jewish usage. On graves and synagogues Jewish and pagan symbols are so freely intermingled that if the menorah appears among peacocks, wreaths, and birds it seems likely that the use of all the designs reflects the same religious attitude. Finally, the location of these symbols suggests that they had value for the entire worshiping group. There is no literature telling of the Judaism that used such symbolism, but there can be no doubt that such a Judaism existed. With the completion and dissemination of the Talmud and the beginning of Christian persecution of the Jews, it is likely that such Judaism was abolished and along with it whatever literature it had produced. It is only the study of the symbols themselves and their use that can inform us of the community that produced them.

The most important of the symbols that became a lingua franca in the Hellenistic-Roman world of religion were originally Dionysiac, but somewhat expanded by symbols from Syria, Egypt, and Mesopotamia. If this lingua franca can be deciphered, it will be possible to identify the basic value which passed with the symbol as long as it was alive. Symbols rather than mythological scenes predominated. "The lingua franca had, apparently, come to speak not necessarily of cult or myth at all, but of something else, and of this in its own right" (*Symbols*, 4. 47).

Goodenough sketches the steps necessary to discover what Dionysus came to mean to the Greeks in terms of religious experience. It would require tracing the development from the myth of a phallic god or fertility through the concept of Dionysus, whose rites promised immortality, each change lineally connected with the older stage until "the process could be carried to the heights reached in Plato's *Symposium* where Eros leads the soul to the Form of Beauty" (*Symbols*, 4. 47). In the succeeding volumes Goodenough traces the history of each symbol. He is confident that the persisting value of the symbols will be as much a historical fact as literary and archaeological data and would be of equal concern to the historian. Also of great importance is the study of the symbols from the point of view of psychology.

Goodenough's psychology begins from the presupposition of the basic human drive for life or "life urge," which is most immediately expressed in eating and in sex. "The great symbols of the life urge are . . . of three basic kinds: they are the symbols of hunting or fighting, the symbols of food and eating (or of the sources of food—the winds, rain, the sun, etc.), and the symbols of sex" (*Symbols*, 4. 50). These themes give the meanings of the majority of religious symbols. The child's relations to parents (primarily the mother) during infancy is another source of religious symbolism. Insecurity, fear, uncertainty, and hunger are all lost in the presence and care of the mother. This blissful experience is eventually lost as the infant matures. The loving goddess now grows stern and imposes incomprehensible restrictions and prohibitions. Monotheism is replaced by polytheism as the infant is now confronted by other great figures, even though the mother is still supreme.

This experience as a whole, first of gratification, then of deprivation, needs to be more fully stressed in discussions of religion. It furnishes the basis of at least one of the most important patterns of religion. It is reflected in the craving for self-realization through absorption of the true Being, the craving for life after death, for atonement and reconciliation, for rebirth and the abiding presence of the comforter. "The 'mystic marriage' in the form of union with the temple prostitute or with the Church, the bride of Christ, is really a union with the Great Mother, a return to her intimate care. We love the picture of the Christian version of this theme, Mary the Mother with her Child, for each of us is the child" (*Symbols*, 4. 52).

In the next stage of development children still need the love and approval they formerly had, but now these no longer come as a free gift. The mother goddess has become a male-female duality. Children now find that the ultimate authority is the father; they must obey the law, which is a codification of the whims and fancies of the father. The sanctions consist of the father-mother displeasure. The "superego" is forming at this time. The mother becomes the intercessor with the father. The fully "compulsory" stage as postulated by Freud goes beyond this. As law becomes more elaborate, mediation becomes less significant. Out of this can come a religion like talmudic Judaism, in which the mother element has become quite obscured. Mercy is not absent from such religion, and there is provision for repentance and reinstatement, but these provisions were never so important in Judaism as to produce a divine personality to execute them. Judaism is a strongly social religion embodied in the family and the entire social unit. In contrast, little of social importance came out of the cult of the Great Mother or of the Virgin. "The social aspects of religion first became important as the father became central, and the tendency reached its logical end when it produced a sense of the Father-God's universal rightness, and of universal Right" (*Symbols*, 4. 53).

This kind of religion gains its hold upon its followers through conditioned behavior. This in Judaism is brought about by the family celebration of the festivals. The ultimate result of such a religion is the binding of the believer to a compulsory pattern of life with the father. Goodenough distinguishes two patterns of religion, the narcissistic mother pattern and the compulsory pattern of legalism, although he recognizes that the great religions contain both patterns. Christianity with its Old Testament heritage and the teachings of Jesus "predicated a relation between a Father and his children, while the Greek contribution of Paul, of the Fourth Gospel, and of the early Greek Christians was in the direction of a personal religion of salvation which in emotional pattern resembled much more the ancient fertility cults than the teachings of the rabbis" (*Symbols*, 4. 53–54). Investigations of Jewish symbolism convinced Goodenough that the Jews who made and used the symbols found in them a meaning that was the most repugnant to the rabbis. He was surprised that the basic value of every symbol was erotic. Consequently, he had to reexamine the role of eroticism in Greek society.[3]

---

[3] This discussion, although evidently based on sound archaeological evidence and upon recognized psychological theory, raises an interesting question. To what degree are Goodenough's analysis and interpretation colored by his own early religious experience and his later partial repudiation of it?

In our own day of sexual repression, said Goodenough, phallic symbolism is usually thought of as arising from a suppressed desire for sexual
experience.[4] In ancient Greece and Egypt with their utter frankness in
the use of sexual symbolism there must have been another meaning.
"Everything indicates that the early devotee wanted by means of his
phallic rites to be gratified with good, and with the perpetuation of his
life" (Symbols, 4. 55). "It was the most obvious kind of sympathetic
magic to try to make a field fertile by setting up a phallus in it, or by
simulating or actually performing intercourse on it or for it" (Symbols,
4. 56). Developing civilization began to distinguish between the spiritual
and the fleshly, between pure and impure, and the symbols lost their
directness. Cupids finally supplanted the satyrs who survived in iconography only as devils—in Christianity as tempters to sexuality, which is
sin and therefore taboo. In this "refinement" of sexual symbolism Goodenough finds the historical antitype of material found in psychoanalysis,
repression of overt sexual symbolism in religion as society demanded.

If the religion of mysticism is to be understood in the image of the
infant seeking to find complete gratification in the mother goddess, why
are the symbols of mystical experience almost universally those of sex?
The answer may be that with the onset of puberty the boy senses the
awakening of the old drive to complete himself in someone else, but now
with a new sense of accomplishing it. The Great Mother, of whom he
still dreams, becomes the Virgin Mother. The immediate projection of
the mother is sought afresh by the mature man in a young virgin. Goodenough believes that this quest for life in the mother produced formal
religious and mystical symbolism, and the symbols of the fertility cults
were the most natural to be developed and perpetuated.

Religion evolves through finding new meaning in old symbols rather
than by developing new forms. This is a three-stage process. First, the sex
symbol is the instrument of literal fertility magic. Later, the sex symbol or
sex acts were used as means for achieving union with deity. Finally, in the
"higher" religions all conscious references to the sexual act were abandoned
in order that religion might achieve "higher" gratification. The sex act is
deplored or despised. This produces an anomaly. "The greatest single tension in most 'higher' religions is precisely the tension between spirit and
body—sex as means to union and life as over against religion, which seems
to achieve its goal in the individual in proportion to his renunciation of the
sexual act" (Symbols, 4. 58). At the same time, in the "higher" religions less
crudely sexual symbols such as the dove and erotic metaphors of mysticism
have lived on. In ancient Egypt there developed the idea of the god as

---

[4] Goodenough stated this opinion in 1954 (Symbols, 4. 55). What might he have said in
the 1980s with the apparent great relaxation in sexual mores in American society?

hermaphroditic. God as father, mother, and child all at the same time is a reflection of this concept.

In halakic Judaism the image of Wisdom as the distinct mother appears so infrequently as to suggest that it marks an invasion of foreign symbolism. In such Judaism the devotee is the son, but the mystical element of identification has been repressed. The way to the father is through obedience. "It is in religions centering not in obedience, but in the birth and death and resurrection of the god or his son, that mystical assimilation of the devotee with the Father, or Father-Mother, is the objective" (*Symbols*, 4. 58–59). In such mystical experience comes the resolution of the "Oedipus conflict" and the problems of the vagaries of the "id." The life urge comes to such full satisfaction that even death loses its terror. It seems likely that such a concept of mysticism lay behind the movement of Orphism, which appealed only to a minority, the majority being satisfied merely with the performance of religious rituals. Yet it is always the devout, the fanatics, who discover the real meaning of the symbols of religion.

Goodenough believes that by means of the foregoing analysis the meaning of the ancient symbolic lingua franca of religion will be seen more clearly. The symbols which both Jews and Christians borrowed from paganism "relentlessly trace back to a common body of symbolic roots . . . used in other religions always . . . as emblems of a certain type of religious experience" (*Symbols*, 4. 59). In the official religions, which expressed themselves in fixed laws and observances, the ideas that the symbols expressed were either ignored, as in the case of the official religions of Athens or Rome, or relentlessly repressed and abolished, as in the case of the Yahwism of the Jews. "These symbols were of use only in religions that engendered deep emotion, ecstasy—religions directly and consciously centered in the renewing of life and the granting of immortality, in the giving to the devotee of a portion of the divine spirit or life substance" (*Symbols*, 4. 59–60). These symbols, which became central to Christianity, had been prominent in the popular religion of both Greeks and Romans. These are the symbols that were found in the graves and used in the synagogues of Jews throughout the Roman Empire.

These symbols indicate the type of mystic Judaism of which Philo is the leading spokesman. This Judaism was superimposed upon Jewish legalism with its code of instructions on how to please God in this life. The mystic form of religion promised a way to renounce the life of the flesh altogether, to rise "into the richness of divine existence, to appropriate God's life into oneself" (*Symbols*, 4. 60). This could be symbolized in a variety of ways, sometimes as achievement of life through death depicted in hunting scenes, or in the sacrificial systems of pagans and Jews, or the Christian image of Christ as the slain lamb. The experience could also be depicted as achievement of victory in conflict. This would account for the various symbols of victory found in Jewish synagogues and on graves.

The mystic quest for appropriation of divine life might also be depicted as birth or as the obtaining of the divine fluid symbolized by the cup for all alike, pagans, Jews, and Christians. For all three religions the vine was depicted as holding manifold symbols of life. The experience could also be represented by the zodiac, the planets, the cosmos with which humanity unites itself. Fruits depicted in the synagogues and on tombs could symbolize identification of one's being with the great cycle of death and resurrection in nature. Although these ideas have no place in normative Judaism, Goodenough finds no surprise in them after his long study of Philo. Philo was one who thought in these terms to find the deepest meaning of the Torah.

Following this statement of his methodology, Goodenough devotes the remainder of volume four to the symbols of the Jewish cult. These include the menorah, the Torah shrine, the *lulab* and *ethrog*, the *shofar*, and the incense shovel. He says that it is striking to note the differences between modern and ancient Jewish practices regarding cult objects. Ritual continues to hold high importance for the modern orthodox Jew, but its symbolic value lies in conformity rather than in any inherent symbolism in the cult objects themselves. In contrast to this, in ancient times after the fall of Jerusalem, symbols of the temple and of temple festivals began to appear everywhere, especially on Jewish graves. He believes that these Jewish objects were transformed into symbols used in devotion and that they took on a personal, direct value. The most arresting fact is that the Jews devised their Jewish symbols for personal use at the precise time when symbols were of the greatest importance in all religions. Not only so, but we find the Jews mingling their own symbols with borrowings from paganism, such as the cup and sheaf of wheat of Dionysus-Demeter, the sistrum of Isis, or the zodiac. Goodenough remarks, "It seems to me incredible that we should find the Jewish and pagan symbols thus together if Jews of that day had not felt that the symbolic values of both were very similar" (*Symbols*, 4. 70).

In the fourth chapter of volume four he examines the menorah or seven-branched candlestick, reminiscent of the seven-branched lamp of the temple. Although the rabbis forbade the reproduction of the menorah with seven branches, allowing only those of five, six, or eight branches, it was precisely the seven-branched type that became almost the universal symbol of Judaism. In spite of a variety of meanings assigned to the menorah by scholars, Goodenough promises his reader that examination of a variety of sources will indicate one underlying deeper meaning. The inscriptions indicate that the menorah was the symbol of God by virtue of its lights. For Josephus and Philo the menorah represents the Light of the world, or Logos, "God's mercy revealed to the Jew in at once a cosmic and a Jewish sense" (*Symbols*, 4. 87). The rabbinic literature generally repeats the command against the use of the seven-branched menorah and with but few exceptions ignores symbolic use of it. In the *Midrash Rabbah* on Exod 27:20 the menorah is interpreted as symbolic of salvation in the messianic age, and later in comment on Num 8:1–2 it tells that Moses was unable to make a menorah until God traced the pattern with his finger, a surprisingly Hellenistic explanation. In the *Zohar* it is said that the menorah is illumined by the "supernal Mother," which suggested to Goodenough Philo's Sarah, who is heavenly virtue, or Sophia, who also is the Logos. He concludes, "The menorah concentrates all Jewish hopes as it manifests God's mercy and forgiveness and his incomparable provision for salvation. It was a popular symbol precisely because, like all good symbols, it could be given so many interpretations" (*Symbols*, 4. 96).

In the fifth chapter Goodenough takes up the symbolism of the Torah shrine. In the rabbinic tradition the sanctity of the shrine derives almost entirely from the scrolls within, whereas in ancient Judaism the shrine seemed to have a sanctity of its own, much as in earlier Israel the ark of the covenant became a sacred object. In the shrine in antiquity the façade had special significance. Goodenough reaffirms a view expressed in an earlier volume that the shrine symbolized the heavenly Jerusalem in the form of the "house of Peace," the "house eternal."[5] He concludes the chapter with an examination of the significance of the scroll. Sometimes Jews of the Greco-Roman period abbreviated the shrine symbol simply as a Torah scroll. This may reflect both Egyptian and Greek custom as demonstrated in little scrolls in the hands of the dead in Roman sarcophagi. The scroll so used would seem to symbolize the hope of salvation through prayer and knowledge. "While gentiles, as is reported, were buried with their sacred scrolls, Jews naturally had the Torah scrolls carved on their tombstones" (*Symbols*, 4. 144).

Chapter six deals with the *lulab* and the *ethrog*. The *lulab* was the ceremonial branch or palm leaves carried in procession during the feast of Tabernacles. The *ethrog* was a particular citrus fruit also carried during the procession. Goodenough traces the origin and practice of the feast of Tabernacles, and he examines the development of its meaning as shown in Jewish and some pagan sources. He finds evidence of Hellenistic influence upon this development. To the Jews the *lulab* was basically a palm branch. It became symbolic of "what the palm branch meant to pagans, and to Christians later—the hope and achievement of immortality or of mystic consummation" (*Symbols*, 4. 165). The *lulab* and *ethrog* together were symbols of hope.

5 Goodenough, *Symbols*, 1. 75–76, 2. 113, 141.

Chapter seven deals with the *shofar*, or ram's horn. Of several interpretations he gives greatest attention to "that which connects the blowing of the shofar with the sacrifice or 'binding' of Isaac, the Akedah" (*Symbols*, 4. 172). The rabbinic explanation of the Akedah is the story of Isaac spared from sacrifice by divine intervention, whereas the Hellenistic Jewish conception is that Isaac actually became the eternal sacrifice "atoning by his merit for all men who blow the shofar" (*Symbols*, 4. 193). Goodenough is quick to suggest the common ancestry in Hellenism of this view and also the Christian understanding of Christ as the atoning sacrifice. He also sees influence of Hellenism upon the thinking of later rabbis, and he concludes that the symbol of the *shofar* carved on Jewish tombs represents the hope for future life.

Finally, in chapter nine Goodenough examines the symbolism of the incense shovel. In his summary conclusion regarding all the symbols treated in volume four he reaffirms his surmise that all the cult objects displayed on either synagogues or tombs in the Greco-Roman world were "Jewish substitutes for pagan symbols similarly used" (*Symbols*, 4. 209). If the question is asked, What kind of people produced all this art? the proper answer is that it was produced by Jews intensely loyal to their faith. However, such Jews lived in the Greco-Roman world, and this encouraged them to raise new questions stimulated by their environment. The first was, How could Judaism take one from the material to the immaterial? The second was, How could Judaism take one into blissful immortality? For Philo and other Alexandrian Jews the answer seemed to be in conceiving Judaism as the true mystery offering release from bondage to the flesh into the freedom of immaterial reality.

Volumes one to three of *Symbols* were not published until 1953, and volume four followed in 1954. A letter to John Barrett of the Bollingen Foundation on 18 November 1947 reveals how publication had become a possibility.[6] Goodenough mentions that he had written to Dr. Carl Jung in Zurich to obtain his endorsement, since Jung, of course, had been instrumental in the establishment of the Bollingen Foundation.[7] Goodenough was writing personally to apply for a subvention from the foundation. His request was successful, and Bollingen ultimately published the entire thirteen volumes. He mentions that on the strength of a single chapter from volume three of *Symbols*, in addition to his earlier publications, in June of 1947 Hebrew Union College had conferred upon him the degree of Doctor of Hebrew Letters. The assistance that he received from Bollingen brought sufficient funds for him to hire a research assistant to type the entire manuscript, verify the thousands of

---

[6] Unpublished letter (Archives of Yale University; Erwin R. Goodenough Papers; Yale University Library). Used by permission.

[7] "Paul Mellon: Great Gifts from Great Fortunes," *Smithsonian* 14 (1983) 101–2.

references, and to have photographs taken, paid for, and arranged. Without this help he would have had to do all such routine work himself. In a particularly moving paragraph he explains why his need is so pressing.

> Years spent in such drudgery would seem all the more tragic to me since with the completion of this work I shall at last be ready to begin the work I have all my life preparing to do, namely to write an equally extensive study of the origin of Christianity in view of all the new material I shall have presented on its Jewish and symbolic background. I am by no means an old man, only 54, but old enough so that the completion of this whole program will require steady application.

He had explained earlier in the letter that he had been engaged in the work on symbols for twelve years. Elsewhere in the letter he presents a concise summary of the entire argument of *Symbols*. It deserves to be printed here.

> The Jews of (the Greco-Roman) period, living for the most part before the Talmud was written, and so with only their Bible (in Greek translation) to go by, kept their devotion to the Torah, to their festivals and Sabbaths and dietary laws as well as they could simply from their Bible and from local and unstandardized traditions. They were certainly loyal to Judaism as they understood it, or they would not have continued building their synagogues in the teeth of pagan, and later Christian, opposition. But the symbols seem to tell us that these Jews were led by the growing Gnosticism, Neo-Platonism, and other forms of mysticism. That is, I believe that in these centuries was laid the foundation for the type of Judaism which later flowered and persisted as Cabala. When a rabbinate based upon the legalism of the Talmud became supreme it suppressed the mystical type of Judaism (or the mystical types, for there must have been varieties), drove it out of general favor, but could not prevent its continuing and reviving in such medieval Cabalism as the *Zohar*. This the borrowed pagan symbols and the biblical illustrations at Dura seem to me to agree in telling us.
>
> Since written texts from the Jews who used this art do not exist, the method of research by which the symbols are evaluated has to be to take the symbols and paintings themselves, but primarily the symbols, and to trace them as they go from one religion to another. These symbols quickly reveal themselves as the essential vocabulary of the lingua franca of most religions of antiquity, one which still survives in Christianity. I limit myself to the historical field, that is I trace the symbols only in their manifestations in contiguous ancient religions from early Mesopotamia and Egypt down to the late Roman Empire and Christianity. I do not consider the problem presented by the appearance of many of these symbols in far-flung cultures which could have had no external contact with the religions of classical antiquity whence they come into Jewish usage. That is a problem which

would take me far beyond my powers, though I am trying to
present what I do in a way which would be of use for larger and
deeper generalizations. But even tracing the symbols from one
religion to another in antiquity forces one to open up the general
subject of the nature of religious symbols. I have reached the
conclusion that while each religion gives symbols its own explanation, in terms of its own gods and myths, there is a constant religious "value" as I am calling it which a symbol never loses in
such transition. The presumption would then be that Jews felt
free to borrow the symbol because they wanted the "value" the
symbols represented for their own religion, and had found a way
to explain that value in terms of their own traditions or biblical
proof-texts.

Critical reviews of Goodenough's work indicate that other scholars found
it difficult to be persuaded that a lingua franca of religious symbols actually existed or, if it did, that Jews would knowingly have used it.

A review in 1955 by Salo W. Baron of *Symbols* 1–4 indicates how the
work was initially received.[8] Baron describes only volume three as "rela-
tively definitive," and he regrets that Goodenough had not included all of
the ancient Jewish symbols and amulets available, although his volume
offers the largest compilation of such material. Baron agrees with Goodenough's criticism of older scholars who tended to interpret archaeological
finds in terms of literary records. Baron sees this work on symbols as largely
a continuation of Goodenough's "daringly brilliant exposition" in *By Light,
Light* of the highly differentiated system of Hellenistic Judaism. Yet Goodenough was not alone, since other scholars, including Baron himself, had
recognized Hellenistic influences on Diaspora Judaism.

Baron's main criticism concerns Goodenough's methodology. Is any
investigator of ancient art and archaeology justified in seeing every synagogue or tomb decoration "as a meaningful symbol with some ritualistic or
mystic significance?" (Baron, p. 198). Goodenough goes too far in denying
the possibility that some ornaments or designs had a purely decorative purpose. A non-Jewish artisan might have supplied a particular object with
decorations which might convey hidden pagan implications of which the
Jewish client was totally unaware. However, Goodenough's "sustained
effort to marshal all available evidence and to set up guideposts for its
uniform and consistent interpretation is a major contribution to learning"
(Baron, p. 198).

In 1958 Samuel Sandmel, one of Goodenough's most distinguished
pupils, published a review of volumes four through six.[9] He begins: "The
appearance of these three additional volumes in Goodenough's great
work ought to excite every student of Judaism and of Christian origins"
(Sandmel, p. 380). He surmises that the series had been noticed by few

---

[8] Baron, *Journal of Biblical Literature* 74 (1955) 196–99.
[9] Sandmel, *Journal of Biblical Literature* 77 (1958) 380–83.

scholars and read and studied by even fewer. He suggests several reasons for this: first, the expense of the volumes; second, perhaps, the daring thesis of these volumes, which is out of the way of much scholarly research (some scholars may prefer to hold to established views rather than be challenged by new ones); third, the fact that Goodenough's volumes appeared at the precise time "that the Dead Sea scrolls changed from a novelty into a fad" (Sandmel, p. 380). He is persuaded that had Goodenough's materials been discovered in a cave rather than assembled from some of the world's finest libraries, their importance would be seen as outshining that of the scrolls, important as these are. When the frenzy over the scrolls passes away, "Goodenough's work will receive the careful attention which it deserves" (Sandmel, p. 380).

Although in his first volume Goodenough discussed the nature of the problem that he proposed to investigate—namely, how the rapid hellenization of early Christianity was made possible through the agency of Hellenistic Judaism, and how the hellenizing of Judaism had to be studied through art and archaeology, since literary evidence is lacking—he did not give a careful statement of his method until volume four. Sandmel believes that in the absence of such a statement, the first reviewers of Goodenough's work did not so much misunderstand it as fall short of understanding it. With Goodenough's statement of his methodology in view, scholars can now discuss the main focus of the work, the meaning of the artifacts and the art. Scholars should debate whether Goodenough's methodology is sound or unsound. Sandmel, although he disagrees with many of the details of Goodenough's interpretation, finds himself in basic agreement with Goodenough's fundamental, principal contentions. Yet, whether one agrees or disagrees, Goodenough's work "represents religious scholarship in its best and most admirable dimensions. Moreover, its focus is not on comparatively remote matters, but on the central problems of early Christianity and Judaism of its time" (Sandmel, p. 383).

6
JEWISH SYMBOLS IN THE GRECO-ROMAN WORLD
Part Two

Because of the massive nature of Goodenough's work, there is the danger that any attempt to report it might degenerate into a catalogue, and catalogues may be dull except for those with specialized interests. However, anyone whose interest in *Jewish Symbols* has been stimulated by what has been described thus far ought to gain some notion of the subjects treated in the remaining volumes. To appreciate truly Goodenough's contribution to scholarship, it is essential to have some sense of the scope of the great endeavor that occupied the last thirty years of his life. Of greatest interest, and perhaps controversy, are his conclusions. These will receive our closest attention.

V

Volume five is the first of two volumes that deal with the symbols of fish, bread, and wine. In the preface Goodenough reviews the first four volumes, stating their contents, their purpose, and some account of criticism by other scholars. In the first chapter he considers creatures of the sea. Although it has long been assumed that the fish was a Christian symbol and a symbol in paganism, few scholars have suggested that the fish might also be a symbol in Judaism. Examination of Jewish monuments of the Greco-Roman period shows that the fish was used by Jews with regularity as a sacred magical symbol. Jewish representations of dolphins and marine monsters must also be included in the category with fish.

In chapter two Goodenough points out that frequently in the West the fish is substituted for the wine in representations of the Last Supper. The eucharistic significance of bread and fish apart from the wine seems clear. He follows the outline of Isidor Scheftelowitz, who in 1911 suggested that the fish symbol had come into Christianity by way of Judaism. In Judaism the fish had four symbolic meanings: (1) the faithful as little fishes; (2) the fish as messiah; (3) the fish as a sacramental or eucharistic food; and (4) the fish as a symbol of the hope of immortality.

Chapter three discusses the symbolism of bread, which on the monuments is represented either as a "round object" or as contained in baskets. That bread is so represented on tombs suggests that the bread was recognized as sacred food. The symbolic meaning of the bread is best considered in connection with the interpretation of the festival of First Fruits. Goodenough concludes that representation of bread on the tombs "marked the true Jew, the accepted Jew, the Jew who had *sōtēria*, salvation or security, even in the face of death" (*Symbols*, 5. 90). The Gospel of John furnishes clues to the symbolic value that bread had for the Jews. Jesus identifies himself with the manna, the bread from heaven. The eating of this bread—namely, himself—grants immortality. Philo demonstrates a similar line of thought. Goodenough says "In his most important passage on the subject, manna is made directly into the heavenly food of the soul. It consists of the *logoi* that God pours out like rain" (*Symbols*, 5. 91).

Chapter four begins one of the most extended segments of Goodenough's study, the symbolism of wine. It occupies the remainder of volume five and all of volume six. He begins with symbols of wine in Jewish archaeology. The problem raised by these remains is whether there was a Jewish sacramental drinking of wine in this period which symbolized (or realized) mystic achievement and brought immortality. The evidence for this cannot be adequately considered until the pagan background is reviewed. Much more than wine itself must be considered. In ancient times other fluids were associated with divinity: water, blood, semen from the gods, and milk from the divine breasts. Most of these symbols eventually coalesced in the later symbolism of the vine and the sacramental wine. The task at hand, therefore, is "to reconstruct from early times the persistent notion of the divine fluid as the source of life and see how in the hellenistic and Roman period especially this fluid came supremely to represent itself in the sacramental cup of wine" (*Symbols*, 5. 113).

Chapter five presents the evidence of the divine fluid in Mesopotamia and Syria, and chapter six gives evidence from ancient Egypt. Goodenough notes that as in Mesopotamia, so in Egypt, some concept of "fluid in general" will be more helpful for our understanding than specifically wine. For the Egyptians the dead must be furnished with fluid of some sort in order to be able to hope for immortality. In examining Egyptian imagery Goodenough gives considerable attention to phallicism in later Egypt. Numerous images and texts celebrate the fructifying, life-giving power of the semen of the god, represented by the erect phallus. The same theme is expressed in hermaphroditic figures. Another common figure in Egypt, which is also observed in Mesopotamia, is that of getting divinity through being nursed by the goddess. Also in Egypt is found the combination of the imagery of light with representations of water, both suggesting ritualistic ceremonies of purification. Volume five concludes with a generous number of illustrations, either in photographic reproductions or line drawings of many of the images that are discussed in the chapter.

VI

Volume six concludes the study of wine symbolism, first in the religions of Greece, next in various forms of religious syncretism, and finally in the Jewish cult and observances. Chapter seven is devoted to examination of the concept of divine fluid in Greece. Goodenough cautions that because of the great diversity of religions in Greece, generalizations about Greek religion are dangerous. Greek religion may be classified according to three types: (1) local cults of great diversity; (2) the religion of the twelve Olympians whose Bible was Homer; and (3) mystic forms of religion, the "religion of the vertical path," by which devotees sought to rise to share in the divine nature and so achieve immortality. This goal was sought chiefly through the cult of Dionysus, whose worship was symbolized primarily through the cup and the grape. Dionysus was *par excellence* the god of fertility. Apart from the wine, the chief symbol of Dionysus is the phallus. Another symbol of Dionysus is fire, and myth refers to his "fiery origin." The modern reader must understand that for the Greek fire was but another fluid.

In addition to the symbols already considered, the Greeks also held a conception of fluid in general. It was thought that this idea came to them from the Egyptians. The thought that all things had their origin in water seems to have arisen from the analogy of water and seminal fluid. Milk, also a symbol of the god, was as closely associated with Dionysus as wine. Goodenough is convinced that the god Dionysus was a product of a sense of superhuman value in fluid, be it wine or milk. The study of wine symbols, the phallus, and hermaphroditism, together with their association with graves, leads Goodenough to the conclusion "that Greeks and imperial Romans had a vivid sense that wine and love represented their chief hope of immortality" (*Symbols*, 6. 59). Moreover, the symbols were more important than the personalities of the god with which they were associated, and the hope of life presented in the symbol had far greater reality than any myth or rationalization.

Chapter eight describes Dionysiac syncretism in Syria and Egypt. Goodenough says that in the effort to trace the symbols of fluid and wine from their early beginning to their use by Christians and Jews we cannot stop with the Greeks. It is important to see with what sorts of gods the Dionysiac symbols came to be used in Syria and Egypt. Goodenough investigates symbols from Baalbek, Palmyra, and the Hauran. In this region the interchange of solar and Dionysiac symbols on graves and temples is clear. They seem to imply the hope of sharing in the divine nature to be assured not only of getting their crops but even more of gaining eternal life.

The hellenization of the Egyptian gods appears to have begun with the earliest contacts between the two peoples. Goodenough traces the evidence through the earliest Greek writers, Plutarch, Philo Judaeus, authors of the Hermetica, and others. The literary evidence is confirmed by the iconography. From the literary and iconographic record of Greco-Egyptian syncretism Goodenough draws two conclusions. First, the Greek symbols are alive, and the Alexandrian tomb symbols are not mere decorations but are poignant expressions of the hope for immortality. Second, the basic symbols are those of sun or light, of bread, and of wine. He says, "It is bread and fluid in the form of light or wine which offer the hope for immortality" (*Symbols*, 6. 92). He surmises that evidence will show that ultimately the Jews also found in the symbols of bread and wine the promise of immortality. However, before turning to such evidence, it is necessary to see how the symbols continued in later syncretism.

In chapter seven Goodenough examines the symbolism of the divine fluid in four areas. The first is in some of the rites and teachings of gnostic sects. Here sexual and phallic imagery is persistent as symbolic both of generation and regeneration of life. The second area, that of later paganism, is represented in the religious experiences of Apuleius, in some of the Orphic hymns, and in Iamblichus. Notable in Apuleius is the sublimation of the sexual imagery. In Apuleius's veiled description of the rites of the mysteries of Isis, Goodenough observes, "With no trace of an overt phallic symbol in all the rites or emblems, the symbolism is obviously based upon the cosmic seminal stream which brings divine life to the mystic, and a new birth" (*Symbols*, 6. 108). Iamblichus likewise teaches the sublimation of sexual imagery. He respects the representation of the phallus because it represents the cosmic power of begetting, but he suggests rising above its material representation to its cosmic symbolism. A third area of the symbolism of the divine fluid is in the ancient tradition of the "Bride of the Nile," a virgin thrown into the rising river to insure an adequate flood. A trace of this appears to have survived in a ritual of the Malkite Christians, who, in a ceremony at the river itself, address the Nile as the "Holy One of God"; this is accompanied by a description that suggests the incarnation of the Logos. Finally, in the language of church fathers like Clement and mystics like Saint Francis de Sales, the imagery of milk and the nursing of infants expresses the conception of salvation.

Goodenough believes that up to this point he has shown three things. First, a living symbol keeps its basic value as long as it lives, even though passage of time and changes in civilization require explanations of the symbols in new terms. Second, in the ancient world a lingua franca of symbols passed from religion to religion. Finally, since in the Greco-Roman world symbols of Christianity were drawn from the lingua franca, it is difficult to suppose that the symbols did not have a similar value for Jews.

In chapter ten Goodenough takes up the question of the significance of wine in Jewish cult and observance. He begins with a study of the Old Testament cultus, and he concludes that evidence is lacking of a cultic use of wine. The great emphasis upon wine symbolism came only after the hellenization of the Jews in the Greco-Roman period.

He next considers the use of wine in later Jewish ritual, looking first at evidence from certain pagan writers. He quotes Plutarch, who describes certain Jewish rites involving the drinking of wine. However, friendly though Plutarch was to the Jews, his description of Jewish worship reads like a caricature of Jewish ritual, so we must turn to Jewish sources for the facts. Goodenough first discusses at length the cup of blessing at the opening of the sabbath ritual. Next he considers the importance of wine and light at circumcision. He finds that rites of circumcision as practiced since rabbinic times have through the use of wine strengthened the two original meanings of circumcision: fertility and the sealing with blood of the covenant between the Israelites and God.

After examining the evidence of the various uses of wine in ancient Jewish wedding ceremonies, Goodenough insists that "the more details we have of Jewish and Dionysiac rites of marriage and wine, the more resemblances appear between them" (*Symbols*, 6. 161). As a parallel suggesting a common origin with Jewish practices, he cites the custom of Christian Arabs in Palestine of commemorating the marriage at Cana in modern wedding ceremonies as the bridal couple drink wine. He also cites the ceremonial use of wine in the Greek church to consecrate the marriage bed, thus making wine explicitly the symbol of intercourse. Although he disclaims any ability to retrace the process, he is convinced that the use of the bridal crown, the canopy or trellis, wine drinking, cup breaking, and suggestions of mourning all came into Jewish practice from the Greeks.

Goodenough next examines the funeral customs of Jews of the period. After describing in detail each step of the funeral, he dwells on the funeral meal. Initially this consisted of bread, eggs, and lentils, but very early the use of wine, the "cup of consolation," became important. Goodenough accounts for the later opposition by the rabbis to the use of wine at funerals by the fact that it must too closely have resembled the Roman and Greek funeral meal to suit the rabbis. To support his view that wine was actively used in the ritual of mourning, he quotes several ancient blessings intended to be said over the cup of wine. He concludes that the study of all this symbolic material, the carved wine symbols, the wreathes, the lamps, and the drinking cups that adorn the Jewish tombs, must have figured in the funeral rites at the tombs. These rites and symbols were very similar to their pagan counterparts.

Goodenough closes volume six with a summary of his conclusions. Fish, bread, and wine rituals must have come into Jewish practice during the Hellenistic period. It is in Jewish mystic writings rather than in the rabbis that evidence appears that many Jews partook of the rites, with the hope of thereby achieving immortality. If the rites were borrowed by the Jews, were they first stripped of their original mystic meaning, only to have these meanings put back into the rites by later mystical Jews? Goodenough thinks this the less likely possibility. It seems to him more likely that the Jews borrowed the rites in the first place because they wanted in Judaism a rite by which Jews, like the pagans, might share in the divine life and ultimately in immortality. Goodenough says that underlying the whole body of Jewish symbolism is "the mysticism, the craving for a sacramental access to life" (*Symbols*, 6. 219). This, he believes, was the basic and original meaning of such rites. The same phenomenon appears in Christianity, namely, seeking the mystical power of the wine and bread to gain for the believer life and the immortality of God. It may be that the rabbis, aware that Christians learned from Judaism to eat and drink their Messiah in a eucharistic meal, ceased to repeat the earlier explanation of the rite since it would seem too "Christian."

Goodenough does not claim to have proved anything, but he challenges those who disagree with him to offer some alternative pattern of interpretation of the data which will explain the interconnection of the elements of symbolism that he has presented. If he has been too eager in pointing out similarities between pagan and Jewish symbols, supposing that the symbols retained their essential meaning in transferring from one religion to another, he believes the case against his views will not be made by those who merely seek to show the differences. He continues to believe that the roots of the symbols "go so deep that food, drink, nature, the fertility of the earth, the paths of the stars, birth, death, water, wine, sex . . . all come to mean the greater security we seek now and in the future" (*Symbols*, 6. 221).

VII

In volume seven Goodenough begins a two-volume investigation of art forms borrowed from pagan religions that had no obvious cultic use as did the fish, bread, and wine. He argues, however, that for Jews to have used them as they did, these forms must have had symbolic value. Most prominent among these are the bull, the lion, and the tree. Study of the Old Testament does not suggest any ancient Hebrew symbolism of the bull; hence, its later meaning must have been borrowed by the Jews from pagan sources. Study of the bull image shows that it was associated with many gods, among them Mithra, Apis, and Dionysus. It appears that the bull illuminated the meaning and power of the god rather than that any god was preeminently the bull. The appearance of the bull image on Jewish tombs suggests that it symbolized the hope of immortality.

The lion and the bull are used interchangeably in much of pagan. symbolism of the period, and the same is true of the two images in the synagogues of Palestine. In view of this, the imagery of lions and other felines is next to be studied. Goodenough identifies fourteen categories of uses of the lion symbol in Jewish iconography. A partial list includes lions guarding inscriptions in synagogues, lions with the Torah shrine, lions with a victim, nursing lions, lions in vines, and the lion on Jewish amulets, etc. Too simple explanations of the meaning of the lion in Jewish symbols are to be avoided, and the basic meaning is to be sought in the symbol as used in the Near East, Egypt, and among the Greeks.

With whatever god of antiquity the lion was associated, the lion symbolized the power of the god, including the sexual power. This power presented itself as primarily destructive, but paradoxically the power could be invoked to ward off danger. "The contour of the lion's face made it an obvious symbol of the sun, and thus of the solar region with its Light-Stream so popular in much ancient thinking" (*Symbols*, 7. 78). This is described at length by Philo. The lion likewise symbolized beneficent power. "The lion gave life especially when love harnessed its ferocity and made it available to men" (*Symbols*, 7. 78). By inference Goodenough concludes that the lion symbol in Jewish use had the same meaning. The images of the lions guarding the Torah shrine are there to protect the scrolls and to indicate the ferocious but saving power of the God of the Torah. The meaning in the other symbolic uses would be the same, whether in synagogue inscriptions, on tombs, or on amulets. "Lions are the protector from evil forces and disease, the savior that takes man to immortal bliss, and indeed God himself with cosmic power" (*Symbols*, 7. 86).

Goodenough now turns to the symbolism of the tree. Usually the palm tree is represented, although occasionally other trees may be used. Tree symbolism appears frequently on Jewish tombs and ossuaries, and also upon coins. On Phoenician coins the palm appears to stand for a source of power and blessing rather than for a political unit. The same must be true for Jewish coins. The tendency for the symbol of the palm tree to appear on Jewish tombs of the period demands for its understanding the study of the symbolism of the tree generally in the ancient world. Goodenough traces this from Mesopotamia and the Near East, through Egypt, Greece, and Rome into early Christian practice. The common thread of meaning throughout is that the tree symbol represents the tree of life, even to its identification with the Christian cross.

This same significance would seem to attach to the tree in Jewish art, which would express the same hope of future life that the tree expressed for pagans. In the period under consideration, roughly during the second to fifth centuries after Christ, the tree of life was a favorite conception and symbol among the Jews. Whether used eschatologically or mystically, it would seem to reflect confident hope of immortality, if not also the expansion and enrichment of life on this earth.

The next symbols to be considered are Victory and the crown. Among the important deities of the Greco-Roman period was Victory, who brought various gifts to humans, especially the crown and the palm branch. The figure of Victory bearing the crown is frequent among Jewish symbols. Study of this design in paganism shows that it came to represent the apotheosis of the person within the sarcophagus upon which it appeared. It would seem to have the same value when represented on Jewish tombs. The crown, frequently used in Jewish art, is the chief abbreviation of Victory in pagan, Jewish, and Christian art alike. Goodenough says, "The crown seems to have become Jewish, as it became Christian, by shedding completely its pagan mythology while it kept its basic value unchanged. . . . [It] still meant at the end what it had meant in the beginning, the award, in one sense or another, of divine and immortal life" (*Symbols*, 7. 170).

The remainder of volume seven includes investigation of miscellaneous divine symbols. A chapter is devoted to rosettes, wheels, and "round objects." Next follows a chapter on masks, and the final chapter deals with the *gorgoneum*, that is, the head of Medusa, or the Gorgon head. Goodenough admits putting this material at this point simply for the sake of variety. These miscellaneous symbols all represent the presence of God but have no other special feature in common. Conclusions concerning them are reserved for volume eight.

VIII

Volume eight completes the study of pagan symbols used in Judaism. The first part takes up symbols that are primarily erotic: cupids, birds, and miscellaneous fertility symbols, the sheep, the hare, the shell, the cornucopia, and the centaur. In each case Goodenough describes the symbols as employed by the Jews, most frequently on monuments, tombs, and synagogues. Study of the use and meaning of the symbols in paganism follows this. Often he investigates the symbolism as used in various forms of Judaism ranging from halakic to mystic Judaism.

In connection with his consideration of the Jewish use of cupid, Goodenough points to a sharp contrast between the stern resistance by halakic Judaism to any hint of eroticism in the interpretation of Israel's relationship to God and the clear presence of the erotic element in the mysticism of

Philo and in the later mysticism of the Kabbalah such as that expressed in the *Zohar*. He says, "With mystic Jews eroticism—that is, the necessity of union with God in love—and fertility—that is, the hope of new life and immortality from such a union—played a conspicuous and basic part" (*Symbols*, 8. 117). He notes, however, that there were varying degrees of intensity in the expression of the erotic element. Less overt symbols were freely used. Cupid appears much less frequently than the bird, the hare, and the cock, although all have erotic implications.

These symbols all strengthen the impression that the hope for immortality was a much more active force among Hellenistic Jews than among those in halakic Judaism. It is to create a false dilemma to suggest that either Jews who used the symbols were conscious of their eroticism or that they were totally ignorant of this element and used the symbols merely as decoration. Goodenough insists that the Jews did not use the symbols merely for gratification of eroticism. The erotic urge, he says, finds its deepest meaning not in physical sensation but in spiritual union with God. The Jewish use of these particular symbols on tombs is ultimately to be understood as the expression of hope for immortality.

The latter half of volume eight is devoted to psychopomps and astrological symbols. The psychopomp is the guide who bears the soul to the next world. Goodenough believes that he is the first to investigate the question of what all the guides have in common. The psychopomp is usually represented as a being with great wings adequate to carry the soul upward. The examples that Goodenough investigates are the eagle, the griffin, Pegasus, the ladder or steps, and the boat. The Jews who used these symbols showed that they were thinking of death as a great migration and that God was providing some kind of means to make the journey possible. Neither of these ideas has any importance in halakic Judaism. The fact that these symbols appear not only on graves but also on synagogues suggests that the values of mystic experience were felt by Jews who attended the synagogue at the same time that the values of the future life were symbolized on the graves. The eagles over the doors of the synagogues suggest that for the Jews who put them there the teachings of the synagogue had the same value as the eagle for enabling them to soar to heaven. It must be stressed, Goodenough said, that the Hellenistic Jews who employed such symbols were no less observant of the law, no less "orthodox," than the later halakic-rabbinic Jews who rejected all of the symbols.

In his investigation of astronomical symbols, Goodenough considers astral symbols in Jewish remains, where he finds abundant use of the symbolism of the zodiac in the period of the late Roman Empire and the Byzantine period. In paganism he studies astral symbolism in religious and philosophic thought and in art. He also examines astralism as reflected in various strands of Jewish literature. A question demanding an answer is, Why, in those synagogues displaying the zodiac, is the symbol

of Helios the charioteer given a central place? In paganism astral symbolism promised immortality as the soul returned to its cosmic origin.
Philo in several passages represents God as the shepherd of the flock of
stars. Philo also represents God as a charioteer, guiding all things in the
cosmos. Goodenough finds these statements to be sufficient basis for
explanation of the use of the Helios symbol by Jews.

In the concluding pages of volume eight, Goodenough recapitulates
the thesis that he has endeavored to illustrate in volumes five through
eight. He also summarizes the contents of these volumes. In so lengthy
and complex a work this is a valuable thing for the reader. His thesis
regarding the Jewish use of pagan symbols has been that the Jews recognized the basic religious message within the common vocabulary of
symbols that migrated from one ancient culture and religion to another.
In this migration the basic message of the symbol might be variously
adapted, but not lost. These symbols as found on Jewish tombs, synagogues, and other artifacts dealt primarily with the aspirations for communion with deity and ultimately with aspirations toward immortality.
Striking analogies can be shown between early Christian assimilation and
adaptation of symbols originally pagan and the apparent adaptation of
such symbols to Judaism in the Greco-Roman world. Jews thereby were
not becoming paganized; rather, through these symbols they sought to
express what they believed to be essential meanings of Judaism. Philo
provides the best literary source for understanding the process whereby
Jews of the Greco-Roman world adapted pagan concepts and imagery to
express the essential faith of Judaism. Each of volumes four through
eight includes a substantial section of illustrations.

IX–XI

Volumes nine through eleven on the synagogue at Dura climax and
complete Goodenough's great study of Jewish symbols. These were published in 1963, the year following his retirement from thirty-nine years
as a member of the Yale faculty. This was thirty-one years after he had
first viewed the photographs of the murals of the Dura synagogue that
had inaugurated his study of symbols.

In volume nine he considers introductory problems. He describes
briefly the astounding discovery in 1932 of the synagogue and its incredible paintings. Investigation showed that the painted synagogue had been
built on an earlier one in about A.D. 245. The implications of the synagogue
for our understanding of Judaism are as radical as those of the Dead Sea
Scrolls, perhaps even more so. At least many scholars were prepared to read
the scrolls, whereas no certain key to the interpretation of the paintings
existed. Goodenough takes exception to the approach of Carl Kraeling and
other scholars who sought interpretation of the paintings in the light of

various bodies of Jewish literature contemporaneous with the paintings. This is to close the door against serious consideration of what study of the Jewish art itself has to teach us. Goodenough is persuaded that such study opens up a whole new phase of Jewish history not made apparent to us by Jewish literature.

Study of the literature alone suggested to some scholars that hellenization affected only a minority of Jews and that the majority rejected Hellenism and remained in what G. F. Moore calls "normative Judaism." This Judaism is thought to have manifested an abhorrence of images, just as image making came to be forbidden in rabbinic Judaism. Suddenly the discoveries at Dura revealed an entirely different attitude and practice. "At Dura the god Ares, for example, could supervise the Exodus from Egypt, Victories bring their crowns on the acroteria of the Temple, and the three Nymphs guard the infant Moses while Aphrodite-Anahita takes him out of the little ark" (Symbols, 9. 6). Nothing suggests that Jews ever worshiped these figures any more than that they worshiped the accompanying figures of Moses and Aaron. If literary evidence gives no explanation of Jewish borrowing of pagan art forms, the art forms themselves must be the evidence of a new segment of Judaism hitherto unknown.

In his study of the Dura paintings Goodenough employs the same hypothesis that he adopts in volumes five to eight to interpret Jewish use of pagan symbols elsewhere. The thesis is that "a live symbol when borrowed by a new religion is borrowed for its value and given explanations (if at all) in terms of the traditions of the new religion" (Symbols, 9. 6). He insists that study of the art itself must precede verbal statements of the meaning. Kraeling and others have insisted that the pagan motifs in the ceiling and dado of the Dura synagogue are purely decorative. Their ideas must be taken seriously, but we must reserve final judgment until further study of the symbolism can be made. Christians of this period employed symbols borrowed from paganism to express purely Christian hopes, just as they expressed these hopes with symbols from the life of Christ and from the Old Testament. It is quite natural to suppose, therefore, that the Jews of Dura were doing precisely the same thing. Consequently, not only the paintings of the synagogue but also its decorations and the plan of the building itself must be treated together, since they express the Judaism of the people who designed the whole scheme. Prior literary study is of no avail for interpretation of the symbols, since no known Jewish literature shows any need of pagan symbols to express itself.

The question arises concerning the possible relationship between the Dura synagogue and Babylonian Judaism. Goodenough takes issue with Kraeling, who suggested that the Babylonian Talmud and Midrash, as well as the targums, presumably shaped the Judaism of Dura. This seems plausible since Dura lies only about 250 miles north of Nedhardea, which at the time was the seat of the great Babylonian Jewish academy. Goodenough's objection is that the Dura paintings must antedate the Babylonian Talmud as well as the halakic reform and, thus, could hardly have been influenced by them. Actually, in their physical setting the Jews of Dura, which was an outpost of Greco-Roman civilization, had much more in common with other Jews of that civilization than with the Jews of the natural ghetto of Babylonia.

Other evidence of the cultural setting of the Jews of Dura is offered by the Pahlavi inscriptions boldly painted on several of the lower panels of the synagogue paintings. Goodenough examines the conclusions of two scholars, B. Geiger and F. Altheim, who studied the inscriptions. His own conclusion is that during the period of Parthian supremacy certain Jews of the area adopted Parthian-Hellenistic civilization to the point of assuming Pahlavi names. The inscriptions then may be understood as records of Jewish building inspectors with such names, who gave their approval of the paintings by putting their signatures on them.

As Goodenough outlines his procedure for interpreting the Dura syn-agogue and its paintings, he states that we must begin with the structure of the synagogue itself. Next the nonbiblical representations must be examined. These are the pictorial graffiti scratched on the plaster before there was any painting, but especially the ceiling and the dado, the lowest band of ornament around the room. These turn out to be symbols found elsewhere in the synagogue and also discussed in previous volumes of the series as representing deep religious feeling for both pagans and Jews of the Greco-Roman world. Both architecture and symbols of the synagogue suggest that the Jews of Dura thought much in the same way as other Jews whose symbolism has already been examined. For the first time at Dura we find Jews using pagan symbols along with biblical scenes, which thus gives a clue to how they interpreted their Bibles. It is important to recognize that in the Dura paintings we have a totally new creation by local Jews. Hellenistic though the paintings show themselves to be, they cannot be explained in terms of the Hellenism that we know from Philo. We must explain the significance of the fact that sometimes figures in the paintings appear in Persian dress but at other times in Greek dress. In addition to the necessity of trying to match the biblical scenes with the episodes that they represent, there remain scenes that represent no biblical incidents at all, and upon them biblical texts cannot be forced. Kraeling takes the position that the didactic element is sec-ondary to the narrative element in the art. This elicits Goodenough's basic disagreement, for he considers the didactic element to be primary. The paintings must be considered in the order in which they were painted on the walls. Circular reasoning is inevitable in interpreting the individual pictures. Shall we interpret scenes in terms of an assumed language of symbols in the art, or shall we first expound the language, then read the paintings in the light of it? The most important single symbolic device in the pictures seems to be the dress of the characters.

Two other considerations remain. Goodenough becomes increasingly convinced that, although the pictures may have been individually painted, they reveal the influence of a master hand. He finds basis for his surmise in an account of how work was done in ancient times in a great sculpture workshop. The skilled artisans who did the actual carving were under the ultimate direction of five "philosophers," men whom today we would call designers. One final detail suggests that not all the Jews of Dura approved of the paintings. This may be shown by the fact that in many figures in the lower registers of paintings the eyes have been gouged out. The clue to the meaning of this defacement is to be found in evidence that among Jews of the ancient world the obliterating of the eyes of an image was thought to annul the effectiveness or the threat of the image. This suggests that the pictures themselves could hardly have been thought of, either by those who favored them or by those who opposed them, as meaningless ornament.

If the reader is to gain appreciation for the scope of Goodenough's studies of the Dura synagogue and of the conclusions that he draws, the briefest possible conspectus of the contents of these three volumes must here be given. Continuing volume nine, chapters two through seven deal respectively with (2) evidence from the structural form of the synagogue and the graffiti; (3) paintings in the first synagogue; (4) the ceiling tiles and dado of the second temple; (5) the Torah shrine; (6) the reredos (with the accidental discovery of both an overpainting and an underpainting); and (7) the symbolism of dress (including examination of textiles, costumes of the Persian and of the Greco-Roman world, and Jewish costume).

The remainder of volume nine contains chapters dealing with the west wall, which was the only wall that remained reasonably intact: (8) Jewish royalty (including the scene of Samuel's anointing of David); (9) the miraculous babies: the infancy of Moses; and (10) the miraculous babies: Elijah revives the widow's son.

Volume ten continues the sequence of the paintings on the west wall: (11) cosmic Judaism: the Temple of Aaron; (12) cosmic Judaism: the Well of the Wilderness; (13) the Judaism of immaterial reality: the closed temple; (14) the Judaism of immaterial reality: the ark versus paganism; (15) two fragmentary scenes; (16) Moses leads the migration from Egypt; (17) the south wall: procession of the ark; incidents of Elijah; (18) the east wall: an unidentified scene; David and Saul in the wilderness of Ziph; the north wall: the dream of Jacob; the middle register (a fragment of the ark in battle); the cycle of Ezekiel. Volume eleven is entirely devoted to illustrations for volumes nine and ten, including 20 magnificent color plates, and 354 figures in black and white: some diagrams and many half-tone plates.

XII

One should hope that there will always be individuals whose interest is sufficiently aroused by the symbols to wish to consult Goodenough's works directly. So massive are these works that summaries can do them no justice. Goodenough was concerned that his work not be overlooked because of its sheer bulk. Consequently, in 1963, with the assistance of his wife, Cynthia, he completed the twelfth volume. This consists of a summary of the work of the preceding volumes and final conclusions drawn from the entire work. Any industrious readers who complete this volume, using the other eleven for reference and for illustration, may come away from the task with a sense of satisfaction that they understand Goodenough's basic thesis and that they are fully aware of how Goodenough endeavors to support it.

Volume twelve opens with a helpful chapter on the literary sources of Hellenistic Judaism. The author explains that the work on symbols is but one part of a larger study that arose from the question, Why in so short a time did the religion that began with the teaching of a Galilean carpenter become a Greco-Roman religion of salvation, of a savior who brought divinity to lost humanity, a religion complete with cult and theology? Goodenough's thesis is that Hellenistic-Judaism provided the bridge between the teaching of the Galilean and the Greco-Roman Christian church. The literary study began with his work on Justin Martyr, and it reached its climax in *By Light, Light*, which he completed just before he began his studies of Jewish symbols. The study of the symbols divides itself into two phases, the first devoted to the tombs, synagogues, and artifacts, and the second devoted to the Dura synagogue and its paintings.

We close with some points from the conclusions stated in the last chapter of volume twelve. He has said repeatedly that he makes no claim to have "proved" anything in his long search However, he proposes that the actual artifacts from Rome and Dura provide more reliable evidence for the nature of Greco-Roman Judaism than do the Mishnah and early rabbinic writings of Palestine. To what extent Jews were abandoning Judaism we do not know, but the archaeological evidence is that they liked to worship in synagogues and they liked to be buried with other Jews. Yet in these places we find such symbols as Helios, the zodiac, and the seasons represented together with Jewish cult instruments. At the very same time in other places rabbis were composing the Gemarah. Evidently different forms of Judaism existed almost side by side. Nothing in the evidence of the use of the images suggests that Jews worshiped the images any more than that they worshiped the menorah. At the same time, however, there is no reason to suppose that the Jews used the images borrowed from paganism unless they associated religious feeling with them.

It appears that throughout the empire Jews continued to worship Yahweh with conscious awareness of their kinship to pagan cosmic worship. Jewish use of astronomical symbols suggests that their piety was oriented in a scientific (or pseudoscientific) sense of God as cosmic ruler. Many types of astral symbols appear: the bull, the lion, or the seasons. This piety could even express itself in a prayer addressed to Helios, yet the worshipers could hardly have thought of themselves as not praying to Yahweh.

o   o   o   o   o

Of the reviewers of the later volumes of *Symbols*, none was more gracious than F. C. Grant. He reviewed first volumes seven and eight, *Pagan Symbols in Judaism*.[1] He discusses Goodenough's work in a larger perspective through his observation that research of the previous fifty years in ancient Judaism and early Christianity "has given us a strange new picture of both religions." He mentions the discoveries at Dura-Europos and those later in Palestine which upset the old notion that Jewish worship had always shown "puritanical simplicity" with total absence of all "worldly" embellishment. Other light is thrown on Judaism by the discovery of the Dead Sea Scrolls, and early Christianity is to be seen in new light because of the Coptic gnostic writings discovered at Nag Hammadi. Goodenough's volumes seven and eight "complete the picture up to the present date of archaeological investigation. He understands these beautiful and lavishly illustrated volumes to be the conclusion of the work, but suggests that there is a hint in the last sentence of volume eight that more might follow" (Grant, p. 61). In any case, Goodenough's work is to be seen as one of the most significant contributions to a half-century of research into the Judaism and Christianity of the Greco-Roman world.

Grant expresses great appreciation for the fact that Goodenough interprets the symbols "with a deep religious understanding of their significance, with no resort to the blasé appeal to superstition or frivolity which some interpreters of ancient religion indulge in" (Grant, p. 62). His illustration is Goodenough's "eloquent exposition of the symbolism of cupids (as) related to Jewish confidence in the love of God, not to something like bourbon boudoir eroticism" (Grant, p. 62). Grant commends this attitude as worthy of emulation by all who study Hellenistic-Roman religion generally, for, he says, "religious symbolism, even pagan, needs

[1] *Journal of Biblical Literature* 79 (1960) 61–64.

to be taken at its highest and best, not as a poor counterfoil to something else." He notes also that "the conclusion of this work (219ff.) opens with a personal testimony, noble in spirit and warm hearted, which goes far to explain the author's success in penetrating the very core of the religious meaning of the symbols he discusses" (Grant, p. 63).

Grant has lifted up in these remarks one of the crucial elements of Goodenough's work. The present author observes that in all of Goodenough's writings on religion, however critical he may be of certain expressions of religion or whatever deficiencies other scholars may find in his theories or his reasoning, of one thing there can be no question: Goodenough always writes with a respect for the values of religion, and he appears always to be seeking for the clearest understanding and the best expression of these values.

In due time Grant reviewed volumes nine, ten, and eleven, *Symbolism in the Dura Synagogue*.[2] He expresses his continued admiration for the work, and he lifts out Goodenough's description of the site where the Dura discoveries were made as "a passage of historical prose that would have been worthy of Gibbon" (Grant, p. 418). It is appropriate to quote it here:

> About A.D. 256 the citizens of Dura, with a little Roman garrison, had been cut off from all help and faced inevitable extinction at the hands of an advancing Persian host. To strengthen the most exposed wall of the city the desperate people tore the roofs from the buildings in the street behind it and constructed a great ramp by filling the whole with quantities of earth. It did no good. The Persians tunneled under, and Dura was never heard of again until, in 1921, a British captain warring against the Arabs camped on the site, and in the course of "digging some trenches in the ruins" discovered the painting of the "Palmyrene gods." (*Symbols*, 9. 3)

Grant remarks that not only the Christian and Mithraic remains had been studied, but also the Jewish, notably by Carl Kraeling. Yet nothing had appeared to match Goodenough's magnificent volumes. Goodenough's vast knowledge of both Judaism and Hellenism gave him special skill in interpretation, "in particular a familiarity with Philo such as very few modern scholars possess—it is like an eighteenth-century Pietist's familiarity with the Bible!" Grant believes that the vast work on the symbols and on Dura supports Goodenough's "mystery religion hypothesis," provided that one does not thereby seek to transform Judaism into a mystery cult. He judges the art of Dura to be amateurish, yet it is the art of the poor and the devout. Since the early Christians with "amazing fecundity of interpretive fancy" transformed great themes of

---

[2] *Journal of Biblical Literature* 83 (1964) 418–20.

the Old Testament into permanent Christian principles, it was natural for Jews to make equal claims.

Grant's final review of volume thirteen, the indexes, maps, and cor-rigenda, some from the author's own hand, appeared in 1969 when Goodenough had been four years dead.[3] He praises its completeness and considers its timeliness in a period when the whole swing of classical and theological (i.e., biblical) study was moving toward the Hellenistic period. Goodenough's studies have uncovered the actual life of ordinary Jews and ordinary Gentiles as never before. In present-day researches, and in the future, Goodenough's *magnum opus* will be an indispensable resource.

[3] *Journal of Biblical Literature* 88 (1969) 370.

7

SCIENTIFIC STUDY OF RELIGION

I

In 1948 Goodenough wrote "Needed, Scientific Study of Religion."[1] Traditionally, he noted, religion has provided answers to the ultimate questions of human existence and of human conduct. He was distressed by a resurgence of popular desire for finalities concerning the nature and destiny of humanity. This desire was turning certain persons back to religious orthodoxies and others to Fascist and Communist ideologies. Many scientists, though they may have renounced religion, do not attack it so much as merely ignore it. In their ignorance of religion they fail to see that the perennial human craving for certainties in an uncertain world confronts them with new enemies, namely, totalitarian ideologies that threaten their freedom of inquiry. For these reasons a scientific investigation of religious experience is urgent.

In spite of the great erudition and industry on the part of modern scholars in the study of religion, true scientific study of religion has not been undertaken. Biblical criticism has had little effect in changing people's beliefs. The humanism of liberal Christianity arose quite independently of Christianity itself. Liberal Christian scholars subjected the Bible and Christianity to historical study "so as to convince themselves that the Gospels' basic message was the promise that Jesus would lead man into the golden age of democracy or socialism" ("Scientific Study," p. 273). Nineteenth- and twentieth-century scholarship, with all of its employment of scientific methodology, aimed at a quite unscientific goal of simply confirming what had already been believed from earlier centuries.

Schools of authoritarian Judaism were involved in nothing except the interpretation of their own great tradition. At just about the same time that the new humanistic ideas of progress and social amelioration through democracy and socialism began to be expressed through liberal Christianity, Moses Mendelssohn laid the foundation of Reform Judaism. The scholarship of Reform Judaism "was essentially dedicated to showing that

---

[1] Goodenough, "Needed, Scientific Study of Religion," *Commentary* 5 (1948) 272–77.

19th-century idealism was the *Wesen* of Judaism, too" ("Scientific Study," p. 274).

Almost simultaneously with liberal Christianity and Reform Judaism arose the fields of psychology of religion and of the history of religion, both with the promise of a much closer approach to the scientific study of religion. Yet, in spite of the initial fruitful work in these respective fields by William James and Max Mueller and others, both disciplines withered "under the same blight that in late years has struck all humanistic study—the attitude that values accuracy of detail above the understanding of larger principle, and small conclusions above large ones, because they are safer" ("Scientific Study," p. 274).

Truly scientific study of religion might make it possible to face some elemental problems such as that posed by Marx: Is religion an opiate for the people? If the correct answer to this question should be empirically demonstrated, "it would constitute the most important empirical study of all time" ("Scientific Study," p. 276). Goodenough declares that the solution of such a question would involve the work of many individuals, and the research might extend over years of study. If the objection should be raised that such study of religion would have little application to today's problems, the pure sciences in the physical realm are vulnerable to the same objection. None of these sciences has shown us the true nature of the physical realm, nor has medical science discovered the ultimate secret of the human body. Yet discoveries made along the way have transformed humanity's relation to nature, and people's health through science has been immeasurably improved. From the scientific study of religion we could expect equally significant discoveries that could have a revolutionary effect on the moral and social life of human beings.

Goodenough insists that the kind of study he proposes must be truly objective and uncommitted. He recognizes that hardly anyone can be completely dispassionate with respect to any human problem, especially problems of religion and morals. Every scholar has individual prejudices. Scientific study of religion could by no means be entrusted to faculties of theology, either Christian or Jewish, since all such faculties "tend to be corporately controlled, and a person whose conclusions might prove to be awkward to the group is simply not made part of such a faculty" ("Scientific Study," p. 277). The research group that he envisages would have to be completely free of such corporate control and prejudice. The group would be in agreement on one thing only: the value of free research in religion. The group would have to be made up of persons of diverse viewpoints. Not one but several such groups should be constituted to counteract any tendency to form a new orthodoxy. Each group would initially be established by an anchor man who would carefully select the ablest scholars from a variety of appropriate fields such as psychology, sociology, and history. Goodenough cites one "great" department of philosophy [Yale?]

which set about deliberately to create such departmental diversity. But, he says, "I know of no religious faculty in the world which has ever operated on such a principle" ("Scientific Study," p. 277).

He deplores the "wastage" of the top 5 percent of Christian and Jewish theological students, who would like to follow a scholarly career in the scientific study of religion but feel that they could not as ministers or rabbis teach the finalities of any one religion. Hence, they abandon religious studies for studies in other fields in which they become leaders. A program such as the one he outlines would attract such persons. Goodenough is convinced that such a program must be developed "if we are not to be swamped by the forces of obscurantism" ("Scientific Study," p. 277).

Whether in the nearly two decades that remained of Goodenough's life he saw even the beginnings of such an enterprise is difficult to know. It is also uncertain whether Goodenough's own personal commitment to the values and goals of religion, albeit of a highly personal and noninstitutional sort, actually allowed him the kind of objectivity that he commends. However, the outline of the method of scientific study of religion that he presents accurately describes the method that he followed in his own scholarship. It is also worthy of note that in his description of a method of scientific study of religion he betrays his distrust of the scholarship of persons related to the "theological establishment."

In 1959 Goodenough was invited to address the founding meeting of the American Society for the History of Religions. His paper, "Religionswissenschaft," presents his most comprehensive statement of his position on the scientific study of religion and of the background out of which it developed.[2] He sees no purpose for the proposed society apart from its contribution to *Religionswissenschaft*, and he asks what its primary concern would be. He notes, on the one hand, that often among scholars religion is distinguished from other aspects of life so that it cannot properly be subjected to scientific study. On the other hand, most believers and practitioners of religion consider that, since religion is a matter of revelation and faith, it cannot be subjected to scientific or dispassionate analysis. He objects to both opinions.

> But the Science of Religion is meaningless unless we see that it essentially breaks this down, and proposes precisely in the realm of the religious to move from empirical data to hypotheses, and from hypotheses back to data, and to correct hypotheses by data, as nearly as possible in scientific fashion. ("Religionswissenschaft," p. 79)

In seeking to account for the decline in *Religionswissenschaft* he traces a century of history. When in the nineteenth century the new

---

[2] Goodenough, "Religionswissenschaft," *Numen* 6 (1959) 77–95.

methods of historical criticism were applied to the Bible, scholars like W. Sanday were most torn by it. American scholars who went to Europe adopted the German solution of Harnack and others that the essence of Christianity was its social and ethical teaching. This facile solution was to be exploded by Albert Schweitzer. The papal bull of 1912 prohibiting critical biblical scholarship was to be expected, since such scholarship did indeed break down the distinction between the sacred and the profane. What had been God's word for the church became instead a collection of historical documents to be scrutinized with critical care. At the turn of the century scholars increasingly studied the myths and rituals of the world with growing detachment. The model of evolution began to be applied to religion, and revelation to many people became progressive revelation, "and scholars delighted to trace the evolution from the crude Yahweh of the Book of Judges to the Christian God, who finally, could 'love' but not 'desire'" ("Religionswissenschaft," p. 80). America's particular contribution to the analysis of religion was by way of psychology. This was encouraged by the fact of the increasing religious pluralism of the United States, which led Americans to regard religion as a purely private matter in which the state should not interfere. In contrast, the psychology of religion did not flourish in Europe, where religion tended to be seen as a unified system of beliefs and practices concerning sacred things.

After the catastrophe of World War I, followed by the depression in Germany in 1918 and in the United States in the twenties and thirties, the scientific study of religion declined radically. Karl Barth, who dominated European and, to a lesser extent, American Protestant theology during this period, decried the scientific study of anything as an expression of human arrogance and presumptuousness before God. Among Barth and his followers science and history became two words for the profane. They taught the complete sovereignty of God, precluding any efforts on the part of human beings to improve their own way of life. As a result of the horrors of Hitler and World War II, an increasing number of people from a variety of backgrounds came to accept the idea of the native sinfulness of humanity and of the futility of analytical and scientific effort. When Goodenough wrote the essay (1959), he noted that most of the theological schools and religious leaders of the time espoused this point of view. On this account he contended that it was exactly at such a time that the proposed Society for the History of Religions should be inaugurated.

It must be said parenthetically that Goodenough never ceased to scorn neo-orthodoxy and to speak out against it. Once he had struggled free from the orthodoxies of his childhood and early youth, he had little appetite thereafter for anything that smacked of orthodoxy. During his years at Yale he suffered from certain animosities, whether real or imagined, that he believed were directed toward him by colleagues in the Divinity School.

Evidently he tended to categorize all of them as "neo-orthodox." It is probably beside the point to argue that had he more closely scrutinized the actual thought of theologians and theological schools of his time, he could have discovered considerable diversity among them. What counts is that he thought what he thought, and he acted and wrote accordingly. In addition, there appears from time to time in his writings the expression of a rather simple, even old-fashioned, kind of American optimism quite inimical to the claims of neo-orthodoxy.

Goodenough confronted his audience with the difficulties that had to be faced in any attempt to revitalize the scientific study of religion. Intellectuals had become more intensely concerned with social problems than with problems of the sacred and the profane. Psychology had increasingly confined itself to asking questions that could be answered by measuring and counting, yet the psyche lies beyond such control. Freud had dismissed religion as an "illusion." Jung tried to keep alive problems which worldwide similarities in religious experience present to us, but Jung had generally been neglected by his generation. Yet a remnant of the old interest still survived, and Goodenough declares that the best scientists that he knew were "deeply devout persons who see the numinous through their telescopes or microscopes, and in their test tubes, not as an 'other,' but as the essential quality of matter, matter as exploding atoms, or galaxies, or as biological processes" ("Religionswissenschaft," p. 85).

Goodenough argues that the only possibility of reviving the study of the science of religion is to recognize that science is itself a religious exercise. Proper understanding of this requires a new definition of religion, although Goodenough recognizes the difficulties in doing this. Religion arises from the universal human experience that human beings live in the midst of a vast external universe in the face of which they find themselves essentially helpless. At the same time, they are involved in social forces over which they have little control. Finally, they know little about themselves as individuals or about the meaning and purpose of life. This concatenation of overwhelming mysteries and forces Goodenough calls the "tremendum." "The conscious mind, and probably even more persistently the unconscious mind, are always confronted by the tremendum, both within oneself and without" ("Religionswissenschaft," p. 86). He finds the essence of religion in the ways that human beings have sought to help themselves live over against this great unknown.

Traditional religions have given two basic answers. The most common has been for human beings to screen themselves off from the tremendum by myths of the origin of the world and humanity, and by rituals designed to placate the unpredictable forces of nature, by divine places and seasons, and by sacred laws. Goodenough frequently uses this image of man draping curtains to screen himself from the tremendum and decorating the curtains with his myths. The second formulation is exhibited in the lives of great individuals who have broken or lifted the curtain "to go alone into the Alone, and to face the numinous tremendum itself" ("Religionswissenschaft," p. 88). Examples are Moses on Sinai, Jesus at Gethsemane, and Buddha abandoning his earthly kingdom. The history of religions examines the ways in which human beings have sought to approach the tremendum, either through the erection of screens adorned by their myths or by seeking directly to confront it. Regarding the tremendum itself, we all create myths "since the tremendum as a whole is utterly too much for us" ("Religionswissenschaft," p. 88).

Goodenough is persuaded that the method of modern science makes possible an objective approach to the value of religious myths and practices. The method of science, whether applied to physics or to religion, is to go out to the unknown with "little questions that inch their way into bits, consistent bits, of knowledge" ("Religionswissenschaft," p. 88). He does not believe that we could have a science of religion as long as we live within apotropaic curtains or live with our critical faculties blurred by mysticism. Moreover, the science of religion cannot consist merely of a cataloguing of data. It must go on to try to discern the principles inherent within them. The science of religion must accept the tremendum and the insignificance and helplessness of the individual before it. Yet without the protection of any curtain, it must seek by its own method whatever relationships and meanings can be found. Goodenough cites the distinguished astronomer Harlow Shapley as an exemplar of this approach. Such a science of religion should not expect to announce the nature of the tremendum, but its practitioners, moving back and forth between data and hypothesis, may have the faith that such study will advance us toward a sounder understanding.

To the question, What will be the data of the science of religion? Goodenough replies that no field of human activity can be considered irrelevant, but important suggestions will come from psychology, sociology, anthropology, and law. The new linguistics will be of special help, and the worlds of creativity in art, literature, and music are worlds of religion. The study of sacred literatures and ethics, as well as myths and rituals of people of all times, will continue to have a place of central importance. If analysis of particular data takes the investigators into strange fields, they will enter them, and it may be that those engaged in the science of religion will have to publish their results, using data beyond their own expert competence. Each step will lead the investigators nearer to the tremendum. The reestablishment of a science of religion will require more than slavishly taking over the various methods now used in other sciences; rather, it may require devising methods never before used. In studying the data of human religion, we must look beyond the data to ask what actually lies behind the values that human beings have found in myths, philosophies, rituals, and symbols. This will be the specific field of investigation of historians of religions. Their expectation should be, using the curtainless procedures of science, to lift the curtain a little and to penetrate a little further in their understanding of the tremendum. As Goodenough, with some poetry and passion, describes the potential goals and procedures of a new learned society for the history of religion, he is merely expounding the ideals of his own scholarship as he had practiced it for four decades. This could have been inspiring to those who heard him, but it might be questioned whether very many could follow him all the way. The intensity with which he combined insistence on exact scholarship with deep personal piety might court the admiration of many who could yet not replicate it in themselves.

In an address to the Institute of Religion in an Age of Science he undertook to define religion.[3] For scientists, religion must be defined in terms of whatever the object of human devotion is. The primary concern of religion is in the source of security that may be found in a fetish, a ritual, love of Jesus, social status, wealth, or creativity. All people seek security in religion from the tremendum, "that which must be feared" ("Historian," p. 9). In religion beliefs are universal. Beliefs do not exercise control through scientific knowledge but through creeds or myths. If we define myth as "an explanation of reality given to conceal from ourselves our lack of understanding, then myths are with us in all aspects of modern life" ("Historian," p. 13). Scientific explanations themselves involve myth.

Fear has been the beginning of all religion, and through various rituals human beings have tried to placate the horror of the tremendum. For most persons for whom love is a religious incentive, it is simply the reverse of fear. Religions that look for a happy hereafter are those in which the "id" or life instinct wishes to preserve itself. Religion expresses itself in various forms. The religion of legalism centers on obedience to a code in which the superego or conscience finds itself spelled out. Another form of religion is orthodoxy, by which one obtains security by means of a scheme of reality. The scheme may be based on the simplest myth or the most abstract theological or metaphysical concept. It is the attitude of commitment that makes an experience religious, not the value or ultimate truth of the belief. The deepest religious experience for many people is found in beauty. For others religious experience comes from striving for social justice and the welfare of humanity. Still others find religion in loyalty to the group. Mysticism, the highest form of religion, in its final form seeks self-dissolution through identification with the tremendum itself. Common to all religious experience are devotion, commitment, service to the tremendum, and the attempt in whatever

[3] Goodenough, "A Historian of Religion Tries To Define Religion," *Zygon* 2 (1967) 7–22.

way to placate it, appease it, or even to declare it to be the source of all that is beautiful and good.

The foregoing statements spell out the method by which Goodenough believes religion should be studied. It clearly is the method that he himself employed in all of his own studies of religion. In the remainder of the present chapter we shall examine several of his shorter essays on various topics of religion in order to see, if we can, what effect his theory of study had upon conclusions that he reached through his study.

In 1942 Goodenough disputed the claim of Nels Ferré that the inner meaning of Christianity is *agapē*, completely self-giving love,[4] and contends that evidence is lacking that this is the core principle of Christianity. His chief objection is to Ferré's claim that *agapē* "is the basic principle, not only of religion, but of society, science, the universe and God. . . . [Ferré] would then have society banish those forms of what he calls 'negative science and philosophy'" ("Scientific Living," p. 8). A society thus purged would be safe for democracy. Goodenough charges that such a program would simply be another form of authoritarianism, no more attractive than that of Hitler. Ferré's presupposition must be scientifically tested rather than acted upon as though it were an authoritative principle.

At the same time, Goodenough warns, we must have no illusions about science, since we cannot live by it alone. "We must live also by ideas and ideals, Beauty, Freedom, Intelligence, Justice, the Good" ("Scientific Living," p. 9). Even though science cannot test these, can we live by them in the knowledge that although they are necessary for our functioning they may not be necessary for the functioning of nature? Can we live by our ideals and yet subject them to our critical instincts and to scientific scrutiny?

Two years earlier Goodenough had criticized a somewhat related thesis of Anders Nygren's *Agape and Eros*, that the peculiarly Christian concept of *agapē* is Christianity's fundamental motif.[5] Goodenough says that Nygren both overstresses his thesis and also tries to support it from too few New Testament texts. What meaning can "love" have, however sublimated, without the element of desire? The Gospels and Paul's letters show that this is not the exclusive New Testament meaning of *agapē*. Nygren is quite wrong in attributing the sexual element only to *eros*. The New Testament refutes this also. On the other hand, the appeal of the mystery religions was precisely the yearning love which their deities showed to human beings and the suffering of the deities which became humanity's way of salvation. Nygren goes too far in making a complete

---

[4] Goodenough, "Scientific Living," *The Humanist* 2 (1942) 8–10.

[5] Goodenough, "The Fundamental Motif of Christianity," *Journal of Religion* 20 (1940) 1–14.

contrast between Christian and pagan motivation.

Because of his oversimplification Nygren fails in attempting to make *agapē* the central motif of Christianity. He is essentially a reformer. He traces the history of the *agapē* concept through the church fathers and the later theologians, finally to conclude that it was Augustine who blended *agapē* and *eros* in the great doctrine of *caritas*. *Agapē* was then throughout the Middle Ages imprisoned in *caritas*. During that time *eros* largely molded the interpretation of Christianity until the rebirth of *agapē* in the Reformation. How, asks Goodenough, could *agapē* have been the fundamental motif of Christianity if it is so infrequently predominant in successive developments of Christian thought? Although Nygren succeeds brilliantly in writing the history of Christian *agapē*, he fails to make it the criterion of true Christianity. This is because no one concept has been central throughout all the varieties of Christian experience. In the end it was not any philosophical or theological conception that furnished Christianity with its fundamental motif. Goodenough says finally:

> If we are to understand early Christianity, we must ultimately do so not as modern philological or philosophical scholars, but as first-century fishermen on the Lake of Galilee who see through the mists the risen Lord. Philology and historical philosophy, our clumsy conveyances to the past, can be of use only in so far as they succeed in bringing our souls back to such places of experience, for understanding of other men, from our own or any generation, is achieved, not in the mind, but in the heart. ("Fundamental Motif," p. 14)

These words stand in strange and haunting disharmony with the agnosticism that Goodenough professes in his later years. They express a depth of feeling for the central Christian affirmation that suggests that, in spite of all his efforts to demythologize Christianity, Erwin Goodenough never succeeded in repudiating its claim.

A 1960 essay is interesting in that it shows what he thought a group of humanistic scholars ought to know about the Bible.[6] He states several reasons for considering the importance of the Bible. Above all, it gathers together more aspects of antiquity than any other surviving writings from the ancient world. Christianity could not have come into existence apart from it. The Hebrew Bible preserves not only the supreme products of ancient Near Eastern literature, but above all it preserves religious idealism. Judaism gave to later civilizations monotheism formed by exclusion, whereas in the ancient pagan world monotheism tended to come about through inclusion, the amalgamation of various deities into a

---

[6] Goodenough, "The Bible as Product of the Ancient World," in *Five Essays on the Bible* (New York: American Council of Learned Societies, 1960) 1–19.

single pantheon. Jews finally came to regard the gods of other nations as mere illusions and the worship of such gods as a travesty of devotion to the one true God. The Old Testament God came to be viewed as the creator and ruler of the universe, yet at the same time as the personal Yahweh of the Jews. This idea was one of the most extraordinary and powerful creations of the ancient world. The Jewish Bible is unique in preserving ancient law, and it kept alive two fundamental concepts concerning law: (1) that law and government are at bottom divine prerogatives; and (2) that human society and law are not totally dependent upon fallible human judgments; therefore, there is a foundation for the human hopes of a better society.

The New Testament, although rooted in the Old Testament, is an utterly different book. Its basic record is of the teachings of an extraordinary person, Jesus of Nazareth, which influenced and transformed the lives of a small group of people who became convinced that Jesus had been raised from the dead. Christian writings became a Bible because the experiences they relate reveal human contact with God that has never been repeated. A fallacy that has persisted in the historical criticism of the Bible is the notion that the earlier the origin of a document, the earlier are its ideas. A related fallacy is that the earlier documents bear the more reliable information. In their ignorance of the past, scholars are in danger of projecting their own desires and patterns on the biblical material, which may lead to another fallacy that must be avoided, that is, the fallacy of consistency. Scholars must conclude that the New Testament writers were not only inconsistent with one another, but with themselves as well. Any effort to produce a consistent biblical theology is doomed to failure.

Recognizing these dangers, one may assume that the New Testament reports some of the life and extraordinary teachings of a single man from Galilee. It tells how this man was crucified and how disciples ultimately numbering five hundred witnessed his resurrection from the dead. The Christian movement arose from the conviction of this group that they had not experienced an illusion but had encountered a real person. They formed themselves into a group and devoted themselves to spreading "the contagion of their conviction that in Jesus man had found the solution of all problems" ("Bible as Product," p. 13) and that his followers would also share in the resurrection. His exact significance and character led to centuries of debate, but there was common agreement that his person and resurrection marked him as God's unique revelation to humanity.

That the New Testament is the product of a pious fraud is inconceivable. To explain Jesus merely as a prophet after the resurrection was too simple. Mark's designation of him as Son of God showing his character through miracles and Mark's forecast of his apocalyptic return—primarily an Iranian conception—show the growth of Christian interpretation. Further, to account for the character of the risen Lord through attributing to him a virgin birth was essentially a Greek or Egyptian idea, but it had become Hebraized in form, probably by Jews long accustomed to thinking of their Jewish heroes in this way. The Hellenistic idea that Jesus was one who existed "in the form of God" and equal to God, a concept typical of Philo, was espoused by Paul, John, and the author of the letter to the Hebrews. Such interpretations presuppose a variety of backgrounds in Judaism itself. The church preserved these books with their different points of view and made them into a single Bible. Once canonized, the books were preserved with almost superhuman care for textual integrity.

Two things about Goodenough become apparent in his essay. The first is that he continually searches out the Hellenistic background of the New Testament. The second is that, scientific as he is determined to be in his approach to biblical studies, he never writes merely as a detached observer but always as an insider to the religious concerns that he seeks to delineate.

These same concerns appear in his 1951 presidential address to the Society of Biblical Literature.[7] He first deplores the nadir to which historical criticism of the New Testament had sunk. Whereas young men of his own generation were led into biblical scholarship by their sense of the importance of the words of Jesus or Paul, at present young men turn to the natural sciences—and theology also—for intellectual challenge. Scholars in these fields are saying things that change human lives, but biblical criticism is not doing this.

In the eighteenth century, as for some still today, the study of scripture was essentially a devotional act. Yet in the eighteenth century the new critical spirit that pointed the way to the age of modern science also led even important thinkers into a sophomoric shallow revolt against the claims of Christianity and the Bible. Even today, although we must look elsewhere for our knowledge of natural science, the values of the Bible are not thereby negated. Earlier biblical scholarship was moved by three assumptions: (1) that the Bible is of ultimate importance; (2) that human beings through understanding the secret of the New Testament could live a better life; and (3) that the new methods of philology and historical criticism would reveal this secret.

Although today's New Testament scholarship has not achieved this goal, there is no reason to abandon hope that better understanding of Christianity will have great importance for the present day. This will require new techniques in order to answer the questions of people who may be ready to accept the Bible. Excellent examples are furnished by

[7] Goodenough, "The Inspiration of New Testament Research," *Journal of Biblical Literature* 71 (1952) 1–9.

Paul's letters of how Paul did this for the ancient world. In the ancient world the only reality was immaterial reality. Paul's message was that through the miracle of incarnation Christ provided the bridge, so that through Christ one could pass from matter to spirit, from death to life. Paul speaks of the fulfillment of this ancient hope of achieving the life of the spirit as *dikaiosynē*. In teaching how the mind can rule the flesh, Paul assumes the Platonic-Pythagorean model of the mind like a charioteer ruling the horses or the king ruling the bodily state. When we reduce Paul's letters to their universal timeless value, the *dikaiosynē* of which he writes "begins to sound amazingly like the desire which we now call 'adjustment,' freedom from 'inferiority complex'" ("Inspiration," p. 7). Paul's dealing with universal and unchanging elements in human problems and aspirations gives us a clue to a new method of interpreting the Bible.

The method involves first of all intensive study of the thought-ways of the ancient world, their aspirations, symbolism, and vocabulary. The New Testament must then be seen as a document written by persons who employed such vocabulary and imagery, presenting Christianity as the one religion of the ancient world which offered the deepest gratification of the needs that they felt. When we understand the problems of the ancient world that found their solution in the New Testament, we can then restate these ideas in a form intelligible for our own generation. Goodenough hints here at what he makes more explicit elsewhere, the demythologizing of the New Testament through the models and concepts of depth psychology.

In 1945 Goodenough challenged the widespread view that John was the latest of the four Gospels.[8] Since John's Christology differs so widely from that of the Synoptics, it had long been assumed that it must reflect a later development in thought. But this is to ignore the fact that Paul's Christology, which antedates that of the Synoptics, differs as widely from theirs as does that of John. The premise that John is the latest Gospel must be tested against internal evidence. The supposed knowledge by John of the Synoptics also vanishes when it is recognized that of the nineteen supposed points of agreement between John and Mark, sixteen can be located in two blocks of early gospel tradition upon which both depend. We are not dealing with documentary interdependence but with the development of oral tradition. In the constant oral repetition of narrative, catchwords and striking apothegms are the most likely to survive. These alone can account for the verbal similarities between John and the Synoptics.

Goodenough tests this on the pericope of the anointing at Bethany

[8] Goodenough, "John a Primitive Gospel," *Journal of Biblical Literature* 64 (1945) 145–82.

(John 12:1–8; Mark 14:3–9; Matt 6:6–13; Luke 7:36–50). The catchwords are "valuable pistic nard ointment" and "three hundred denarii." The apothegms are that the ointment is a premonition of Jesus' burial and that the poor are always with us. Luke's version seems to be the most primitive. A woman revered as a saint in Mark's version would hardly have been later transformed back into a streetwalker as in Luke. John's version appears to be later than Luke's. Mary of Bethany is no sinner, nor does she weep. Thus, it is ridiculous for her to wipe the ointment away with her hair, for it is intended to remain on the skin. The ointment now becomes of great value in preparation for Jesus' burial. This is more important than a single act for the poor. In Mark, the latest version, the value of the ointment is retained, but it is now applied to Jesus' head as a messianic sign with no reference to the woman's hair.

The story of the Feeding of the Five Thousand and the Storm on the Lake (John 6:1–21; Mark 6:30–52) presents a different problem. Striking verbal similarities between the two versions suggest a literary relation. Yet, in light of the differences between these two Gospels, why should John have reproduced just this sequence? Goodenough suggests that the two conjoined narratives came to both authors from an earlier written source. Similarities of John's story of the mocking of Jesus (19:2–5) to Mark 15:16–20 show dependence on a common oral tradition rather than John's dependency on Mark.

Close similarities between John and the Johannine Epistles suggest common authorship, although denunciation of heresies in the Epistles and their pastoral tone suggest later problems of the church. However, it is quite conceivable that a later writer of the Epistles was steeped in the phrases and ideas of the Gospel, which itself came earlier. John's conception of the church as the vine (chap. 15) is likewise not late. Far from representing an advanced ecclesiology, it represents a primitive stage "where the notions of paganism were being borrowed without adequate digestion or full sense of their implications" ("John," p. 167). John probably received his figure from Hellenistic Jewish sources.

That John's Gospel is early is demonstrated by its interpretation of the Eucharist. Evidently John had no knowledge of the institution of the Lord's Supper as presented by Paul and the Synoptics. The discourses in chapter 6 indicate that John's community believed in the real presence, but knew only the story of the miracle of the loaves and fishes to justify their practice. Early Christian art shows that fish were included in early eucharistic observances. John's story of the miraculous feeding is analogical to Moses' miraculous feeding of the Israelites with manna. For Christians, Jesus takes the place of Moses. Mark's account of the Eucharist supplanted John's story. Although the multiplication of the loaves was preserved as a sacred story, it was no longer the story of the institution, and the story of the supper in Mark and Paul became the official one.

A new hypothesis is needed to account for John as the primitive Gospel. What is most obvious about early Christianity is the amazing diversity of viewpoints from which the New Testament expresses it. It is unlikely that any one of the New Testament writers read as a close guide the writings of any other. The endeavor to arrange the New Testament writings in order according to the supposed development of ideas among Christians is futile. It is more fruitful to identify the common denominator of all these documents, which is the proclamation of the incarnation, crucifixion, and resurrection of Jesus, together with the messianic implication of these events. This provides the basis upon which each writer constructs a theory of the person and work of Christ. "Stirred by the amazing story of Jesus . . . each person . . . saw in the stupendous phenomenon the fulfillment of his hopes" ("John," p. 180). Each writer finds in Jesus the fulfillment of his own spiritual longings, and each uses a theological vocabulary without explaining its terms. The message of each writer is the fact that Jesus saves, and not the nature of salvation. This makes it perfectly plausible to think that John is a primitive Gospel and that the author could have been a Hellenistic Jewish Christian, perhaps in exile.

Sharp criticism of Goodenough's article was leveled by Robert P. Casey.[9] Casey comments primarily on Goodenough's methods rather than his conclusions. He faults Goodenough's main argument that John need not have known the Synoptics to have derived the elements that his Gospel has in common with them. Casey contends that an oral tradition which influences to the point of reproducing in identical fashion peculiar words, phrases, and turns of style is, in a sense, already a text, whether written down or not. Goodenough's attempt to substitute the impact of oral tradition for the documentary hypothesis to account for close similarities among the Synoptics and to ignore evidence of editorial procedure in the development of Matthew and Luke out of Mark "is the substitution of complexity for simplicity as the mark of truth" ("Professor Goodenough," p. 537). To assume the existence of lost originals to explain the known evidence is only to push the problem one stage further back.

The fallacy of Goodenough's method is shown, according to Casey, in his explanation of the story of the anointing of Jesus. On the presupposition of documentary interrelationship, Casey offers his own analysis of the pericope to demonstrate the priority of Mark's version because of its greater simplicity in form. A further example of arbitrary criticism is Goodenough's claim that verbal similarities between Mark and John in the story of Jesus' crossing the lake could arise from oral tradition. By

---

[9] Casey, "Professor Goodenough and the Fourth Gospel," *Journal of Biblical Literature* 64 (1945) 535–42.

what "inner compulsion" would an early Christian, whenever he told the story of the miraculous feeding, be moved immediately to add that of the walking over the sea? To add to the difficulty, "in John the connection between the two miracles is forced, and their association is one of the least felicitous instances of Johannine compilation" ("Professor Goodenough," p. 540). Goodenough's theory that the early Christian eucharistic tradition arose from Jewish mystic thought is likewise open to serious question. As early Christians "partook of the Messiah in the form of fish, bread, and wine, in anticipation of his coming and of the great Messianic banquet of the future life,"[10] what would have induced them to begin thinking that they were partaking of Christ in the blessed elements? The Christian eucharistic tradition arose nowhere else than in the story of the Last Supper itself. The development of thought, feeling, and practice is quite adequately displayed in the appropriate texts in Mark, Matthew, Acts, 1 Corinthians, and Luke when read in that order.

Casey concludes: "With Goodenough's method the whole earliest stage of Christianity disappears in a fog of vain conjecture. Where documents appear most plausible they must be most suspect. Where they appear primitive, this must be due to the refashioning of less plausible material. This is the point of his article" ("Professor Goodenough," p. 541).

Goodenough's reply followed immediately.[11] He faults Casey for failing to define what he means by the "documentary theory." "His remarks imply that he thinks Mark, and presumably Q, spring fully formed from their authors' minds with no developments of consequence between the events themselves and their being recounted in one of these documents" ("Reply," p. 543). By failing to penetrate this unknown background, Casey enters the same "fog of unverifiable conjecture" of which he accuses Goodenough, who sees nothing in the issue to debate. Casey did not read carefully enough Goodenough's statement on the sequence of the stories of the feeding and the crossing of the lake, where he had admitted that oral tradition alone was insufficient to account for the juxtaposition of the two stories. Goodenough admits that his section on the Eucharist is the least satisfactory part of his essay, yet Casey is unfair to accuse him of not considering the question of why in the meal the Christians found themselves partaking of Christ in the blessed elements. It would have been more fair simply to say that he had not answered it. This is the kind of scholarly debate that Goodenough sought to encourage. He engaged in it graciously and without rancor, yet he was always ready to give sturdy defense of his own positions when he considered them to be positions of strength.

---

[10] Goodenough, "John a Primitive Gospel," 172.
[11] Goodenough, "A Reply," *Journal of Biblical Literature* 64 (1945) 543–44.

In a brief article in 1966 Goodenough shows the direction of his thought with respect to Christian origins as shown in the New Testament.[12] He shows how the portrait of Jesus in Acts is strikingly different from that of Luke's Gospel. Acts shows nothing of the great teacher of parables and ethics that the Gospel shows. The mention in Acts of the disciples' breaking of bread gives no implication of its being a sacramental meal connected with bread and wine. Although Acts tells of Paul's establishing "elders" in the churches he had formed, it gives no indication that Luke recognized them as priests in the new Christian sense. Baptism mentioned in Acts seems simply to be the rite formerly practiced by John the Baptist, although now it is given in the "name of Jesus." In contrast, Paul's teaching of baptism as a participation in Christ's death and resurrection that makes of the one baptized a new creature in Christ opens up an entirely new conception of baptism. Although theological and sacramental teaching about baptism was fully alive in the time of Acts, Acts does not mention it.

The most striking differences are to be found between the portrait of Paul in Acts and Paul's representation of himself. Paul emphasizes the genuineness of his Judaism (Phil 3:2-7), but he indicates nothing to support the claim that he had been tutored by Gamaliel (Acts 22:3; 23:6) as a Pharisee. Paul's familiarity with the Septuagint rather than the Hebrew Bible tends to refute the claim. Talmudists have consistently despised Paul's attitude toward the law and have seen nothing in common between themselves and Paul.

Paul's claim in Acts that he was a Roman citizen appears to be without foundation. One detail in Acts 21:28 seems genuine: "This is the man who is teaching everywhere against the people and against the law in this place." However, Acts implies that such an accusation is pure slander. "Yet it is at the core of Paul's letters that keeping the law, even circumcision, is not only misleading but quite wrong for one who has died to the old law and been saved in the new law of the Spirit in Christ Jesus" ("Acts," p. 56).

The Paul of Acts seems to be a pure invention of its author. Why would such a "romance" be written? There is no good reason to assume as late a date of origin for Acts as that usually assigned to it. Neither the Gospels nor Acts suggest that their authors are talking about a lost temple and civilization. Even Luke's warning of armies surrounding Jerusalem need not have been *post eventum* (19:43-44). Many persons must have been constantly aware of the possibility of seige and destruction of Jerusalem by the Romans. Chronological arrangement of

---

[12] Goodenough, "The Perspective in Acts," in *Studies in Luke-Acts: Essays Presented in Honor of Paul Schubert* (ed. L. E. Keck and J. L. Martyn; Nashville: Abingdon, 1966) 51-59.

New Testament writings in terms of supposed developments in Christian thought is impossible. The more fully developed thought of Paul, John's Gospel, and the Epistle to the Hebrews, which integrates eschatology with sacramental mysticism, could exist side by side with the more elementary teaching of a book such as Acts.

Although Luke both in the Gospel and in Acts retreats from the more ardent expectation of the return of Christ, his solution is nevertheless that of Jewish Christianity. "He sees Christianity not as a new covenant, which superseded the old by offering a mystic and sacramental body of Christ, but as the fulfillment of the old covenant itself" ("Acts," p. 58). Acts may have been written in the early sixties to reassure Theophilus that, despite possible disturbing rumors concerning Paul's teaching, "Paul was actually a very great man who preached and lived for what Paul, like the author of Hebrews, actually considered the childish milk of the gospel (1 Cor 3:1-2)" ("Acts," p. 58). Although such fiction could have been written at any time, it is likely that it was written before Paul's death while the issue was still acute. This merely reinforces Goodenough's earlier argument concerning John, that in the great diversity of early Christianity both sophisticated and simple theologies could exist side by side, which does not give much clue to the time of their origin.

Goodenough never abandoned his "grand plan" of writing an extended study of the origins of Christianity. By the winter of 1964-65 he recognized that his illness precluded the possibility of completing such a work. When it became clear that time would not permit completion even of a first volume, he wrote a long article to suggest the methodology and to indicate conclusions that might be reached in the long-projected longer work, could it have been written.[13]

In this article he suggests that the understanding of Paul has been confused by the fact that practically all older lives of Paul have been based on Paul's story in Acts. If Paul is to be understood correctly, he must be approached through his own writings. Where these disagree with Acts, Paul's word must take priority. To illustrate, Goodenough translates Gal 1:16 as ". . . was pleased to reveal his son within me (ἐν ἐμοί)" ("Paul," p. 26), which indicates an inward mystical experience, rather than "to me" as in the RSV, which presupposes the Acts story. Phil 3:4-6 merely indicates that Paul followed the Pharisees, not that he was himself a Pharisee, as clearly indicated in Acts 26:5. Paul's story in Acts makes clear that for an unspecified time Paul preached along with the Jerusalem apostles and that it was the Hellenists who wanted to kill him.

[13] Goodenough, "Paul and the Hellenization of Christianity," with A. Thomas Kraabel, in *Religions in Antiquity: Essays in Memory of Erwin Ramsdell Goodenough* (ed. J. Neusner; Leiden: Brill, 1968) 23-68.

The "Jerusalem Conference" of Acts 15 is the same as the consultation with the apostles that Paul reports in Galatians 2. It is incredible that the Paul of Acts 15:28–29, meekly accepting the laws of kosher meat, is the same as the Paul of Gal 2:11–21 who openly repudiates all such ritual law.

The main objection to using Acts as a source for Paul's ideas is that "the essential preaching of Paul in Acts is a Jewish-Christian message . . . [and] what appears in *most* of the letters to be the *essential* Paul is not there" ("Paul," p. 33). Each of Paul's letters conveys a separate impression. In the light of this diversity, is it legitimate to attempt to extract Paul's essential message from a single letter? Goodenough thinks that it is and that the letter is the Epistle to the Romans. In Romans, Paul "is provoked by no outside vagaries or problems, he is expounding the message of Christ, the theme of which is salvation" ("Paul," p. 34).

In Romans 1 Paul's commission is to bring about "the obedience of faith for the sake of his name among all the Gentiles" (1:5). This is in no sense obedience to the law of Moses. Paul's reference in 1:16 to the gospel as the power of God reminds us that Philo regarded God's power as extended through a series of powers, which taken together were the Logos. It would not be a bad guess to take Paul's meaning to be that the gospel is "the Logos of God which works salvation" ("Paul," p. 37). Paul also runs parallel to Philo when he says that the nature of God has been revealed in the created world (1:20).

In Romans 2 Paul says that nature reveals not God's *law*, but rather *God himself*. In 2:14–15 he uses law in two senses. Clearly a Gentile never had the *Jewish* law, "but a few righteous Gentiles have known the *natural* law, the real law, the law of the spirit, and have obeyed it" ("Paul," p. 39). The real law is in the spirit, not in the written code (2:29). According to Philo the spirit-law is revealed in the great patriarchs, the *nomoi empsychoi*, or incarnate laws. Philo is referring not to the Torah but to a higher general law which basically was the source of Platonic reality, which could never adequately be represented in matter. "This understanding of the true law as a kind of Platonic Real, a basic thesis of Philo's whole writing, is carried over directly in Paul's contrast between the law of the letter and the higher law of the spirit" ("Paul," p. 42). This higher law issues in the higher principles of morality which throughout his letters Paul exhorts Christians to follow.

Romans 3 expounds the advantages the Jews have over the Gentiles. The written law at least brings the Jew to knowledge of sin, and 3:2 answers on a deeper level. "The Jews were given a share in the great *pistis* (of God) by being given the formulated laws of God, *ta logia*" ("Paul," pp. 43–44). The Jewish law is a great revelation of the righteousness of God, and of his faithfulness, his *pistis*, his stability. The second gift was the Mosaic code given specifically to the Jews. *This* is their great advantage. The third revelation of the "law-abidingness" of God is made in Christ. Although all human beings are sinners, this gift is available to all. "We are made righteous because this faith *of* Christ is given us" ("Paul," p. 44). Emphatically Goodenough says, "It is crucial to note that 'faith' in this passage (3:22 and 26) is not faith *in* Jesus Christ but the faith *of* Jesus Christ, πίστις 'Ιησοῦ Χριστοῦ. . . . By this faith *of* Christ, transferred to us, we have hope of immortality ourselves" ("Paul," p. 45).

On the basis of the lower and higher law, Paul must explain why "boasting" must be excluded. Spiritual pride results precisely from an approach to righteousness by deeds, acts, and obedience. However, Christians have nothing to boast about, for they follow not the law of precepts but the law of faith.

In Romans 4 Paul's interpretation is Philonic as he uses Abraham as the great example of one who is saved by faith. The promise was made to Abraham not through law but "through faith that brings *dikaiosynē*" (Goodenough's translation of 4:13 ["Paul," p. 49]). In 4:17 and 23–25 Paul brings together *our* faith, the faith *of* Christ, and the faith of Abraham. Each is a faith in the God who raises the dead, which results in righteousness. It seems incredible to Goodenough "that the raw experience of Christ should have suggested to Paul this extraordinary rationalization through Abraham, unless he had had considerable association of religious experience with Abraham already. It could not have come simply from the Genesis story of Abraham" ("Paul," p. 50). It would be extreme to say that Paul took over totally from Hellenistic Judaism the tradition of the patriarchs as *nomoi empsychoi*. Yet Paul demonstrates clear traces of Hellenistic Judaism. If Paul seldom deals with patriarchs apart from Abraham, the reason may be that for him "Christ, as revealed in the resurrection, was so supremely the *nomos empsychos*, the incarnation of the higher law, that he had no need of the others and so passed them by" ("Paul," p. 50).

Romans 5 declares that righteousness *out of faith* brings us peace with God. A whole new problem is raised in 5:12–14. How could the righteousness of *one* lead to the salvation of the human race? Paul is quite Jewish in his argument that because all are descended from Adam, all must die because of Adam's sin. The fact of the universality of sin was not Paul's invention. But "the suggestion that the sin of Adam vitiated Adam's character in such a way that 'original sin' came to all men as guilt, and that all men shared in Adam's sin . . . is a contribution of Paul himself" ("Paul," p. 51). Christ the "New Adam" can gather to himself a new "body" or community to whom, through his atoning death and resurrection, he brings *dikaiosynē* and *zoē* (life).

Only a Jew could have written the allegory of Adam, but in

Romans 6 Paul deals with the problem in a Greek sense. Rom 5:5–14 "opens the whole problem of the identification of sin with the body, something as recognizably Hellenistic as it is foreign to essential Jewish thought" ("Paul," p. 53). The new criterion here is that of the corruptibility of the flesh and the subversiveness of the flesh over against the spirit. It is the old problem brought out by Plato in the allegory of the cave (*Republic* 7.514ff.). "Those who have gone outside the cave and seen the glory, seen the truth, seen reality, must still return to the cave and sit on its inner bench again, seeing only the shadows and living the life of the shadows" ("Paul," p. 54).

Romans 7 declares that the death we have shared with Christ annuls any obligation to the Mosaic law. Paul's analysis of the effects of commands upon the human psyche, that they induce us to do the very thing that they prohibit, is extraordinary. Goodenough observes, "It is a common saying that the *id* knows no negatives, that every negative command is for the *id* a suggestion; we are coming pretty close to Freud's *id* in this matter of the members and their special life" ("Paul," p. 55).[14] Paul agonizes over the identification of his authentic ego (7:14–20). Is the self the person Paul knows that he ought to be, or is it the person he actually is? In 7:21–25 appears an array of laws which create despair in anyone trying to understand Paul in terms of the Old Testament and later Judaism. The law of doing evil when we want to do good may be the law of nature, but it is no part of the code of Moses. The law of the spirit may be the Torah. Beyond these is the evil law that resides in the flesh, Paul's thought here cannot be understood in terms of the Jewish "evil impulse" versus the "good impulse."[15]

Philo, seeing incarnation in the body as the great tragedy of human existence, interpreted the great patriarchs as incarnations of the higher law through whom we could gain access to lives of value and virtue. The Mosaic law was but a shadow of the higher law toward which we should aspire, not stopping with the precepts of the written law. Goodenough believes that Paul was thoroughly acquainted with the Jewish mystery, of which he gives a masterful summary in 1 Cor 10:1–4: "Those who had passed through the sea and the cloud were baptized *into Moses*; he was a personal revelation of this higher entity. Baptism *into Moses* exactly parallels Paul's idea of baptism *into Christ*" ("Paul," p. 59). In saying

[14] In a footnote on this passage Goodenough denies that he intends to reduce Paul to Freud's categories. He wishes only to note that both Paul and Freud may be stating the same truth. Similar interpretations of Romans 7 appear in *Toward a Mature Faith* (p. 119) and in *The Psychology of Religious Experiences* (pp. 58–63).

[15] Goodenough refers to "Law in the Subjective Realm" (*By Light, Light*, pp. 370–443) where he traces out at length the origin in Orphism of the idea of the body as the corrupting agent of the soul. He is emphatic that the law of sin as a part of the body is Hellenistic in origin.

that the Israelites were fed with the same "pneumatic" food and drank the same "pneumatic" drink, Paul is saying only what Philo often says about the manna in the wilderness and the water from the great rock (Exodus 16–17). The stream of water from the rock was the Logos. Paul makes a simple change: "The rock was Christ." A Hellenistic background underlies the passage, and Paul certainly did not invent the idea that the passage of the Red Sea was a baptism *into Moses*.

The same theme continues in Romans 8. We can rise from the lower to the higher law which Christ embodies, just as Moses did. We fulfill the just requirement of the law not through doing the law of Moses but through the higher law which we obtain through Christ. This is just what the Jews did who were baptized into Moses. Paul here has the difficult task of describing Christian existence until the Parousia. Pre-Christian legalism is an impossibility; therefore, we must set our minds upon the spirit. We have entered a new order, although not yet perfect, since *dikaiosynē* in the fullest form belongs to God alone. To arrive at that full perfection our bodies must be transformed into spiritual bodies. We must die to our whole selves, to our physical nature, and come to live in the law of the spirit of Christ.

Romans 9–11 present further points of comparison between Paul and Philo. Like Paul, Philo identifies as the true Israelites those Jews "who live not by the laws of the commands, but by the Logos and the powers of the higher law. But unlike Paul he does not say that those who are doing the best they can (the ordinary Jews with the Mosaic code) are a rejected people" ("Paul," p. 62). Philo accepted as a matter of course that the true Israel was a spiritual elite that was necessarily to be distinguished from the great mass of Jews to whom mercifully had been given the law of Moses by which to live. Paul, on the other hand, found the higher law made so vivid and so accessible through Christ, that "he took the step that Philo would never have taken; he rejected those who tried by their own efforts to be saved" ("Paul," p. 63). All may pray to God equally for the gift, "for everyone who calls on the name of the Lord will be saved" (Rom 10:3).

Paul's predestinarianism is not specifically Jewish or specifically Greek, but rather reveals a problem that arose out of Paul's particular experience of Christ. Nothing compares with it either in Philo or in rabbinic texts. This raises a question concerning the whole of Goodenough's endeavor to show fundamental influence upon Paul by Hellenistic Judaism. It would appear that Hellenistic elements in Paul are not determinative for his thinking. Paul's theology is incarnational in a way that Philo's doctrine of the *nomoi empsychoi* could never be. On the one hand, the goal for which Paul longed was achievement of fellowship with God through Christ. For Philo, on the other hand, the goal was the mystic vision and ultimate absorption into God himself. Paul hoped for the final fulfillment of selfhood through relationship with Christ, whereas Philo aspired toward the final merging of the self into Ultimate Being.

Romans 12–16 suggest that Paul's ethical statements in his letters often resemble those of the Sermon on the Mount, yet with a difference. Jesus as a Palestinian "came to the higher meaning by generalizing the laws of the code themselves; Paul, on the other hand, worked to establish a morality that rises above specific precepts altogether, one that is based instead on the higher perception of right and wrong, on the higher immaterial law" ("Paul," p. 65). Paul thinks in Hellenistic rather than Jewish terms. Comparison of Paul's thought with that of Philo in *The Special Laws* shows this. In the law of nature Philo sees the first great revelation of God's law. This was followed by its embodiment in the patriarchs and, finally, in the giving of the Ten Commandments elaborated in the Torah. Unlike Paul, Philo never lost his reverence for the literal Mosaic code.

Goodenough points out that "once the specifics of the law have been explained, Philo leaves detailed laws behind altogether" ("Paul," p. 66). Paul's view is similar: "For him the only way to avoid the sins of the flesh is to let the light of God so shine into us that the body with its desires and passions fades out of existence" ("Paul," p. 66). Paul's great difference from Philo is "that he has been so engrossed, encompassed, engulfed by the vision of Christ that he no longer needs to defend the specific commands; indeed he rises above them altogether and looks toward a state where the higher mind, the higher vision, the higher self illuminated by God, is governing us, so that the body has become dead" ("Paul," pp. 67–68). In spite of differences between Paul and Philo, "both of them are trying to lead man into a life in which the higher part, the part engulfed by God, takes over and the fleshly impulses are no longer in control" ("Paul," p. 68).

The question of Paul's mysticism has been much discussed, and Goodenough is not the first to raise it. The influence of Hellenism on Paul has long been recognized; however, the present writer is left with doubts that Paul was as heavily influenced by a "Jewish mystery" of a Philonic sort as Goodenough claims. His claim that Paul, like Philo, rises above the specific commands of the law does not seem to be borne out by Paul's letters. To be sure, Paul insists that salvation does not come by doing the law and that the entire ritual law is nullified by faith in Christ. Nevertheless, the Pauline *didachē* is surely rooted in the moral teaching of the Torah. Paul nowhere teaches the relaxation of any of the Ten Commandments. Moreover, in Col 2:8–23 he teaches against the very kind of asceticism that Philo's "higher mystery" might tend to promote. Although in 1 Corinthians 7 Paul expresses preference for the single life, he justifies this view by the nearness of the parousia rather than because of any scorn of the flesh. Moreover, in 1 Corinthians 9 he affirms his right to marriage, and he does not claim any spiritual superiority over the other apostles because they have wives and he does not. Throughout his writings Paul's moral and ethical teachings have a concreteness that we normally associate with law.

The most fundamental difference between Paul and Philo lies in their objectives. Philo's highest goal is the achievement of spiritual enlightenment, which is accessible to only a few choice individuals. Philo's highest concept of religion is a religion of an elite from which the great mass of ordinary individuals is excluded. Paul's highest goal, on the other hand, is so to proclaim the gospel that all persons, whether Jew or Gentile, male or female, bond or free, are afforded the opportunity to participate as members in the body of Christ. Paul becomes "all things to all men, that [he] might by all means save some" (1 Cor 9:22). If that meant borrowing something from the language of the Jewish mystery, Paul was capable of doing that; yet his goal was set by the gospel of Christ and not by the mystery.

The questions that Goodenough raises are always significant, and out of the riches of his very great scholarship he has much illumination to offer. Yet the questions remain open, and, if we do not always find it possible to agree with his conclusions, we are always in his debt for stimulating us to consider seriously the questions that he raises.

8

THE PERSONAL RELIGIOUS QUEST

In the opening chapter we traced the biography of the young Erwin Goodenough, observing how his early life was dominated and shaped by Methodist pietism. We saw also how in his early maturity he came under strong intellectual influences that eventually were to draw him away from the orthodoxies of his youth. His rather natural decision to prepare for the ministry remained apparently undisturbed during his studies at Drew and Garrett theological seminaries. But at Harvard his immersion in historical and critical studies in religion led him across the threshold of a new world of intellectual excitement from which he never retreated. His subsequent years at Oxford opened this world out to him, and upon his return to the United States he exchanged the ministry for scholarship and university teaching.

Throughout his life of scholarship the power and values of religion nevertheless beckoned and sustained him, and he sought to interpret the nature and meaning of religion in new ways which seemed to him to be better suited to the modern scientific era. His early research in religious symbolism provided him with one way of reinterpretation, and his discovery of depth psychology provided him with another way, which he found highly compatible with the study of symbols. For him psychology furnished the golden key to unlock the resources of religion for the modern mind. Toward the end of his life he wrote two small books in which he expounded the religious insights and convictions of his late maturity. The first is a kind of spiritual biography in which he shows the power of myth and symbol to express the deepest meanings of religion. Although Goodenough professes not to be a scholar in psychology, he nevertheless makes bold to show how the essence of religion over the centuries has been to serve a psychotherapeutic purpose only now correctly to be understood in the light of modern scientific psychology.

In these two books Goodenough dismisses as meaningless in any literal sense much of traditional Christian doctrine about the nature of God and salvation through Christ. He declares that religion is our most powerful wish projection, and we must resolve in these modern times to be our own saviors. Yet traditional forms of religion can still be of value if they are infused with new meaning compatible with the thinking of the modern age. Of the various forms of religious experience, he finds legalism and orthodoxy the most prone to the fostering of "blueprint religion," and he holds these forms in the lowest esteem. In this judgment we can perceive the young Goodenough as he finally cast off the orthodoxy of his parents.

Beyond legalism is supralegalism, its highest exemplar being Jesus, who teaches us to live above the standards of human society, to live rather in the social context of God himself. Supralegalism among the Greeks made almost superhuman intellectual demands as its devotees sought to live by the law that is above and beyond all human law. Only the greatest religious geniuses have dwelt in that realm. Most if not all religious traditions and forms of religious experience may be of service to modern persons if their symbolic value and their psychological significance are properly understood. Ultimately they fail to achieve their goal. In the final analysis, religion must be understood as a perennial search. In its highest form religion is the mystic striving toward the indescribable, the incommunicable, the darkness which is light. Goodenough's term for this is "the *tremendum*." Acceptance of the tremendum he calls agnosticism. Here it is possible to see the mature Goodenough, further and further separated from traditional religion. Although he feels a sense of isolation from others who profess conventional religion, he is convinced, nevertheless, that he is engaged in the highest form of the religious quest, which is reserved for the very few.

Throughout all of Goodenough's discussions of religion there emerge frequently the expressions of earnest piety. He declares that even though Christ's image must be recreated in every age, Christ is the one to whom we may turn for spiritual guidance and comfort. He is the very embodiment of our highest ideals. Prayer is still a very live option, even for the most intellectual. Into his final days Goodenough professed that he prayed and found great benefit in it. He readily commended prayer to others. Although he was constantly critical of traditional forms and expressions of religion, the sense of religious awe and the spirit of devotion never failed in Goodenough's life. In spite of the wide universe of thought that separated them, with his Uncle Charlie he could say concerning spiritual resources, "Drink deep! Drink deep!"[1]

I

The second chapter of *Toward a Mature Faith* tells of Goodenough's introduction to depth psychology. In 1938 he met Carl Jung during Jung's visit to the United States. Jung expressed great interest and

---

[1] Goodenough, *Toward a Mature Faith* (Englewood Cliffs, NJ: Prentice-Hall, 1955) 180.

gave strong encouragement to Goodenough's beginning studies of religious symbols. In Jung's concept of "wish projection" Goodenough found one of the most important ideas for religion, an idea that had permanent influence on his later studies. Through projection of dreams of God and right, great religious leaders truly helped those who accepted them. Freud's dismissal of religion as an "illusion" must be rejected. Much truth resides in religious projections. Scientific theory is projection of patterns upon nature whereby we can better relate ourselves to it. Much of the modern person's sense of meaninglessness derives from abandonment of the great projected wishes of traditional religion, of a God in whom people can have faith and into whose hands, even at death, they can commend their spirits.

Goodenough says, "This discovery was to me not paralyzing at all, any more than the discovery of the implications of the historical criticism had been ten years earlier. For if man has always lived on projections he can continue to do so" (*Mature Faith*, p. 44). The world we actually see is a projected illusion, and "in the illusion there is a large element of truth" (*Mature Faith*, p. 44). He illustrates, as he recounts with great warmth of feeling, how his mother gently led him beyond his childhood belief in Santa Claus to the larger concept of light and hope emerging out of the darkest days of the year as a new baby is born. This is a parable for modern intellectuals who need to recognize the truth that lies behind the old stories. "God is no illusion. He is a marvelous form of projection by which we perceive the truth, as is the law of gravity" (*Mature Faith*, p. 47). If a new civilization is to emerge it will have new dreams and new projections. Depth psychology can greatly help us to distinguish between bad dreams like fascism and communism, and assist us to cultivate the better dreams by which we may live.

The third chapter treats symbols from the viewpoint of depth psychology. Our most important thinking is done in pictures and symbols in the subconscious mind. Putting thought into the right words is difficult, and facile speech or writing is often shallow. At the same time, nonverbal thinking is often excellent thinking. A great complex of symbols operates in our lives, arousing many different feelings, and the symbols by which we live exercise great power over us. Just as we can control nature for our own benefit, we can also through understanding of the irrational symbols that influence us use them for constructive ends.

Symbols are of three kinds: private, social, and religious. The private symbol of the child's security blanket becomes almost universal. Speech and dress are powerful social symbols. The only universal social code is prohibition of killing within the group. Conformity to the social code is essential to society. The distinction between social and religious symbols is not always clear, and to understand religious symbols we must begin with the most distinctive ones. For Christianity it is the cross. The paradox of a symbol of death giving us hope for life helps to heal the inner division between guilt and the desire for life. The infant and the nursing mother are powerful symbols of our desire to be reborn and to share in divine life. Born as we are, naked and helpless into the world, most of our social symbols are designed to conceal this fact and give us security against it. Nowadays leaders in science and literature reject traditional symbols, yet even in the age of the new science we must live by the simple older symbols which put the mystery of life into workable terms.

The next three chapters are devoted to the traditional Christian graces: faith, hope, and love. We must discuss the old symbols since new symbols cannot be custom-made. From old symbols we must derive new meaning, not by credulity to creeds but through a skeptical and critical attitude. We must doubt not the ends of our predecessors but their means to try to achieve them. Doubt is such an important means to truth that we must have faith in it. Faith is the first religious symbol to discuss, and it must be considered in connection with myth. Answers to all important questions are myths which are indispensable to our having a sense of security in the world. All the security and confidence of early humans came through confidence in their myths and the rituals that grew out of them.

Myths are still important to us today, because through myths the unpredictable becomes manageable and endurable. Myths of weather, love, and war live comfortably with an overall myth such as of a universal creator, because human beings have particular as well as universal problems. Moral codes are sustained by the myth of the universal right. Modern science has added the myth of evolution, since we cannot live without an explanation of origins. Social stability requires the support of myth. Stable marriage requires the myth of the right in marriage. Stability also requires the myth of the state. Goodenough argues that he is not using "*myth*" as something fictitious, but rather as the way that people can piece together experience and knowledge into a connected whole to which they can adjust themselves. Science, which functions to increase human knowledge of reality, is a threat to myth because new discoveries cannot be restricted to old conventions. Yet, since science gives only partial knowledge, the need for myths is not replaced. Christianity earlier used the word "faith" for fixed acceptance of a stability that resides in God alone. Faith leads to the danger of smugness, rigidity that must be "spaded up" by doubt. Goodenough finds that his own life has been stabilized by such "spading."

Modern people must challenge the old myths through intelligence, yet also must formulate creeds and codes to make life bearable. Relativism is not adequate for this. By looking at life's experiences and drawing conclusions from them, people must create myths in which they can believe. New codes cannot be simply invented. Traditional codes to which the majority of persons conform cannot deliberately be abandoned for other codes that are foreign to them. Observance of seasonal festivals such as Christmas need not be abandoned. Acceptance of the basic traditions of society can give life meaning. If seasonal festivals are based on myth, they in general have formative power for people.

In the fourth chapter he discusses hope. Christianity could not survive without hope, and hope is necessary for a strong personality. Hope for the future requires adequate knowledge of the past. This is demonstrated in the survival of Judaism. A vivid sense of the past that showed that human problems could be solved made hope for the future possible. This was absorbed into Christianity as a part of its heritage. Paul, the great psychologist, saw this. Hope is looking forward to the unseen and waiting for it patiently. Neo-orthodox denunciation of history as a basis for human confidence strikes at the roots of the Christian message. Christianity tells us that we may have hope because of the experience of Abraham, of David, and of early Christians, and gives us the realization that humanity on the whole has had a successful history. Goodenough's essential optimism shows itself quite strikingly here. He declares that despair of this world and complete centering upon the future have never been the living hope of the majority of Christians. Most have believed that the experience of Christ should mean the spreading of Christian virtues and raising the level of human existence.

When Goodenough wrote *Toward a Mature Faith*, he believed that the obsession with despair and disillusionment was an occupational disease of the upper classes and had little effect upon the masses. He identified not with the frightened intelligentsia but with the common people with their expectation that society for all its faults is slowly improving. Scientific developments make modest hope in progress reasonable. America was founded not so much on our forebears' belief in God as on their basic humanism, their confidence in the possibility of achievement through their own efforts. Goodenough deplores an attitude of dependence upon inherited wealth or prestige exhibited in unwholesome conservatism with its resistance to change. The church has too often catered to such attitudes, thereby bringing out the apostles of doom in the churches.

The shallow optimism of science of a previous generation must be rejected. We have in fact achieved real progress through science. However, we have had to realize human limits in understanding and the continuing mystery of the universe. Yet we can continue in the tradition of hope. The survival of humanity indicates that we do not live in a hostile universe. Even if we do not look for individual future life, we can face the world with the traditional confidence of Christians and Jews of God's saving power in the future. In spite of our increasing effectiveness in warfare, history can either be written in terms of the increasing destructiveness of humanity or in terms of people's increasing respect for one another and the promotion of human welfare.

Nations or people who have lived by justice and cooperation have survived, but others who have lived by arrogance and force have not. The survival value of basic virtues is revealed in history. They must have survived because they are in accord with the basic nature of things. This is a basis for hope. Here our religious traditions can help us more than anything else, and we can continue to live in hope.

The sixth chapter treats love. Self-love is our deepest instinct. The Christian commandment comes that we love not simply those closest to us, but all fellow human beings in the same way. Christianity has for the most part considered the Great Commandment and the Golden Rule to be possible only for "perfect" people. Yet their very seeming impossibility has spurred people on to more adequate ideas of justice and social cooperation. Therein lie their power and value. They are still useful in modern thinking. To say that Christian *agapē* disregards self-interest is a modern error. It and the Golden Rule are important precisely because they do not disregard it. Christian teaching does not submerge the individual in social obligations. The libido (= *agapē*) that rules our lives must also be "the ruling principle in our reflection to others" (*Mature Faith*, p. 114). This goes far beyond Freudian individualism.

The modern sense of the value of the individual is largely inherited from the Christian tradition. The implications of the Bible gradually undermined slavery, and in warfare armies of Christian nations cannot use the term "expendables" as readily as the Soviets or the Chinese. The Christian spirit demonstrates itself in the gradual extension of universal human rights. Although regard for the individual is strong in Judaism, and humanity as the image of God is an Old Testament idea, the idea of concern for all individuals was carried out in the name of Christ in Gentile society. Statements of Jesus about God's concern for humanity offered the first step in Christianity toward creating self-love in human beings. The great mass of people in the ancient world were hopeless, and paganism offered only a philosophy of resignation or esoteric mysticism unappealing to common persons.

Too stark and too basic to be adequate, Jesus' statements were scorned in later New Testament teaching. Paul and John accept the fallenness of the individual as the natural state. Yet Paul shows amazing insight into the psychological problem of self-rejection in Romans 7, a premonition of later Freudianism—namely, the theory of the conflict between the "id" and the "superego." The psychological insight of the early theologians showed them that our only salvation is in strengthening our superegos until we can live without inner "condemnation." This is "dying and rising with Christ" (Paul) or "rebirth" (John). Whether we take literally this gospel of salvation through faith in Christ, the early

Christians converted the world with this message and brought people for the first time inner healing and basic self-love. Whether we accept Jesus' teachings literally, we must learn from them that human beings must accept themselves as persons with a place in the world and in history. Too often the churches have given only lip service to Jesus' teaching of the equal value of all persons. Yet even non-Christians have held this teaching to be the greatest contribution of Christianity.

Christian self-love must recognize the dignity of others. Only those who lose themselves in concern for others can find themselves. Happiness is never achieved except through creative activity. Teachers, spouses, parents to be true to their roles must identify with pupil, spouse, or child. Good-enough stresses the necessity of the woman's identifying fully with her husband and with her children if she is fully to realize herself. A father who tries to make his son into his own image fails to follow Jesus' teaching, which is to love our children as ourselves, not for ourselves. So in marriage neither partner should seek to dominate the other. Self-sacrifice for its own sake is a sort of perversion. Albert Schweitzer's service to the blacks in Africa, Clifford Beers in reform of psychiatric institutions, and Alcoholics Anonymous all exhibit the acts of persons who so identify with the needs of others that serving these needs becomes the fulfillment of the lives of those who serve. Recognition of the essential unity of the race is the consequence of Jesus' teaching. Presenting the value of the individual together with the individual's obligation to society has been Christianity's great contribution to the development of Western civilization.

In chapter seven Goodenough treats salvation. Basic Christian doctrine is that although human nature is flawed it can be put right by the grace that comes from Christ's death and resurrection. Even if we do not believe in the historical and metaphysical basis of this doctrine, the acceptance of it by many believers has enormously improved their lives. The concept is still of great value even though some prefer to put it in other terms. The conception of human guilt has never been universal, yet a proper sense of guilt is as wholesome as insensitivity to it is unwholesome. In recognizing human guilt Christianity recognizes one of humanity's deepest problems. Many lives have been renewed by the Christian doctrine of salvation. Such a change is the purpose of psychiatry, although it uses other myths and means. The difference is more of means than of substance. Christianity, like all religions, has been the psychiatry of the ages.

Salvation means radical psychotherapy, elevation of life through mastery of life's problems and impulses. Not only Christians but Jews and pagans also felt inner tension and guilt. The Jews spoke of the good and evil impulses. The Greeks thought of the "higher mind" as perceiving true moral principles. This eventually became conscience. Both ancients and moderns recognized the conflict between the demands of society and our urge to gratify our senses and exercise aggressiveness. Throughout life we have to find a balance between these forces. Throughout the centuries this has been a religious problem, and psychiatry is a newcomer to this field. The "good impulse" has always seemed to be of divine origin, the revolt against it requiring to be forgiven or overcome by God. The Christian version of the problem goes back to Paul. Although Paul never questioned the rightness of the law, he was not able to keep it. He did not challenge the law as Jesus did. Paul discovered that every prohibition is a positive suggestion to do what is prohibited. In this dilemma we know that pleasurable yielding to temptation brings the pain of guilt. Healthy-minded people can refrain from forbidden acts but cannot escape the impulse to do them and so experience guilt.

It is usually "good" people who suffer most acutely from guilt and experience the inner dividedness of which Paul speaks. This is still universal human experience, and although modern people have difficulty with Paul's other doctrines—human perversity inherited from Adam, or predestination—we must nevertheless recognize this inner division as inescapable in human nature. Paul need not be belittled because of the inadequacy of his doctrines, for he saw that mere moral teaching is not enough. The whole person must accept what the conscience says is right. The pagans attempted psychotherapy in two ways. The Greek approach arising out of Platonism was to train the mind to contemplate superhuman reality until it mastered the lower desires or impulses. The mystical approach was to find means to rise to mystical association with higher reality, essentially training oneself. This approach is too rarified for the average individual.

Modern psychology teaches that our consciences are not the voice of God but the standards of our parents represented to us as children. These become a part of ourselves. We project them upon a spouse, or priest, or God. We have to experience conscience in personal terms, not under the images of animals as did ancient people. Protestants may reject images as "idols," yet the Protestant stress on the "personality" of God is only the Protestant version of the same phenomenon. The ancient representation of personal experiences of the gods in myths may be seen in the myth of the divine family and the birth of the divine child by union of the human and the divine. Usually the divine child was destroyed by wicked forces and then restored to life. Yet the ancients found such divine persons hard to reach and only vaguely personal. Only Christianity announced that a truly divine person had entered into history, had conquered death and sin, one with whom ordinary persons can identify and experience new birth.

The violence of Paul's language in describing the experience of overcoming the lower nature and achievement of rebirth and salvation is unique. Nothing before Christianity offered this idea with such concreteness and conviction and has brought the solution of the problem of guilt to so many people.

This help of the ages has been abandoned by many intellectuals. True intellectuals may find the solution in the ancient yet perennial philosophy of mysticism, but such mystics are few. The mass of intellectuals have turned to the ancient solution of self-help, but for them the saving person becomes the ego. Contrary to Christian teaching their hope is in themselves, but the self-sufficient personality is as mythical as the creedal Christ. Younger intellectuals are increasingly demonstrating the desire for conversion. The myth that we can become our own saviors is widely challenged, yet Goodenough accepts it and finds it constructive. American democracy is built on it, but it can only be held in faith. He declares that participation in American society requires it. Belief in America is actually belief in ourselves collectively as the savior. Yet this one myth is not enough; we need another as the basis for our private morality. We need faith in our ideal person to tell us what to do and to love us and to help us. Can we make such a person to order and project into that one our ideals? Yes, and we can do what others throughout the ages have done and call him Jesus.

In the eighth chapter Goodenough discusses "Jesus in the New Age." The average modern person is ignorant of Jesus. Historical data about him is scanty, but the Christian movement arose from the conviction of Jesus' resurrection. Surely he was crucified for political reasons, was the son of Mary, and had brothers and sisters. He taught and healed, but only some healings are credible; and the originality of Jesus' teachings is uncertain. The Jesus of history is obscured behind what people have projected upon him. The vision of the resurrected Jesus was the crystallizing agent, and each group made a Jesus for itself. Goodenough finds this praiseworthy. Jesus took on all the successive forms of the Christ myth, and each new form meant a great human achievement and source of power. As Jesus became freshly meaningful, people felt their own lives take on meaning and direction. This is the best psychotherapy for the mass of people. Nothing can take the place of such a personality.

The effort to idealize some living person turns out to be stultifying, and the "great leader" of a people will become their destruction (Mussolini, Hitler, Lenin, Stalin). The power of Jesus in Western civilization has been precisely his power to change from age to age. Modern technology does not give life meaning, nor does it develop spiritual power. This comes only from our dreams. The best dream to save us from guilt and give us new power is the perfect human embodiment of our ideals, one who loves us and lifts us rather than one who condemns us. The present age has the power to dream, but we cannot return to the nineteenth-century Jesus.

Modern historical and psychological study forces us to recognize that our objects of worship have always been images of our own making. We cannot go back. Only by experiment can we recover a new Jesus who will become a saving power for us all, perhaps through selecting biblical passages that appeal to us. Analogous to this is the continual reinterpretation of both English and American law to make them relevant to the times. The same is true of Judaism, for whom the Talmud provides reinterpretation of the Torah to suit later situations. The rise of historical attitudes and techniques in the study and practice of religion has led to modern feelings of insecurity. This results from the loss of our sense of right through continuity with traditional standards. However, we cannot solve modern problems with ancient solutions. We cannot modernize the historical Jesus and invent a Jesus for ourselves. We must discover the best of the old by use of the best of the new.

The best of the old was not the belittling of humanity and human hopes but rather the deepening of faith and hope, and growing confidence in the constructive aspects of life. This is best expressed in the incarnation. The gospels show that the divinity preeminently demonstrated in Jesus is manifest in many other people. "Jesus came to be the incarnation, and so the source for others, of the stability of faith, of the promise of hope, of the creative potency of love" (*Mature Faith*, p. 174). Mythic though Jesus as Savior may be, this myth has been the source of comfort, stability, and inspiration of countless people.

In the final chapter Goodenough urges our need for prayer. People have always prayed to the extensions of their highest ideals and have been strengthened by doing so. We can still pray in the name of God or Jesus, and when we do so he comes to us. We must pray not for things but for strength, generosity, and love. Our prayers may be directed to an unknown reality, but we cannot get beyond our projections. Yet it is more important to use spiritual reality for our own strengthening and inspiration than it is to understand the nature of the reality that strengthens and renews us.

II

Ten years later than *Toward a Mature Faith* Goodenough published a further summation of his understanding of religion in *The Psychology of Religious Experiences*.[2] In it themes recur that are to be found in all of his preceding writings. The question of the first chapter is "What is Religion?" It is an attitude of trust coupled with a sense of helplessness before what Goodenough calls the "tremendum," that collective sense of

---

[2] Goodenough, *The Psychology of Religious Experiences* (New York: Basic Books, 1965).

threat from all forces that make life precarious. Through magic and ritual human beings try to gain some sense of assurance in the face of the tremendum. Goodenough questions whether we can draw a sharp line between magic and religion. Both appear to function powerfully in modern life. He declares that even the knowledge and power that we obtain through modern science "have by no means put an end to invasion of the uncontrollable tremendum" (*Psychology*, p. 14).

The second universal in human religion is belief. Creeds, myths, and philosophical and theological systems give humans the illusion that they understand the tremendum. Myths serve to prevent our feeling of helplessness before the unknown. Goodenough confesses:

> I know myself as a religious man. In very few aspects of my own life do I really have evidence of the validity of what I am living by. Yet my life would indeed have been chaos if I had not taken certain "truths to be self-evident.". . . Life has meaning if we give it meaning. Accordingly, all men are religious . . . for all men must live by a set of values. (*Psychology*, p. 19)

In the light of this conviction Goodenough believes that many intellectuals in losing their religion have lost their stability as politicians and international lawyers. This has sobering consequences. "Those who in our own past wished to secularize law never wanted to divorce society and its ethics or law or regimentation finally from the idea of the holy or sacred" (*Psychology*, p. 22). The state itself must have a certain sanctity if we are to have protection from the tremendum in society.

We also have to face the tremendum within ourselves. We claim to understand our inner world, yet we know even less about it than we know of the world of nature and society. The "censor" within us protects us against this ignorance. Psychiatry and depth psychology created guilt within us without offering a superhuman salvation. They do this by making us aware of the mixed character of our motives, and our revolt against what society has called "good." The old myths no longer sustain us. We need a more objective understanding of human nature. Yet we cannot hope that through sheer knowledge we can create an adequate base for conduct. Finally, humanity will have to live by religious truth.

In the second chapter Goodenough explores the ways in which the problem of the divided self was treated in Greco-Roman religion. In the religious tradition beginning with the Orphics, the human personality appeared essentially as a unit, but made up of various, often conflicting parts. Plato describes the psyche as composed of three parts which he compares to a charioteer trying to control two horses. The horse of "desire" gives the charioteer the most trouble. The "spirited part" of the psyche is symbolized by the second horse, where the emotions appear to be central. Reason or intellect is the charioteer who is required to bring order to the various parts of the psyche. Such order is called *dikaiosynē*, which ordinarily means social justice. "This is the theme of Plato's *Republic*, wherein Plato discusses psychological justice, not social justice" (p. 33). Aristotle holds a position similar to that of Plato. He conceives of a lower mind and a higher mind. For him the question becomes "Can we so strengthen and clarify our highest mind that it will at all times give us a vivid sense of the true values of life . . . that the desire for the higher values will steadily dominate lower and destructive desires" (*Psychology*, p. 37).

Although the Stoics professed a materialistic pantheism in which multiple parts of the psyche were denied, in practice they were as dualistic as Platonists and had to deal with the conflict between desire and intellect. For Stoics the soul ruled by emotional impulses was in a pathological state. Goodenough sees this view as close to the basic notions of Freud. The ideal of the Stoics was the Wise Man in command of the wisdom necessary to rule his passions. But they failed in explaining how one can get this saving knowledge.

Goodenough concludes that Pythagoreanism was the one Greco-Roman philosophy that had the most influence upon Hellenistic Judaism and early Christianity. Basic to this philosophy was the idea "that man is a composite whose supreme virtue or goal is subjective harmony. The virtue in its logical sense was defined as justice, the regulation of the lower parts by the higher reason" (*Psychology*, p. 46). Their chosen method for approaching the ideal state of soul was through study. The agency that would bring one into direct connection with the *orthos logos,* or right reason, was the divine king, sometimes identified with an actual ruling king. Goodenough declares that the modern world is still haunted by the dream of the ideal ruler despite the failure of modern dictators.

The Hellenistic mystery religions provided a popular version of the quest for saving knowledge. Under the influence of the mysteries Philo joyfully announces that saving knowledge is to be found in "divine men," namely the patriarchs of Israel, most notably Moses. In Philo's dualism the ego is the integrating factor between the soul and the body with its insistent demands. Only one's higher mind has access to the truth, the law of God. "But man's higher mind can function only as the ego unites with it to dominate the lower mind or functions" (*Psychology*, p. 52). The achievement of the harmony within the soul to which Philo aspired required increasingly the identifying of one's higher mind with the divine mind. To assist in this process God had brought to humanity the patriarchs, who were either born in this perfect condition, as Isaac and Moses were, or came to it by migration, as Abraham did. By identifying with them, "which we could do much more easily than we could identify with the metaphysical God or law, we could win the same victory, make the same migration" (*Psychology*, p. 55).

Paul took for granted the scheme of salvation or psychology of the Greeks, that the parts of the soul must be brought into harmony. Like Philo, Paul considered that God himself took initiative in sending the Logos to earth in human form, although for Paul the incarnation was in Christ rather than in Moses and the patriarchs. For both the Greco-Roman philosophers and the early Christians salvation was bringing the "higher mind" to such "saving knowledge" that it would rule the lower mind, taking the ego into itself and giving one inner harmony. "The difference between religion and the rationalist psychiatry of the ancients has proved to be a difference of means rather than of ends" (*Psychology*, p. 62).

After Paul, Christians lost interest in and even understanding of this psychological tradition and developed a new psychology in which the human person was regarded as being made up of "faculties": intellect, feeling, and will. The Christian fathers took literally Paul's allegory of the fall and created out of it the doctrine of original sin. "Sin became primarily not maladjustment but disobedience, and salvation, a problem of restoring to the will the power to obey . . . God as revealed and made available in revelation" (*Psychology*, p. 61). Goodenough concludes that "Paul transferred to Christ the psychological ideas that thoughtful hellenized Jews used in explaining religious experience" (*Psychology*, p. 62).

In chapter three Goodenough considers how modern psychology has returned us to much of the ancient point of view. In this chapter he states his psychological assumptions. Modern psychology recognizes the strong determinative force of the unconscious. It also recognizes the independent centers of emotional compulsion of which the personality consists. The personality of the newborn infant is constituted by the id, which shows itself "as a quite irresponsible craving for direct gratification of purely selfish urges" (*Psychology*, p. 66). The influence of parents on the developing individual eventually brings under control the urge of the id for self-gratification. By ingesting the personality of the parents until this becomes a part of the child's own inner self the child becomes socialized. Various influences upon the individual may create within him or her a number of social centers not always in harmonious relation to one another. The uneasiness that begins with fear of parental disapproval and extends to apprehension of social disapproval leading to inner disapproval we term "guilt."

Guilt may arise from conflict between the id and the dictates of the social center. It may also arise from conflict among the various social centers, each presenting a different standard of action in a given situation. Recovery from psychological illness may require abandonment of one scale of values for another. For the modern person, as for the ancients, the healthy soul is one whose parts are so adjusted that conflicts are minimized and "the personality as a whole . . . can move freely in creative activity" (*Psychology*, p. 72). Goodenough believes that modern psychiatry has returned to the technique of the ancients for the attainment of psychic health, not exhortation to follow precepts but education. Most notably today this means self-education, in which patients come to understand the nature of their inner conflicts and thereby become able to free themselves from destructive compulsions.

Goodenough's primary interest is to show how this new–old theory of the soul illuminates religious experience. The commonest type of religious experience is that of employing religion to obtain something highly desirable that we might not otherwise be able to obtain. This has psychotherapeutic value because it stabilizes our emotions by assisting us to overcome a feeling of hopelessness in a hostile universe. Goodenough believes that we are in a quite new type of religion when instead of seeking objective goods we look for healing of our own distraught personalities. He believes that religion has light to throw on the Oedipus problem, which he describes in some detail. It appears that the very young child's jealousy of his father as chief rival to the mother's affections very early becomes repressed. Yet even though repressed, the problem manifests itself in all sorts of apparently irrelevant associations in the form of a sense of guilt. In Freudian theory the residual guilt in an adult must be appeased by punishment, so a man tortures himself in various ways, often to the detriment of his ability to exercise sexuality in constructive ways. This suggests salvation from guilt offered by religion. In both the Jewish and the Christian tradition the source of reconciliation and freedom from guilt has been in reconciliation with the father.

Goodenough interprets the Genesis story of the expulsion of Adam and Eve from the Garden in terms of sex. Adam and Eve were innocent because of sexual ignorance. Through their disobedience in eating the fruit they learned the shame of exposing their sexual parts. Although Jews through the ages have honored sex through the begetting of children, Orthodox Jews have continued the sense of shame in exposure. Although the Greeks, in contrast to the Jews, practiced freedom about nakedness, it was they who found in the flesh the inherent center and source of human sin. Although the early Greeks made use of phallic symbols in their most sacred and religious rites, Plato exhorted against lust and taught the sharp contrast between body and spirit. After Plato, sexual continence was often the price of spiritual attainment. "If the old sexual symbols and language were still used, they were made into the language of union with the divine female principle or into replacing the divine creative masculine—that is, it became the language of mysticism" (*Psychology*, p. 80). Philo adopted this method and called it the true Judaism.

In the Jewish acceptance of the fatherhood of God through the complete and detailed obedience to the law, Goodenough perceives one of the solutions to the Oedipus complex. In some later rabbinic expansions of the story of the sacrifice of Isaac, the sacrifice is not stopped, but rather Isaac becomes the willing victim. Since the sacrifice was at God's command, it was God who killed the boy, and God's "judgment against mankind is replaced by mercy and forgiveness" (*Psychology*, p. 82). What is only hinted at in Judaism is made central in the Christian tradition: that guilt is removed by the father who kills his son. "In Freudian language, man through Christ loses his feeling that he is condemned by the father because the sense of guilt is removed" (*Psychology*, p. 83).

Goodenough refuses to believe that Christian theories of how guilt must be removed do in fact confirm Freud's Oedipus complex theory. He declares that both are symbolic myths. Yet both indicate that sensitive people living in our Greco-Roman civilization of censured sex, if they are to find freedom from conflict and guilt, must find fresh orientation to some great reality of which they are a part. This both Freud and the early Christians symbolized as a father. The underlying problem is that the lusting id must be restrained and civilized in order to become acceptable to humanity. If Freud has described the problem better, "theology has better shown the way to peace of mind and freedom from guilt" (*Psychology*, p. 86). Peace lies in taming the assertiveness of the id and conforming to the universal. Goodenough believes that Freud spoke for the new age, employing a mythology that belonged with Nietzsche's superman. He believes further that we must find a middle ground between the way of assertiveness and what Freud and Nietzsche both considered the "Jewish-Christian solution of submission, slavery, death" (*Psychology*, p. 87).

The fourth chapter treats the psychological meaning of types of religious experience, beginning with legalism. Individuals grow up in a complex society governed by many rules, taboos, and folkways. Because these are not organized into a system, people find themselves constantly in conflict with one or the other of the rules with no sense of what is "right." Religion of legalism aims at the solution of this problem. Catholicism is not the only legalistic religion, for legalism is to be found in many forms of Protestantism. Examination of history shows that Jews, Greeks, and Romans all attributed a divine origin to their laws. Evidences of this attitude toward law can be found in the modern state. Goodenough declares, "In general, secular and religious laws blend so indistinguishably together that the legal structure of a society becomes one of the most important elements in the religion of a society" (*Psychology*, p. 93).

Goodenough defines legalism as "a religion based on specific definitions" (*Psychology*, p. 93). He recalls his devout Methodist childhood, when his parents placed in his room a large motto, "What would Jesus do?" This gave him specific direction that he must obey his parents in the same way that Jesus did. If this led to self-righteousness, it also dissolved doubts and led to inner peace, which disappeared only as he grew older. Religious legalism constantly recurs. Calvinistic legalism emerged out of the Protestant revolt against the legalism of medieval Catholicism. Legalism has its full value only in unified societies such as those of Orthodox Judaism. Legalism produces the caste or group. This can be seen not only in the religious caste system of India but also in monasticism. The British "code of a gentleman" produces caste as readily as formal religion. Indeed, Goodenough concludes that "the code of a gentleman can be as sufficient a religious approach to life" as any overtly religious code (*Psychology*, p. 99). Goodenough states that "some element of legalism is a necessity of human nature . . . and to deny that legalism has any place in religion is to deny one of the facts of life" (*Psychology*, p. 101). Yet, if legalism is pushed to its logical extreme, although it may lead its proponents to a sense of peace and security, this, according to Jesus, was bought at the price of spiritual degradation.

Beyond legalism Goodenough defines supralegalism, which is most fully exemplified in Jesus. It is illustrated in the episode of the Rich Young Ruler whom Jesus advises to go beyond customary Jewish legalism and to take up the formless self-directed life that Jesus himself lived. In legalism the individual delegates moral decisions to a ready-made code. "The heart of supralegalism, on the other hand, is that a man's own ideal world has become so vivid and self-sufficient that it subordinates both the id and the negative agents of his social urge alike, and he identifies himself with the ideal" (*Psychology*, pp. 103–4). Although the supralegalist does not flout the codes of society, in more important matters a higher law takes command. The supralegalist usually leaves his followers a code which in turn becomes for them a new legalism. This is illustrated in Lutheranism and in the rule of the Franciscan order, both founded by supralegalists.

The teachings of Jesus afford one of the few schools for supralegalism, and the Sermon on the Mount is one of the best sources. In spite of the fact that Jesus' followers repeatedly have sought to transform Jesus' teachings into a new legalism, to treat them so is to mistake their intent. The Sermon shows that what Jesus proposes does not go against the legalism of the Pharisees, but quite goes beyond it. Jesus does not merely destroy the technicalities, but the very foundations of Jewish law. Jesus teaches that people must live not by human standards but by the standards of God himself. But how do we know what these are? Goodenough answers, "Psychologically, Jesus is saying we should come into a higher life in the social context of God himself. Only there do we envisage the life of God in contrast to the standards given us by human society. . . . [We must] be perfect as God himself is perfect" (*Psychology*, p. 108). Goodenough calls this the new supralegalism.

The Sermon teaches that we cannot through calculation achieve full ethical conduct. One must find God for oneself. "We live by the right as we construct visions of it, not by the blueprints of human society" (*Psychology*, p. 112). Yet, however much we may strive, we will always sense that we have failed to achieve the right. Nevertheless supralegalists, though they hate their failures, must never despair but only be made more determined by them. Although the church could find no place within itself for supralegalists, those who could live in no other way, namely the Old Testament prophets and the later Christian saints, have greatly enriched organized religion.

The Greeks approached supralegalism in another way. The Greek idealists considered that to live only by the laws that society could sanction led only to the most meager ethical achievement. To give the individual some sense of creative ethical responsibility they taught the middle way, the way of moderation—"Nothing too much." True bravery is conduct midway between cowardice and foolhardiness. Generosity is midway between stinginess and profligacy. Finding the middle way requires rational analysis of oneself and the circumstances. The middle way is for the few only, for the intelligent and the heedful. People of antiquity turned gradually away from the quest of the middle road and increasingly sought an orientation to the law of nature, the great law to which all laws made by humans were secondary. Yet this again made demands on the intelligence that were almost superhuman. Who could ever actually know this law beyond laws? Goodenough says that supralegalism is beyond most of us, yet "its difficulty must not blind us to the fact that many of the greatest religious geniuses of all ages have found their religious experience in it" (*Psychology*, p. 115).

From the viewpoint of psychology supralegalists have gone completely beyond socially conditioned compulsions and projected a new society, a right, or an ideal with which their egos so totally identify that they completely transcend the urges of the id and pressures for social conformity. Woodrow Wilson's ideal of "peace without victory" for the outcome of World War I is a positive example. A dangerous perversion of supralegalism is demonstrated in Adolf Hitler's destructive acts in response to his visions of a right beyond the accepted rights of society. The problems of the potential excesses of supralegalism and the difficulty of knowing the validity of our own visions suggest that society is safe only when the majority of us are reliable legalists.

Goodenough next turns to analysis of orthodoxy, a position that gives us a sense of freedom through assuring us that we have possession of the truth. The key words in a religion of legalism are "believe" and "obey." Freedom thus attained is "actually release from the crushing chaos of the tremendum" (*Psychology*, p. 120). One of the most notable persons of recent history to seek freedom in orthodoxy was Cardinal Newman in his pilgrimage from Anglicanism to the Roman Catholic Church. Many highly intelligent persons of our own times have sought and found the same peace without criticism in various religious orthodoxies. The orthodox of all kinds have a common hatred of the liberals, all those who seek a middle ground between atheism and claims of absolute certainty. The common denominator among the orthodox is not what they believe, but that they have accepted a "blueprint" pattern of thought as true. But that there are doubts hidden in the unconscious of the orthodox "appears in the murderous savagery with which the orthodox usually face heresy" (*Psychology*, p. 124).

Next to be examined is supraorthodoxy. Persons of this class crave total metaphysical patterns but cannot accept those given by tradition. The supraorthodox must make their own new patterns. For such persons religion commonly begins with an emotional experience which quickly comes to express itself as an idea. Goodenough offers two examples of the supraorthodox. The first is Benedict de Spinoza, who because of his nontraditional thinking and acting was excluded from the community of his native Judaism. Central to Spinoza's religion was the love of God, the way to which, according to Spinoza, was not through the emotions but through the understanding. For him the creating of new true ideas gave the same sense of security that Newman found in orthodoxy. Goodenough's second example of supraorthodoxy is Søren Kierkegaard. Kierkegaard achieved certitude from a faith that demanded the rejection of all orthodoxy and through exercise of reason the apprehension of truth revealed by faith. He developed no system, and he gained certitude through rationalization of the paradoxical character of life, the very resolution of which seemed to him to be a direct revelation of God's grace.

A further type of religious experience that Goodenough examines is aestheticism, which he characterizes as the search for form, one of the chief goals of religion. "To create form or to share in the created forms of others gives a real experience of form within oneself and hence a real religious experience" (*Psychology*, p. 136), although it must be recognized that the experience is much more intense for the creator of form. Such experience can be obtained through participation in athletics, whose aesthetic dimension has long been recognized. The same can be said for the dance, for architecture, and for language as exemplified in the prose of the King James Version of the Bible. Goodenough cites George Santayana, who identifies poetry with religion. One of Goodenough's boldest suggestions is that a beautiful sex act can be an aesthetic experience that "conveys its own benedictions" (*Psychology*, p. 138). He would find it extremely interesting to treat sex as a type of religion, but doubts that it could be presented to the general public.

He next considers the approaches to religion through symbolism and sacramentalism, defining psychologically any rite or object capable of conveying religious benefit as sacramental. He cites Augustine, who recognized that every traditional religion had its visible signs and sacraments. Goodenough believes that sacraments have an inherent power whether or not they are understood by their participants. Reconciliation with the *tremendum* through symbols may take all forms, from the most primitive to the most profound and beautiful. To understand the religion of the vast majority of people everywhere requires us to recognize that most human piety is directed through sacraments and symbols. He defines the church as "a corporate body, superior to the individual, itself the medium of revelation, in which the individual can find divine guidance, protection, and the means of grace" (*Psychology*, p. 147). The church provides another blueprint type of religion, which rests on assurance through something given.

Goodenough considers conversion to be a type of experience that differs from the others previously considered in that it is a temporary, rather than an overall, experience of adjustment. If his reader is at all surprised by his distinction, this may be dispelled by Goodenough's recollections of the annual revival meetings of his youth in which certain persons were annually "converted." He describes conversion as the surrender of the id to the highest social relation, namely, Christ. In traditional Protestant revivals the preacher usually stimulates anxiety or guilt, which in Goodenough's view may have little relation to what human society would actually consider wickedness. The new power which seems to control the individual after "surrender" in a conversion experience, the power which is defined as "grace" and which Goodenough recognizes, he does not pretend to define in psychological terms. Apostasy no less than acceptance is conversion, and conversion may be sudden or gradual.

Mysticism is demonstrated in the more creative type of religious experiences when the worshipers tend to identify themselves with the object. The traditional "blueprint" religions provide horizontal paths showing the worshiper "the way he should go." Considered psychologically, these religions seem to continue the ideal life of the boy with his father. Religions of mysticism provide a vertical path which much more suggests the infant's relation with the mother. Goodenough finds that in mysticism the sexes become figuratively and extraordinarily mixed. The nun as the "Bride of Christ" reflects an essentially Freudian relationship of the little girl fully accepted by her father, rather than the relationship of the spouse of Jesus. In mystic initiations the candidate often experiences death and rebirth into new life in which the initiate is reborn as the god. This is reflected in the Pauline phrases "to die with Christ" in baptism in order that we may "live with him." In Christian mysticism Christ becomes more than a guide. The mystic must "take on Christ" or "live in Christ."

Popular mysticism tends to express itself in terms of a return to the mother; hence it is not strange that Christians very early began to direct their prayers more to the Mother of God than to either the Father or the Son. Goodenough declares, "Protestants who have rejected what they call Mariolatry keep the same figure and the same confusion of sexes as did Clement of Alexandria" (*Psychology*, p. 155). To illustrate, he cites favorite evangelical Protestant hymns: "Safe in the arms of Jesus, safe on his gentle breast"; and "Jesus, lover of my soul." Goodenough recalls his own youth, when, like Brother Lawrence, he "practiced the presence of God." He compares this with Socrates, who said that within him was a *daimonion* always guiding his life. Mysticism can move away from a sense of personal relation and can express itself in much more abstract terms. The Hindu, by bathing in the Ganges, can identify with the quite extrapersonal, immaterial reality. Mystics achieve their goal when they find the essence of reality in the extirpation of their own or any other human categories. Although few in our civilization actively cultivate the mystic state, many have passing experiences of it.

In the final chapter Goodenough treats "Religion as Search." He points out that he has viewed with detachment the various types of religious experiences that he has been discussing. Like Ernst Troeltsch, he finds religion to be polymorphic, not only in phenomenology but psychologically as well. He admits showing less sympathy for what he calls "blueprint" religions, such as religions of legalism, orthodoxy, of sacraments or traditional symbols, or of an ancient and organized church. Yet he admits that he is not able to reject many of these elements, since they are part of his total adjustment to society and the universe—in short, since they are inseparable from his own religion. For him the primary question is How can the modern person who is still *homo religiosus* live in the new age of science? Although the old myths may not be useful, can modern persons fit themselves into the old psychological patterns of religious experience? The modern person is the one who, although recognizing values from the past, must live in "the modern world of exploding knowledge and of congealing, leveling humanity" (*Psychology*, p. 161).

From the time of the Greeks, we in the Western world, in order to find meaning in the universe, have had to think in terms of first cause or creator, and of teleology or cosmic resolution, which we call eschatology. Yet the world as envisaged in today's science appears as a world of perpetual mutation such as Heraclitus proposed, and "a first cause and teleology both seem to have disappeared in a universe of evolution" (*Psychology*, p. 163). Goodenough declares that modern persons accept the *tremendum* rather than impose upon it a mythological scheme, and instead of living by "truths" they live in a world of hypotheses that can be tested—and, if found wanting, can be replaced by better hypotheses. Goodenough is

scornful of the intelligentsia—theologians, poets, novelists, and play-
wrights who "try to take us back to ultimates which are only thinly dis-
guised traditional patterns" (*Psychology*, p. 163). In contrast to them he
likens the modern person to a steeplejack climbing to dangerous heights or
to a mountaineer climbing beyond Everest. "To the modern mind, there is
no ground any more, no fixed level or point of meaningful reference. Such
a world is not for cowards, but such is the world in which modern man
lives" (*Psychology*, p. 164). The reader may agree that a considerable
number of persons in the modern world share this point of view, although
many do not. Yet the statement is a quite ringing affirmation of Goodenough's own viewpoint and consistent with other statements in which he
betrays a sense of his being a solitary pioneer in the scholarly fields that he
has chosen to explore.

He insists that even in such a world religion still has a valid part to
play. Mysticism provides us with the necessary basic concept that the
ultimate is the Indescribable, the Incommunicable, the Darkness that is
Light. These are terms that we can use to show our direct acceptance of
the tremendum as such. Goodenough defines this acceptance as "agnosticism." Even the abandonment of the concept of a homocentric universe,
with its eschatology of the human race as the final victorious hero, need
not cause people to remove themselves from religion. Can one still have
a sense of meaning and purpose "if he must accept himself as a rela-
tively late form of mutation whose survival definitely depends on this
planet's enduring under conditions fairly well established in their present
form?" (*Psychology*, p. 167). Expectation of individual survival after
death seems to have no support from science; therefore, if life is to have
any meaning for modern people it must be within the universe of which
science gives us the best understanding.

Historical techniques do not make the modern person's predicament
any less stark. They give no evidence that either Moses or Jesus broke
through the natural order to reveal to humanity a supernatural order of
existence. There is no more reason to doubt the historicity of Jesus than to
doubt it for Socrates. But that he was the incarnate Logos or the Second
Adam has no historical claim. Historians are quite cognizant of great peri-
ods of the past—classical Athens, the Hebrew prophets, Buddha, Con-
fucius, and the later beginnings of Christianity and Islam—but they have
no need of divine intervention to explain them. In their turn modern sociology and anthropology have shown that the frameworks of social right
and wrong in which people find security appear to be largely local adjust-
ments rather than the results of divine decrees. Likewise, experimental
psychology tends to show that human beings are automatons responding to
their experiences. Beyond this, depth psychology sees the human person as
almost fully conditioned by early experiences later deeply buried in the
unconscious. Goodenough rejects the assumption of total determinism

which emanates from the common foible of scientists that T. Dobzhansky pointed out, "that the little truths they discover explain everything rather than something" (*Psychology*, p. 173). Psychologists are far from establishing a simple cause-and-effect relation between Shakespeare's boyhood experiences in Stratford and his later creativity, or between Hitler's youthful frustrations and his later cosmic enormities. Even if in fact human beings have no freedom, they must act on the assumption that they do, if they are to be human beings of moral judgment, individual creativity, and reality. Although we must accept the findings of science, at the same time we must accept its limitations.

The real question is how the modern person can be religious in the world of science. We need not deny what appears to be reality in order to be religious. Thoughtful persons today are concerned with studying the tremendum rather than with creating fanciful stories about it. A new understanding of it may emerge as a new scientific law or a new conception of the meaning of some historical period. A creative theorist such as Einstein may penetrate some distance into understanding the tremendum without presuming even to come close to full understanding. The pursuit of truth by scientists is a religious experience for them. Goodenough believes that we have returned to the Greek awareness that virtue is knowledge—not of myths or religious dogmas, but knowledge of ourselves as total persons. To do this requires our maintaining faith in science. The use of scientific hypotheses instead of the old traditional symbols can give one consolation and meaning.

Goodenough asks if with this approach people can express themselves in worship. It will certainly not be worship of a traditional sort. Worship may consist of "earnest discussions of the latest discoveries or hypotheses about some aspect of reality with a seriousness that registers in a sacred code of honesty" (*Psychology*, p. 181). For the modern person, the eager search for truth is a form of prayer itself. Scholars are usually polytheistic, and, in addition to the form of religion that Goodenough describes, they may find stability in traditional orthodoxies and rituals. Scientists must avoid confusing their hypotheses with final truth, and science cannot be restricted simply to those investigations that can use measurements and mathematics. Here Goodenough exhibits his own understanding of science as it may be applied to study of religion. "Commitment to the quest for reality can never become 'the religion of the future,' since it can never be a popular one. . . . But increasingly the quest will become the way millions of trained minds continue in religion" (*Psychology*, p. 183). In the meantime, we should all seek to practice tolerance in religion, cognizant of the many ways in which it may be experienced.

Earlier articles show that Goodenough's ideas of personal religion had been long developing. A short article of 1945 provides a lucid kernel of the material later developed in the two books just reviewed.[3] Good-enough's two-year-old daughter experienced a peculiar phobia during the temporary absence of her mother. This was gradually relieved by the frequent telling of the story of a little girl who went away but came back, always emphasizing the happy return of the girl. The make-believe of the story furnished the cure. One benefit of sleep is in the make-believe of our dreams. Experiments in pschotherapy have encouraged mental patients to extemporize daily an act on stage. When we witness a drama or view a film, all of us may experience the "catharsis" of which Aristotle speaks. The religion of humanity furnishes this type of experience. On the primitive level the devotee gains psychological benefit from the magic of ritual or from the wearing of a talisman. Similarly, many Christians find great power in the image of the cross. Acts of ritual in religion are essentially make-believe that enable the worshiper to gain a calm not obtainable in any other way.

"Make-believe or myth, in story or ritualistic act is the basic pattern of all religion. . . . Behind religious make-believe there is presumably a reality which makes the make-believe work" ("Make Believe," p. 98). Immanuel Kant and William James both affirmed that we can act *as if* there were a God, feel *as if* we are free, or *as if* nature operates by design, or that we are to be immortal. These words can have important effect on our moral life. Some make-believe is better than other. Even if all believing is make-belief, we must believe, must make-believe to keep our sanity, "for make-believe and rational study of the world are man's only approach to the universe, its meaning and its power" ("Make Believe," p. 98).

Goodenough has written that throughout the ages religion has been the psychotherapy of the common people. In 1951 he illustrated this in a brief essay.[4] Religious people have expressed varying attitudes toward the mentally deficient. One view is that the afflicted one is possessed by an evil demon which must be exorcised. In contrast to this is the idea that the indwelling demon is a good demon and that the one possessed by the demon is dear to God and may be consulted as an oracle. The image of the simple fool for Christ has its basis in the New Testament and has recurred frequently in Christian legend and tradition. Another religious view is that the mentally deficient one has inherited the sins of the parent. Often, however, religious people have given solicitous care to

---

[3] Goodenough, "Make Believe," *The Deke Quarterly* (October, 1945) 97–98.

[4] Goodenough, "The Place of Religion in the Treatment of the Mentally Deficient," *Crozer Quarterly* 28 (1951) 120–26. That Goodenough's views had gained the respect of psychologists themselves is demonstrated by the fact that this paper was originally deliv-ered in Boston in 1948 before the International Congress of Mental Deficiency.

the mentally deficient, and in the name of religion many institutions for their care have been established.

Goodenough observes with approval the overtures that religion and psychiatry have been making toward each other and the increase in theological education of training in psychiatric techniques. Even though in extreme cases of mental deficiency religion has little to offer, it has much help to offer to the large and varied group called the feeble-minded. The Christian tradition that religion functions well with childlike minds is well founded. Through simple stories, myths, or legends religion has taught very childlike truth. This mode of teaching can be effective with many of the mentally deficient, even though it may not satisfy the mature intellect. If patients are to benefit from simple formulations of religion, these must be presented by those who themselves are sincere believers in the stories and find direct value in the accompanying religious rituals. However, this teaching must be done under the supervision of the doctor or psychologist, so that the teacher may understand that what may greatly help one patient may be detrimental to another.

Mentally deficient persons who are sweet-tempered, cooperative, unimaginative, and practical can best be served by religion presented as legalism with clear distinctions between right and wrong. Some mentally deficient persons are quite unstable, with deep streaks of negativism and hostility. Let them be taught to transfer their problem from the superintendent of the institution to Christ. They should be assisted in apprehending the great loving Person in Christ, or Mary, or Moses, or Abraham. Still other mentally deficient persons can find in the scheme of sacraments great help for adjustment to life. Some of the feeble-minded, like some children, are extremely imaginative. For such persons stories of the saintly figures of religion, Jesus, or Blessed Mother Mary can have great appeal. Goodenough deplores the fact that, after a brilliant beginning around 1900, the study of the psychology of religion had become almost dead; but he was encouraged by the increasing receptivity to the newer scientific approach to mental problems.

In *Mature Faith* Goodenough urges the importance of doubt in apprehending the truth about God and the universe.[5] In 1959 he spelled this out in a short essay.[6] He objects to the popular notion that attendance at formal religious services identifies a person as religious. Many of the intelligentsia live in great religious doubt, yet they are not without faith. This is true even though the professors among them may to their students seem to be irreligious. It seems clear that Goodenough includes himself within this latter group. He calls himself an agnostic, but he

---

[5] Goodenough, *Mature Faith*, pp. 72–73.
[6] Goodenough, "Honest Doubt," *Yale Alumni Review* 22 (April, 1959) 19–21. This is an address that in the late 1950s Goodenough presented several times before student groups.

sharply distinguishes agnostics from atheists, who deny the very existence of God. There are persons who need to be shown the possibilities of honest doubt. If they are "honest doubters" can they have the value of faith? "Can there be ethical conviction (i.e., faith) without a sense that our moral values correspond to the *summum bonum* of the universe?" ("Honest Doubt," p. 19).

Agnostics must first admit that they are human beings having to adjust themselves to a mysterious environment and an equally baffling inner life. Traditional religion meets these needs with myths, yet these do not accurately describe the universe. Even if agnostics can no longer accept the myths, they need them nevertheless. Freud thought that the new scientific knowledge would do away with the need of "illusory" myths. Yet Freud "really belonged to the succession of arrogant nineteenth-century scholars and philosophers who created the myth that man through science could become supermen and leave the childish orientation of ordinary humanity behind" ("Honest Doubt," p. 20).

Myths are necessary. Agnostics as pragmatists should admit that myth is the basis of all social and personal order. "It is itself a myth that men must have some ethic, but it has been a constructive myth which I would see no reason for discarding" ("Honest Doubt," p. 20). The agnostic sociologist or lawyer, by asking the questions of what do we or should we mean by justice and how should we apply it, and rigidly practicing the best he knows, truly lives a life of faith. Parents similarly must have mythical convictions about the values they wish to instill in their children. In this we can see a genuine and beautiful religious life that has no loyalty to any creed or tradition as such. "It demands the same strong faith in the value of life when lived right as do all the higher formulations of religion, and seems to me no less valuable a religion for its questing and openmindedness" ("Honest Doubt," p. 21).

Finally, can an agnostic pray? Even though we know that the gods of all peoples are projections, nevertheless "the agnostic is not an atheist precisely because he knows that human projections often correspond to external reality, or involve a reality component" ("Honest Doubt," p. 21). All historical reconstruction involves such projection, as do the sciences. Scientific theories continue to be modified as some projections or theories fail even though others succeed. Even though modern depth psychology is correct in calling all concepts of deity projections, through communion with them individuals have been strengthened, ennobled, and inspired. Agnostics, if they can have faith in this realm, may find help in their sense of humility and ignorance quite as much as in any creedal formulation. In prayer agnostics may deliberately use the symbolic terms of childhood. Agnostics have access to the Unknown that is uniquely their own. The very asking of questions about any realm of human experience, when rewarded by even the smallest new insight, gives the questioner a sense of relating to the tremendum comparable to the ecstasy of a devout Christian communicant. "Questioning and research even at the edges of this Unknown will make us walk humbly and intimately with something greater than ourselves, whether we call it God or admit we do not know what to call it at all" ("Honest Doubt," p. 21). We do not find a clearer *apologia pro vita sua* from Goodenough than this.

Goodenough is notable for his celebration of the spiritual value of scholarship. In an eloquent essay on the subject he lifts up a largely unrecognized goal of scholarship, the saving of the scholar's own soul.[7] Goodenough declares that in scholarship the scholar finds fulfillment that other things do not offer. It is a truly spiritual calling, and those few "chosen ones" who pursue it for its own sake do so without regard for distinction or prestige. It is evident that Goodenough counted himself among the chosen. He affirms his own scholarly conclusions with boldness against his critics, and he appears to be content if his views do not gain a wide following. He reminds us of Socrates—up to the very point of his death asking questions in order to come to better understanding of ultimate reality. He also reminds us of Plato himself in the *Republic*, trying to devise a technique of education to free human beings from the dimness of the cave into the true light of understanding. It must be that this understanding of scholarship for the younger Goodenough came to fill the vacancy in his life that had initially been filled by his youthful religious piety. He declares that, whether we are Platonists or not, in scholarship we seek patterns within the welter of phenomena under our investigation, and "the greatest discovery of all is that in spite of our many errors, there actually is . . . some correspondence between the form of our mind's creation and the external world" ("Scholarship," p. 222).

There is no gulf between the scholar and the mystic. Scholarship is in the pattern of religion, since the most important function of both scholarship and religion is to make sense of the ordinary world of experience. With great warmth he counsels that the most helpful minister is one who can go to those tortured by grief and soothe them by answering the inevitable question, Why? Religion does more than tell of a greater world of meaning outside life's present chaos, it leads people into it Scholarship has a parallel to this: it appeals to the initiated because it is a sacrament. It is a religious experience that offers "the sense of achievement and relaxation which comes through having a pattern, a form into which we may fit our own lives and the activities of society" ("Scholarship," p. 224).

Such scholarship is of great social value. All types of human interests and activities yield their greatest rewards only as they are cast in their

---

[7] Goodenough, "The Mystical Value of Scholarship," *Crozer Quarterly* 22 (1945) 221–25.

religious form. Religious leaders have impoverished religion by forcing it into too few exclusive patterns, so that many who practice scholarship would fail to recognize the scholar's experience as truly religious. Religion would be wise to make room for scholars, whether or not they accept traditional patterns of formal religion, simply because they are scholars. Scholars in turn would be enriched by learning what other mystics have to teach. Young scholars would be enormously clarified if they were taught not to become their teacher's faithful pupil, but to find forms of universal validity within the material because they find them within themselves.

Expressions of Goodenough's personal religion appear in his letters. In a letter of 3 March 1937 to the Reverend Fay Campbell, Goodenough defends a little book on Christianity that he had recently written.[8] Campbell had criticized it because it emphasized the mystical and intellectual rather than the social aspects of Christianity. Goodenough frankly admits that the religious position that he states in the book is primarily for intellectuals rather than for the common run of believers. In the letter Goodenough makes a statement that is arresting in view of the position he was to profess only a few short years later, namely, that he was an agnostic with no connection with organized religion. The italics are the present author's.

> *I shall never stop being a Methodist, little as the Methodists are aware of it.* To me a religious ethic is only possible as it comes from personal religious experience. The Methodists have been socially conscious to the point of being ethical busybodies, but I am sure that their ethical drive is so real because in the Methodist churches themselves the start has always been with the individual discovery of spiritual reality.

Although Goodenough dissociated himself from organized religion, nevertheless, for him religion must always be the basis of moral and ethical action.

In a letter of November 1939, Goodenough answers some objections to his religious point of view that had been raised by Mr. M. D. Follin.[9] He assures Follin that the essentials of religion will not be shattered by critical study, for critical scholars are concerned both for the essentials of religion and for the welfare of humanity. He says:

---

[8] Unpublished letter from the Erwin R. Goodenough Papers, Yale University Archives. Used by permission. Fay Campbell was at that time the director of Dwight Hall, the student Christian association at Yale. The book in question was probably Goodenough's *The Church in the Roman Empire* (New York: Henry Holt, 1931). It passed through several reprintings.

[9] Unpublished letter from the Erwin R. Goodenough Papers, Yale University Archives. Used by permission. The correspondence was occasioned by the fact that Goodenough, then editor of the *Journal of Biblical Literature*, had rejected a manuscript that Follin had submitted for publication.

> Unsettling as is the immediate effect of the historical and psycho-
> logical study of religion, truth must prevail, and that man in the
> long run is going to be better off if he is adjusting his life to the
> facts than to however beautiful dreams. But let me assure you
> that we scholars dream of beauty, truth, justice, redemption, and
> all the other varieties of human experience in religion, and not
> only dream of them, we experience them in our hearts. How our
> dreams or experience are to benefit mankind we have not yet
> worked out. Be patient with us, and be sure that we are far more
> concerned for the mass of humanity than the mass is for us.

On 19 September 1957 Goodenough replied to a letter from Mr.
G. R. Elliott in response to questions about Jesus' resurrection and the
empty tomb.[10] This is especially interesting because of the aptness with
which it expresses the paradox of Goodenough's personal religion. It
speaks for the viewpoint of the scientific historian, yet at the same time
it expresses Christian conviction in surprisingly traditional terms.

> I cannot, and never shall *deny*, that Jesus rose from the dead in
> the traditional sense, and that there actually was the "empty
> tomb." But I think this less *likely* than that the resurrection expe-
> rience occurred in Galilee. The idea of a "spiritual resurrection"
> seems to me useless—a question-begging formula. Jesus either
> rose from the dead or he did not. There either was an "empty
> tomb" or there was not. Since I have no way to resolve either of
> these dilemmas I just say I do not know, but insist that the origin
> of Christianity is inconceivable if the early Christians did not
> sincerely believe they had seen him in a fleshly condition. This is
> as near as I can come to answering your letter—to say that when
> a true historian does not know something he admits it.

If it must be said that Erwin Goodenough never resolved the paradox of his own personal religion, it must also be said that none of his
readers are any more likely to be able to do so. The least that can be said
is that during his long intellectual journey away from the theological
inadequacies of his youthful piety, Goodenough never abandoned the
sense of the holy. It illuminated the long course that he set for himself.
The conviction of the worth of religion and the sense of the holy, the
tremendum, gave him strength for his labors and lent ultimate meaning
to his life.

---

[10] Unpublished letter from the Erwin R. Goodenough Papers, Yale University Archives.
Used by permission.

9

THE UNFINISHED JOURNEY

I

Goodenough's most compelling interests have already been shown in his major writings, but these do not exhaust the total diversity of his interests. In a letter he explains that, unlike some scholars, he did not find the energy to continue his work into the evenings. Rather he was more inclined to turn to the reading of poetry, and it is reasonable to suppose that he continued his piano playing, which had begun in his early youth. Information is lacking to tell of other diversions that might have engaged him, but it seems safe to say that most of his interests were intellectual.

He was generous in sharing his interests and expertise with others outside his own field. An example of this is reflected in a letter to him in 1950 from Professor George R. Andrews of New Haven, presumably from the faculty of the Yale Medical School.

> Dear Dr. Goodenough:
>   This is a word of appreciation for the talk that you made to the psychiatry staff today on the general subject of symbolism. It was an unusually stimulating and helpful presentation, and something very much needed by a comparable department where perspective tends to be lost in the absorption with the immediate data accepted as essential. . . . In addition to physiology, neurology, and the rest of the sciences, there is the equally great need to learn what one can of philosophy (and) epistemology. There is a great desire to know which can only be partially satisfied due to all the exigencies of life, limitations of time and energy, and the fact that it is seemingly true that knowledge of whatever sort is always so limited itself, and we are so peculiarly though wonderfully constructed in these brains and sense organs and minds of ours that it is hard to say what we really know when we do seem to know. Because of all this I enjoyed your talk very much. I would like to hear a great deal more along the same lines.[1]

After Goodenough "discovered" psychology and began to see the interrelatedness of psychology and religious experience, his interest in

[1] Unpublished letter of 7 December 1950 (Erwin R. Goodenough Papers; Yale University Library). Used by permission.

these interrelationships continued unabated. In the spring of 1956 there was correspondence between Goodenough and Monroe Stearns, editor of the tradebook division of Prentice-Hall, who in 1955 published Goodenough's popular book *Toward a Mature Faith*. The correspondence makes clear that Stearns had encouraged Goodenough to write another book for the popular religious market. Goodenough had submitted a number of chapters on which Stearns gave encouraging criticism. In a letter to Stearns of 10 April 1956, Goodenough includes the following outline of a partially completed manuscript.

> Foreword
> Chapter 1, "What is religion?"
> Chapter 2, "The structure of the psyche: depth psychologies"
> Chapter 3, "The structure of the psyche, my own working theory"
> Chapter 4, "Legalism"
> Chapter 5, "Supralegalism"
> Chapter 6, "Orthodoxy, the relation of the religion of the ideological blueprint corresponding to legalism in ethics"
> Chapter 7, "Superorthodoxy: the religion of ideological inquiry, especially as manifested in metaphysicians and theologians"
> Chapter 8, "Fear, and its place in all religions"
> Chapter 9, "Conversion, various types of conversion and their psychological meaning"
> Chapter 10, "Religion of the church and sacraments, with parallels outside Catholicism"
> Chapter 11, "Symbolism: its place and function in religion"
> Chapter 12, "The Religious experience of asceticism"
> Chapter 13, "Personal mysticism, that is mystical experience of union with a person like Christ or Krishna"
> Chapter 14, "Abstract mysticism, the mysticism with nature with purely abstract relations with the Ultimate"
> Chapter 15, "Religion of the quest, my own approach, that of scientists and researchers in all fields"[2]

Goodenough's bibliography fails to show that Prentice-Hall ever did in fact publish a book as he had outlined. However, most of the proposed topics of chapters 4 through 14 of the outline appear as subsections of chapter 4, "Types of Religious Experience," in his book *The Psychology of Religious Experiences* (1965). He completed this book at the end of 1964, just three months before his death. It is fair to assume that the substance of the book that he had planned nearly a decade earlier finally appeared in this later form.

In 1958 Goodenough had the opportunity to read a paper in Tokyo at the ninth international congress of the International Association for the History of Religions held from 27 August to 9 September. His topic

[2] Unpublished letter of 10 April 1956 (Erwin R. Goodenough Papers; Yale University Library). Used by permission.

was "The Evaluation of Symbols in History."[3] Since he expounds at
length in *Jewish Symbols* the significance and proper mode of interpreting religious symbols, only a brief account of this paper need be given
here. The mass of human beings adjust their lives "to what seem to them
immediate realities of great impact" ("Evaluation," p. 519). These produce "symbolic acts, rites, and designs or images, which have had the
merit of relating the immediate with the universal" ("Evaluation,"
p. 519). These rather than theological or philosophical explanations bear
the meaning of these realities. History offers the most promising technique for understanding the symbols. Goodenough defines a symbol as
"any object that brings to the observer's conscious or unconscious mind
more than the object inherently is" ("Evaluation," p. 521). A national flag
is a good example. The value of a symbol must be distinguished from
"the mythical or philosophical explanation of the value. . . . In the passing of symbols from one religion to another they amazingly keep historical continuity in their value, although new names and stories come to be
associated with them" ("Evaluation," p. 522). Even within the same civilization a variety of stories may be offered to explain a symbol, which
indicates that the stories are secondary to the symbol that inspires them.

"The value of the symbol is its subverbal impact which no words properly explain" ("Evaluation," p. 523). Goodenough asks "if the truths
brought to us by symbolic words or forms are not more important to our
actual living than anything we can precisely formulate" ("Evaluation,"
p. 523). Because of the importance of symbols, he believes that their study
should be a primary concern of historians. Yet "we enter a world where as
men we are all deeply experienced, but as scholars have no techniques at
all" ("Evaluation," p. 523). He proposes that historians can trace any particular symbol "through a series of historically consecutive civilizations and
diverging mythologies within a single region, to see whether behind the
divergencies of explanation the values of the symbols do not give us a new
constant" ("Evaluation," p. 523). It is the determination of this constant
that is of the greatest importance. Symbols must be taken one by one to see
how each was used in its historical context. It is possible for symbols to die.
In that case the form becomes a mere decoration. "Within a given environment, a live symbol can never be separated from its value, can never be
used as a mere decoration" ("Evaluation," p. 524). If historians can establish that a symbol is alive within one religious group, "its adoption by the
followers of another religion in that civilization has real significance. It
indicates that followers of the second religion have aspirations and experiences like the first, even though we must presume that the explanations in
the second would, if we had them probably speak of other deities, other

---

[3] Goodenough, "The Evaluation of Symbols in History," *Proceedings of the IXth Congress for the History of Religions, Tokyo and Kyoto, 1958* (Tokyo, 1960) 519–25.

mythologies, use distinctive rites" ("Evaluation," p. 524). This has been the central thesis of Goodenough's massive study of symbols of the Greco-Roman world, and one to which he would repeatedly refer.

A personal sidelight of Goodenough's reading of the above paper in Tokyo appears in a letter of 8 October 1958 to Robert Blum, president of the Asia Foundation.[4] In it he thanks Blum for the kindness of the Asia Foundation in making it possible for him to give papers in Tokyo at the meeting of the International Association of the History of Religions and at a UNESCO symposium on East–West relationships which was held after the congress. Goodenough's enduring interest in the history of religions made him very open to the revival of interest in world religions, which was gaining momentum in the 1950s.

In 1962 an article was published in which Erwin Goodenough and his wife, Evelyn, collaborated. His interest in symbols combined with her interest in child development.[5] Evelyn Goodenough was director of the Eliot-Pearson School, which was the experimental school of the Department of Child Study of Tufts University. Professor and Mrs. Goodenough had nearly completed the rearing of two children, a girl and a boy, who were at the time of the writing nineteen and eighteen respectively. The Goodenoughs were evidently writing out of strongly shared interests and a good deal of personal experience. The analysis of the significance of symbols is clearly that of Erwin Goodenough. The article is in response to a question that had been raised at a meeting of the Unitarian-Universalist Committee on Education and Liberal Religion: "Since very young children do not understand abstractions, is it appropriate to introduce into church schools myths and symbols they do not understand?" ("Myths," p. 172). The authors argue the following points.

"There is nothing abstract about either myths or symbols, but only in adult explanations of them, explanations always secondary to the concrete myths and symbols themselves" ("Myths," p. 172). A symbol is a concrete image, object, ritual, or word that operates upon us directly, although subverbally or subrationally. A myth is an allegorical story. As far as stories are concerned, stories told either to the child, or by the child, become for the child "psychic experiences realized through the imagination" ("Myths," p. 172). In earliest childhood Santa Claus can be just as real as Daddy. At that stage the child does not make the same distinction between the real and the imaginary world that most adults eventually tend to make. The Goodenoughs disagree with those students

---

[4] Unpublished letter (Erwin R. Goodenough Papers; Yale University Library). Used by permission.

[5] Goodenough and Goodenough, "Myths and Symbols for Children," *Religious Education* 57 (1962) 172–77, 236. Following her divorce from Erwin Goodenough in August 1962, Evelyn was married to Robert B. Pitcher. From 1965 to her retirement in 1980 she served as chair of the Department of Child Study at Tufts University.

of children who hold that stories of evil fairies or giants or stories of anger or deceit exert a harmful influence on children. They state as their own guess, unsupported by scientific evidence, that such stories may have therapeutic value for the child as safety valves for the child's emotions. It is best to meet the child where he actually is psychologically, that is, "in the world of concrete, if imaginative violence" ("Myths," p. 172). To the universal popular stories that have survived the centuries, it may be well to add an abstraction such as, "How good of Cinderella to do her work so well" ("Myths," p. 172). But this will be primarily for later association.

Symbols are not abstractions. They carry within themselves the power to move us. "Symbols are such as they create emotions within us, not as they convey ideas" ("Myths," p. 174). To the little Catholic children at Mass, making the sign of the cross in imitation of their parents exerts power in their lives well before they understand its meaning. In addition to specific religious symbols there are universal symbols that come out of the elemental experiences of life. "A child of parents who like abstract generalizations grows up in a world of concrete symbols quite as really as a little Catholic or an Orthodox Jew" ("Myths," p. 174). Among these universal symbols are the mother figure and the father figure. Drinking water and eating food have a similar symbolic significance. "The family table becomes everywhere a concrete symbol of the indescribable spiritual or psychological complexities (call it what you will) of the family unit" ("Myths," p. 174).

Seasonal symbols can mean much to a child. Children associate the celebration of spring with jumping ropes and first ball games, and fall with football and burning leaves. "Our Christmas is a medley of symbols, few of which have any Christian reference at all" ("Myths," p. 175). The pagan baby reappears as the baby New Year. Gifts, the lighted tree, feasting, family reunions, the myths of Santa or Jesus, all intensify the symbolism of the new life marked by the winter solstice. Some individuals mourn the loss of specific religious references in these celebrations. However, this is loss only of some abstract explanations, and the ancient power of the symbol still remains. "If coming into a larger life in tune with Nature be not religion for us, it is hard to know what we are talking about" ("Myths," p. 175). For the Unitarian child, Easter likewise has a proper place. "Its symbolism as little began with the story of the empty tomb as did Christmas at Bethlehem" ("Myths," p. 176). The eggs and Easter flowers and new clothes are "means by which the child becomes a part of the great new life of nature" ("Myths," p. 176).

Symbols clearly are of profound importance to children. "The child's life is enriched chiefly not by teachings but by experiences, real in themselves at the time, which, by their early reality, can become also symbolic in later years" ("Myths," p. 176). A few symbols deserve particular mention. One of these is going to church, "the symbol of the family's looking beyond itself to a greater reality" ("Myths," p. 176). The Goodenoughs warn, however, that this symbol becomes effective for the child only if the parents themselves attend the church service. Moreover, parents must enter into churchgoing sincerely and must not afterward engage in gossip about members of the congregation.

"The chief symbols of all, however, are those we furnish our children in our own characters as parents or teachers or ministers" ("Myths," p. 176). This is a return to the father figure and the mother figure, which finally exert the greatest influence on the child's life. There is little need to talk about morality and ethics to the child if these are exemplified in the lives of the parents. "The symbol the child gets is what we actually are, not what we profess to be" ("Myths," p. 176). "Even though we cannot offer our own lives as perfect ethical patterns to our children, we can present them with the image of honest and earnest struggle toward ethical virtue" ("Myths," p. 177). Church and Sunday School should provide the place where children interact with other people engaged in this same common struggle.

In liberal religion the child needs to be led into the conception that "religious experience consists in discovery and inquiry rather than in the discovered and revealed" ("Myths," p. 177). If we no longer revere the old myths, we may be all the more reverent before the mystery of existence which still remains. "Religion lies in the sense of reverence, not in its object. . . . The Western Liberal . . . feels his greatest reverence which he knows he does not understand at all" ("Myths," p. 177). In his more extended works defining religion, this is what Goodenough designates as the tremendum.

It is not possible to symbolize this sort of religious experience with any fullness to a small child. "But he may have the concrete experience of adults approaching life and its mystery thoughtfully, and this will register with him as a symbol long before the abstract merits of the problems being discussed are understood" ("Myths," p. 177). This form of religious experience can be fostered in children through simple explorations of nature. Not only school but also Sunday School should offer such opportunities. The child's simple experiments with planting seeds and watching them sprout and grow or experiments with water, air, and fire provide concrete experiences which become symbols of the wonders of nature and stimulate a lifetime of intellectual curiosity. "A liberal church brings people together to stimulate one another in asking questions, not for the common recitation of ultimate creeds" ("Myths," p. 236). This article provides us with further good evidence that, although Erwin Goodenough had long since abandoned religious orthodoxy, he by no means advocated the abandonment of religion or, in particular, the practice of it.

Between 1960 and 1962 there was an exchange of correspondence between Goodenough and Samuel Sandmel concerning the possibility of publishing a *Festschrift* in Goodenough's honor. Goodenough resisted this idea and, in a letter of 22 February 1962, expresses to Sandmel with characteristic pungency the reasons for his objection. He then offers a counterproposal.[6]

> Dear Sam,
>
> It appears to me, as I intimated to you, that the idea of a Festschrift is impossible. I have to decline contributing to such volumes two or three times a year (terribly embarrassing), because they constitute such an invasion of my plans for writing. A Festschrift really has no point, since it contributes only to the vanity, or memory, of a person whose claim to such an honor must still rest in his own publications.
>
> What I suggest you might consider, if as I believe you do want to pay me such an honor, is to start a movement to publish a rather fat volume of my collected articles, since some of my most important contributions lie scattered in a wide variety of places. Many of these should not be reprinted, for they were preliminary sketches of notions later worked out for *Symbols*. I doubt if even you have heard of them all.

Then follows a list of twenty-seven titles of articles, the earliest published in 1925, and continuing throughout the remainder of his life. In the bibliography of Goodenough's works by A. Thomas Kraabel, which appears as an appendix to the present work, the list in Goodenough's letter corresponds almost exactly to those articles starred by Kraabel as the ones that later on Goodenough considered to be his most important. The letter concludes:

> Perhaps some of them could be omitted, but if the range of my interest and contribution is important, nothing could present it better than these very divergent essays. You might well write a brief preface in which you say that his pupils had thought of a Festschrift, but had decided that a collection of his own writings would be a more appropriate monument. The work involved would be minimal. The printing could mostly be done from old printed pages (which I myself would have to edit for typos), and a bibliography of my writings could be appended, which I have on cards all ready for typing. I suspect Bollingen would be glad to cooperate, as well as the Yale Press.
>
> The suggestion is probably nonsense, and don't be afraid to say so.

The suggested project to publish a collection of Goodenough's articles was never undertaken. The plan to publish a *Festschrift* was not

---

[6] Unpublished letter (Erwin R. Goodenough Papers; Yale University Library). Used by permission.

abandoned, and under the editorship of Jacob Neusner the volume appeared in 1968 entitled *Religions in Antiquity*.

On 24 November 1964, Ralph W. Burhoe wrote to Goodenough, inviting him to become a member of the Scientific Advisory Board of a forthcoming conference sponsored by Meadville Theological Seminary in Chicago. Burhoe had just been appointed by the seminary to head a new department, Theology and the Frontiers of Learning. He continued as Research Professor of Theology and Science at Meadville until his retirement in 1974. This invitation was consistent with Goodenough's interests. He had served on the Advisory Board of the Institute of Religion in an Age of Science from 1956, and he became vice-president in 1964. Also in 1964 he read a paper at the opening session of the Star Island Conference of the Institute, which was asking the question: What is Religion? Goodenough's paper, "A Historian of Religion Tries to Define Religion," was published posthumously in 1967 in *Zygon*, the journal of religion and science of which Burhoe was editor.[7] Just at that time there was a mounting interest among American scholars both in theological and scientific studies in the exploration of interrelationships between science and religion. Since this had long been one of Goodenough's particular interests, if he had lived he would have plunged with enthusiasm into this dialogue.

The variety of Goodenough's interests is clear, and he sought to pursue each one in as much depth as the primary focus of his own scholarship would permit. He participated actively in many scholarly organizations. He was a long-time member of the Society of Biblical Literature, and from 1934 to 1942 edited the *Journal of Biblical Literature*. For many years he represented the SBL in the American Council of Learned Societies. He served on the Committee on the History of Religion of the ACLS. In this role he had a large share in the organization of the American Society for the Study of Religion, and he served as its first president. This is a representative but not an exhaustive listing of the many ways in which he served the world of scholarship.[8]

II

Erwin Goodenough was a private person, and he was not much inclined to make public the details of his personal life. However, some insights into his private life are helpful to illuminate attitudes expressed in his writings. During most of his adult life he apparently was not a robust person, and his career was periodically interrupted by bouts of illness. In a letter of 25 February 1954 to the Yale provost, Edgar

[7] See above, chap. 7 n. 3.
[8] Morton Smith provides a more complete list in "In Memoriam," *Religions in Antiquity: Essays in Memory of Erwin Ramsdell Goodenough* (Leiden: Brill, 1968) 2.

Furniss, Goodenough explains his current illness, which he had previously experienced in 1929, 1938, and 1945. "The fact is that I have a disaffection of the nervous system that controls the intestines so that periodically from the time I was six months old I have gone into these rather terrifying skids. On those dates I went to the hospital for observation because it did not seem possible that so much could be wrong without my having cancer or something to account for it. But always these tests have given negative results, and I see no reason why we should worry in this case."[9]

Two years later he reports an astonishing resolution to this long-standing problem. In a letter to Frau Olga Fröbe-Kapteyn of Ancona, Italy, on 15 May 1956, Goodenough tells of a summer trip he planned to make to Europe in 1957. He offers to read a paper at the Eranos Conference. Following this he explains an amazing improvement in his health. "My health is incredibly improved. A pediatrician finally found that an illness of babyhood, corliac disease, had lingered on with me all these years, and at sixty I was put on a diet that I should have had at six months. The result is that I am well for the first time in my life and enjoying myself immensely."[10]

From an entirely different direction comes further insight into Goodenough's personal life. In 1960 Goodenough was asked to contribute an article to an anniversary volume published by the Groton School, which his two older sons had attended and in which his youngest son was then enrolled.[11] In this brief essay it is possible to see something of Goodenough as parent and also to gain some sense of his philosophy of education. He leaned heavily on the reminiscences of his older sons for his own information. One of the strongest influences of Groton School was its characteristic of welding its students and faculty into a "family." The school had been founded in 1884 by the Reverend Endicott Peabody (1857–1944), who served as its first and only headmaster until his retirement in 1940. The familial characteristic of Groton was but Dr. Peabody's lengthened shadow. Goodenough writes of this with great warmth: "I learned to call the school a family from one of my older sons, who, I am sure, feels himself more deeply a part of that family than any I ever provided him with. He cannot escape being my son, or from the father image I impressed upon his early years. But the great father image by which he now tries to live is the old Rector, as the supreme example he ever knew of the Christian gentleman" ("Groton," p. 335).

---

[9] Unpublished letter (Erwin R. Goodenough Papers; Yale University Library). Used by permission.

[10] Unpublished letter (Erwin R. Goodenough Papers; Yale University Library). Used by permission.

[11] Goodenough, "A Yale Professor and Groton Parent looks at the School," *Views from the Circle: Seventy-Five Years of Groton School* (Groton, Massachusetts, 1960) 335–46.

Goodenough commends many aspects of the school. A student might take part in dramatics, write for the literary magazine, or try to write poetry, and not be looked down on. There was a strong sense of participation of all the students in the various activities of the school. Goodenough's investigation showed him that Groton provided Yale consistently with approximately ten or a dozen boys, about 1 percent of the Yale freshman class. Yet this modest number within the Yale student body earned a surprisingly high number of the most distinguished prizes Yale had to offer its graduating seniors. In view of the wide variety of learning opportunities that Groton offered its students Goodenough has only one complaint to make. Although the school encouraged musical participation, it made no provision for learning to play a musical instrument. His own personal interests are reflected here.

Against the background of Goodenough's high commendation of Groton in most respects, he is direct in the criticisms he feels it necessary to make. After World War II new admissions techniques were devised by Directors of Admissions not only at Yale but also in many other colleges. These included in particular the evaluation of prospective students by academic aptitude tests. Whereas formerly any "Grottie" might go to any college he chose, the new admissions practices created a new situation, and more and more boys from Groton were being turned down by colleges of their first choice. Goodenough says, "There is a vast labyrinth of personal relations to be established with the admissions offices, involving stratagems and negotiations in which Groton seems not sufficiently skilled" ("Groton," p. 343). Ever more boldly "as an outsider," he addresses what he considers to be the most crucial problem, namely, what boys to admit in the first place. "The best of American aristocracy, to speak tautologically, has always had great intellectual interest" ("Groton," p. 343). The most outstanding preparatory schools, of which Groton is one of the latest and best, owe their existence to the support given them by this aristocracy. "As a result the preparatory schools have a double reputation; one for splendid educational training, and one for exclusiveness. . . . Groton is generally known much more for the latter than for the former" ("Groton," p. 344). He urges, therefore, that if Groton is to maintain its reputation for intellectual supremacy, it must be willing to draw on a wider background of students. "The problem of how to educate young gentlemen *qua* gentlemen has never concerned me, for my own sons or for other boys. How much it is in the mind of those conducting Groton I have not the least idea" ("Groton," p. 345). He argues that his proposed greater democratization of Groton will not stifle any boy's genius. "It is highly important, however, not only that the young genius develop his special gifts, but that he learn to live in human society and adjust to his fellows by appreciating their merits" ("Groton," p. 346).

For Goodenough there was only one kind of elite; it was constituted by those whose minds were cultivated by learning. In earlier writings he occasionally refers to it as the intelligentsia, and he apparently associates himself with it without embarrassment. He himself seemed to be free enough of intellectual pretense that the word did not, as it does to others, suggest possible intellectual snobbery. His word of advice to the directors of Groton also reflects the rather simple and sturdy democratic attitude that he exhibits elsewhere in his writings. He knew himself to be the son of common parents without social pretensions, but with strong personal ideals. Out of such a background he knew that many persons could rise to become members of the intellectually elite, and he thought that persons with pretensions of wealth or social status should be fully aware of this, and experience it. However, the advice is kindly meant, and he concludes the essay with a warm word of praise for Groton's excellence, illustrated by the enthusiasm of his youngest son for return to the school following the summer vacation.

Goodenough was twice divorced and thrice married. In his more personal writings, as we have seen, he indicates that he valued the warmth and bonds of marriage, family life, and the rearing of children. The reasons for the dissolution of his first two marriages must remain private, but it seems apparent that he did not believe in either case that the causes lay with himself.

Those who were his students soon became aware of estrangement between himself and the faculty of Yale Divinity School. Sandmel, who knew Goodenough more intimately than most other students, may be the best qualified to speak to this point.

> It was never clear to me whether his estrangement from the Divinity School was a cause or effect, whether he was an ex-Christian first, and then estranged, or first estranged and then an ex-Christian. Though he insisted over and over again that he had not been reared in that orthodoxy against which his students often rebelled, I always suspected that unresolved rebellion had something to do with it; I never knew how much his first divorce occasioned or accentuated that estrangement; and while there was no doubt that he was relatively more unorthodox than many of the people at the Divinity School, the Divinity School itself was scarcely a center of orthodoxy.[12]

III

Goodenough never lost sight of his ultimate goal to write a history of earliest Christianity. His study of Justin Martyr at the beginning of his career gave impetus to his plan, although that study likewise sent him on

---

[12] Sandmel, "An Appreciation," *Religions in Antiquity*, 4.

his lifetime research of Hellenistic Judaism, which in fact became the major substance of his scholarship. Yet again and again he took steps that were calculated to bring him to his ultimate goal. Separate shorter writings give us clues to the theses he would develop in a larger work. These have been examined above in chapter 7. We see Goodenough flying in the face of widely accepted theory concerning John's Gospel as he presents evidence and argument to support the conclusion that John is a primitive rather than the latest Gospel. He finds that the portrait of Paul in Acts is completely inconsistent with that which Paul's letters provide. The Paul of Acts is a primitive Jewish Christian rather than the radically hellenized Paul of the letters. His article on Paul indicates how powerfully Goodenough believes that Paul's thought had been influenced by Hellenism.

We are fortunate to have in a letter from Goodenough to Mircea Eliade on 11 October 1958 a tentative outline for the study of the origins of Christianity that Goodenough still proposed to write.[13] In the letter he thanked Eliade for a copy of his book *Birth and Rebirth,* and he made some critical comments which led him to giving a synopsis of his theory of how Hellenism influenced Christianity by way of Hellenistic Judaism. He lists the major facts that seem to him to be established, facts which any historian of Christianity must take into account.

1. Moore's Normative Judaism (as one aspect of Judaism, at least).
2. The various other sorts of Judaism, including the Qumran group and the apocryphal writings.
3. The definite witness for the hellenization of Judaism: in Philo, in my archaeological material (mostly later than Christian beginnings but apparently nascent during the first century), and in the hellenistic group of synagogues and early Christians mentioned in Acts.
4. The tremendous impact of Jesus as an historical person, and as one whose followers sincerely, passionately, believed they had seen him [*sic*] risen from the dead. This gave a new historical orientation to Christians orientation not in a shadowy, even mystical, past as with the Patriarchs and Moses, or Orpheus, but with the immediate past. The first Christians felt they had experienced a fresh invasion of God and revelation in history.
5. The obviously different way various early Christians interpreted this, probably reflecting varieties of interpretation within the Church itself, and varieties of previous patterns within Judaism:
    a. Jesus as the Nazarene Miracle worker of Mark.
    b. As the teacher of eschatology and the Kingdom.

[13] Unpublished letter (Erwin R. Goodenough Papers; Yale University Library). Used by permission.

    c.   As the Teacher of "Q," or, I prefer to think, of the various logia of teaching circulating in the Church, mostly in an unhellenized vein.

    d.   The several beginnings of hellenized interpretation:

        1.   The Birth stories added to Mark and Q by Luke and Matthew

        2.   The Theological and Soteriological approach of Paul.

        3.   That of the Fourth Gospel.

        4.   That of the Letter to the Hebrews.

    e.   The fitting of Jesus into the gnomic tradition of Sirach by James.

    f.   The steady growth of the sacraments (extremely interesting of how little importance the Eucharist is in Acts, or the Apocalypse or James) and the growth of Church organization and discipline centered in the protection of the sacraments.

This is a complicated outline—roughly the preliminary outline of the books on the rise of Christianity I hope to write when I finish *Symbols* (by the way VII & VIII came out this week—I have an advance copy). The trouble with all my approach is that it is too elaborate, and cannot be tucked into a few pages of judgment and pronouncement.

A paper that Goodenough read in 1951 gives us a further clue to the direction his history of early Christianity might have taken.[14] The occasion was his participation in a symposium on the Age of Diocletian at the Metropolitan Museum of Art. He discusses the various avenues by which the ancients of the time sought through the many religious options available to them to achieve a sense of security in an increasingly uncertain world. The emperor as a divine figure, the mystery religions, religious philosophies, astralism, mysticism, or a syncretism of elements of these—all promised salvation in some form to their pagan devotees. For Jews, in addition to its rabbinic form, there was a widely popular Judaism much augmented by elements appropriated from Hellenism. Into this world Christianity was born and in a remarkably short time prevailed over all other forms of religion in the ancient world except Judaism. Goodenough explains why this occurred.

"First, I remind you that Christianity is to be understood only if we think of it as the omnium-gatherum of all the different religious values, including Judaism" ("Aspirations," p. 47). He describes new Christian amulets that were only slightly altered from pagan-Jewish amulets. Local deities were transformed into local saints. Pagan ritual sacrifice disappeared, but the symbolism of the slain lamb became available through the sacrifice of the Mass. Neoplatonism provided the church fathers with

---

[14] Goodenough, "Religious Aspirations," *The Age of Diocletian: A Symposium* (New York: Metropolitan Museum of Art, 1953) 37–48.

a foundation for theology. Continuity of Christianity with earlier forms of religion is "epitomized in the fact that the symbolic *lingua franca*, first of the pagan religions, then of Judaism, was—and to a large extent still is—also the symbolic language of Christian devotion" ("Aspirations," p. 48).

> To become the exclusive religion of the Empire, Christianity had, however, to do more than reaffirm the values of the religions it displaced. As to what this "more" was, we shall never agree. . . . Still we can all agree that the Christians were deeply convinced that the incarnation was indeed an historical fact, and they see in that conviction a power whose absence was the greatest lack in even such lofty pagan formulations as those of Porphyry and Julian. ("Aspirations," p. 48)

He concludes by noting that out of this conviction a church organization arose to keep believers in line, to administer the consolation of the sacraments, and offer a gratifying liturgical cultus.

Finally, one brief source demonstrates Goodenough's defense of the historical Jesus. In a letter of 9 May 1955 to Samuel Sandmel, Goodenough both praises and criticizes the manuscript of Sandmel's book, soon to be published.[15] The criticism is leveled primarily against Sandmel's conclusion that, although there can be no doubt of the historicity of Jesus, the nature of the Synoptic Gospels is such that no narrative or saying of Jesus reported in them can be accepted as historical. This view has been widely held by liberal Protestant Christian scholars. Goodenough writes:

> I have the haunting feeling (this I learned from Conybeare who constantly returned to it) that while the picture of Jesus is too much made up of pericopes of which we are not sure—indeed we cannot put our finger on a single one and say that Jesus pronounced it as it is recorded—still there is a creative, poetic body of teaching—the supralegalism I was speaking to you about, which adds up to a sense that behind the screen there was not only a real person, but a person who essentially created this sort of doctrine.

Supralegalism to which Goodenough here refers is a form of religious experience that he was to define and describe at length in his *Psychology of Religious Experiences* (1965, pp. 101–18). Goodenough appears to find supralegalism one of the most compelling forms: "I can be inspired by an impractical law—never by one that I can literally obey. The traditional Golden Rule in the 'negative form' seems to me to be a deliberate break from the possible." Goodenough cites other examples of the striking

---

[15] Unpublished letter (Erwin R. Goodenough Papers; Yale University Library). Used by permission. Sandmel's book was probably *A Jewish Understanding of the New Testament* (Cincinnati, OH: Hebrew Union College, 1957).

absurdity of Jesus' teaching: on adultery, the treatment of the older brother of the Prodigal, the abandonment of ninety-nine sheep in favor of one.

> Jesus was taking man not to a metaphysical law like Philo and Paul, but was in a very pragmatic way breaking with any attitude of calculation. Was it Jesus who did this? I cannot believe that the early gentile church invented it. It is the product of a supreme ethical-religious genius, and if we are not to call him Jesus, we must, as the Harvard Freshman said of Homer, say that it was composed by another man of the same name.

In the end Goodenough did not live to write what for forty years he had anticipated as the climax of his scholarship, a history of the beginnings of Christianity. Thomas Kraabel reports that when Goodenough finally accepted the nearness of the end of his life, he attempted in his article, "Paul and the Hellenization of Christianity," to indicate the methodology and some of the conclusions of the projected larger work.[16] On the basis of the fragmentary material available to us we can make only educated guesses about what the completed work might have been like. Had Goodenough survived a few short years, with his dedication and determination he might have indeed accomplished his purpose, but one question remains. What contribution would such a work actually have made? Samuel Sandmel is probably the best qualified to make judgments in this matter. These are contained in his fine memorial essay dedicated to Goodenough.[17]

Goodenough had no more loyal pupil than Sandmel. They respected each other as scholars, and they depended on each other's judgments. Sandmel above anyone else is qualified to criticize his mentor. His most telling criticism is that Goodenough showed himself not to be familiar with the most current New Testament scholarship of his time. "So thoroughly had he immersed himself in materials outside the New Testament that in inner New Testament problems he often seemed to me either a quasi-Fundamentalist or else even a tyro, for he was not *au courant* with the material which finds its way into introductions. He knew primarily the older introductions" ("Appreciation," pp. 6–7). Goodenough was almost unacquainted with the work of Bultmann in form criticism. When he criticized Sandmel's book, *The Genius of Paul*, because its conclusions ran counter to his own presuppositions, Sandmel inquired what these were, and he comments as follows: "It seemed to me that he had scarcely moved beyond the proposed solutions of the 'synoptic problem' at the turn of the century. The New Testament scholarship was for him a challenge for the future, to be met at that time with all his

---

[16] *Religions in Antiquity*, 23n.
[17] Sandmel, "An Appreciation," *Religions in Antiquity*, 3–17.

thoroughness" ("Appreciation," p. 7). With all of his interest in the Hellenization of Christianity, he apparently was unacquainted with nineteenth-century scholarship on this subject, such as is reflected in the work of F. C. Baur and Bruno Bauer. "Not only was he not a rabbinist, but he was also not a New Testament specialist. . . . He seemed to me not to have an organic grasp of the heft of New Testament problems. He knew a great deal that was outside the New Testament; he did not know comparably what was inside it" ("Appreciation," p. 11). But Sandmel asks, how could he? He was so deeply immersed in the voluminous literature of Hellenism, and in his own writing, that detailed study of the New Testament had to wait until he had finished his preliminary studies.

Sandmel marvels at the quantity of scholarship that Erwin Goodenough had produced, yet the paradox was that he considered the work that he had done to be only the prolegomenon to the work he yet intended to do. Poignantly Sandmel describes how this paradox was illuminated during his last visit to Goodenough, two weeks before he died. Goodenough described his moments of pain but indicated that at times he was free from it. He thought it possible that he might be spared two or three more years to complete the work on the history of Christianity which he was just beginning. Sandmel comments:

> I think also that I was impressed by this, that it was my opinion, and still is, that what he took for the major chore was not nearly as important as he thought it was. The "prolegomena" seemed to me, and still seems, to be more significant for scholarship than still another theory, and not a new one at that, on the rapid hellenization of Christianity. . . . No, in a lifetime of scholarship he carved out for himself his own niche. He had devised his own field, and had penetrated it with comprehension, depth, and thoroughness. He had accomplished something so signal that it worried me that he seemed to feel that he might be prevented from what to his mind was the major task incumbent upon him. . . . I could have wished there was some way to tell him that I saw no tragedy in his leaving unfulfilled his wish to write the history of early Christianity, and that his accomplishments in hellenistic Judaism were a monument of his own creation to his own spirit. ("Appreciation," pp. 15–16)

The conviction grows on the present writer that Goodenough's persistence in his plan to write a history of early Christianity reflected a sense of obligation to Christianity which he might have denied, but which seems most plausible. He ultimately abandoned the house of faith in which he was reared. Yet in all his scholarly journeyings through the myriad modes of expression of religion by myth and symbol in the ancient world, and through his psychological observations of the ways in which religion may be experienced, he never disavowed the values that Christianity professed and sought to promote. Rather he affirmed them fervently. The myths and doctrines of the old house of faith became increasingly useless to him, and he finally professed to be an ex-Christian. At the same time, it can be argued, the personal benefits that he derived from the scholarship were better materials, and a better design, for a new house of faith. Hellenist that he was, Erwin Goodenough might not reject as uncharacteristic of himself the image of aspiration and hope expressed in the very Hellenistic epistle to the Hebrews (13:14).

"Here we have no continuing city, but we seek one to come."

APPENDIX:

A BIBLIOGRAPHY OF THE WRITINGS
OF ERWIN RAMSDELL GOODENOUGH*

BY

A. THOMAS KRAABEL

Introductory Note

Within each year, the following order is used: First, books; second, sections of, or articles in, books, annuals, Festschriften, etc.; third, articles and review-articles in periodicals, listed chronologically; fourth, book reviews, listed alphabetically by author.

The twenty-three entries marked with an asterisk are those Professor Goodenough considered "my more important articles," according to a list drawn up in 1961 and last revised in 1964. Some substantial articles do not appear on the list, probably because they were incorporated into later publications, e.g., parts of *The Psychology of Religious Experiences* (1965) had their beginnings in the paper, "Religion and Psychology" (1947).

Abbreviations often used: *H.T.R.* for *Harvard Theological Review* and *J.B.L.* for *Journal of Biblical Literature.*

1915

"Christianity and the War" (The Sixtieth Clark Prize Oration), *Hamilton Literary Magazine* XLIX (1915) 344–48. (Published with a picture of the author in the year of his graduation from Hamilton College; other undergraduate writings have been omitted from this bibliography—A. T. K.).

1923

The Theology of Justin Martyr, Jena, Verlag Frommannsche Buchhandlung, 1923.

*From *Religions in Antiquity: Essays in Memory of Erwin Ramsdell Goodenough* (ed. J. Neusner; Studies in the History of Religion—Supplement to *Numen*, 14; 1968) 621–32. Used by permission of the author, the editor, and the publisher.

1925

* "The Pseudo-Justinian 'Oratio ad Graecos'," *H.T.R.* XVIII (1925), 187–200.

1926

"Philo and Public Life," *The Journal of Egyptian Archaeology*, XII (1926), 77–79.

1928

* "The Political Philosophy of Hellenistic Kingship," *Yale Classical Studies*, I (1928), 55–102.

1929

The Jurisprudence of the Jewish Courts in Egypt. Legal Administration by the Jews under the Early Roman Empire as Described by Philo Judaeus, New Haven: Yale University Press, 1929.

"Paul and Onesimus," *H.T.R.* XXII (1929), 181–83.

* "Kingship in Early Israel," *J.B.L.* XLVIII (1929), 169–205.

1931

The Church in the Roman Empire (The Berkshire Studies in European History), New York: Henry Holt and Company, 1931.

1932

* "A Neo-Pythagorean Source in Philo Judaeus," *Yale Classical Studies*, III (1932), 115–64.

Review of:

H. Schneider, *The History of World Civilization from Prehistoric Times to the Middle Ages*, New York, 1931, 2 vols. In: *The Saturday Review of Literature* VIII, no. 40 (April 23, 1932), 690.

1933

"Introduction" to Stewart Means, *Faith: An Historical Study*, New York: The Macmillan Company, 1933, xi–xiii.

"Philo's Exposition of the Law and his *de vita Mosis*," *H.T.R.* XXVII (1933), 109–25.

Review of:

I. Heinemann, *Philons griechische und jüdische Bildung*, Breslau, 1932. In: *The Journal of Religion*, XIII (1933), 93–95.

1935

By Light, Light. The Mystic Gospel of Hellenistic Judaism, New Haven: Yale University Press, 1935.

1936

"Archaeology and Jewish History," *J.B.L.* LV (1936) 211–20 (Review-article on J.-B. Frey, *Corpus Inscriptionum Iudaicarum, IIIe siècle de notre ère* [volume I], Rome–Paris, 1936).

Review of:

S. Belkin, *The Alexandrian Halakah in Apologetic Literature of the First Century C.E.*, Philadelphia, 1936. In: *J.B.L.* LV (1936), 319f.

E. Eyre, *European Civilization: Its Origin and Development*, New York, 1935, Vols. I–III. In: *The Saturday Review of Literature*, XIII, no. 15 (Feb. 8, 1936), 16f.

Philon von Alexandrien *Von den Machterweisen Gottes: Eine zeitgenössische Darstellung der Judenverfolgungen unter dem Kaiser Caligula*, über. H. Lewy, Berlin, 1935. In: *J.B.L.* LV (1936), 245f.

R. Schütz, *Les idées eschatologiques du Livre de la Sagesse*, Paris, 1935. In: *J.B.L.* LV (1936), 318f.

1937

Religious Tradition and Myth, New Haven: Yale University Press, 1937.

* "Literal Mystery in Hellenistic Judaism," in *Quantulacumque: Studies Presented to Kirsopp Lake by Pupils, Colleagues and Friends*, eds. R. P. Casey, S. Lake and A. K. Lake, London: Christophers, 1937, 227–41.

"New Light on Hellenistic Judaism," *Journal of Bible and Religion*, V (1937), 18–28.

"Symbolism in Hellenistic Jewish Art: The Problem of Method," *J.B.L.* LVI (1937), 103–14.

Review of:

W. Schubart, *Die religiöse Haltung des frühen Hellenismus* ("Der Alte Orient, XXXV, 2"), Leipzig, 1937. In: *J.B.L.* LVI (1937), 279f.

1938

The Politics of Philo Judaeus, Practice and Theory, with a General Bibliography of Philo by H. L. Goodhart and E. R. Goodenough, New Haven: Yale University Press, 1938.

Review of:

P. Boyancé, *Le Culte des Muses chez les philosophers grecs: Études d'histoire et de psychologie religieuses*. ("Bibliothèque des Écoles Françaises d'Athènes et de Rome, 141"), Paris, 1937. In: *American Journal of Philology*, LIX (1938), 487–90.

J. R. Marcus and A. Bilgray, *An Index to Jewish Festschriften*, Cincinnati, 1937. In: *J.B.L.* LVII (1938), 106f.

W. O. E. Oesterley and H. Loewe, eds., *Judaism and Christianity*, London–New York, 1937, 2 vols. In: *J.B.L.* LVII (1938), 345–48.

A. Parrot, *Le "Refrigerium" dans l'au-delà*, Paris, 1937. In *J.B.L.* LVII (1938), 104–06.

1939

"Problems of Method in Studying Philo Judaeus," *J.B.L.* LVIII (1939), 51–58. Review-article on W. Völker, *Fortschritt und Vollendung bei Philo von Alexandrien: eine Studie zur Geschichte der Frömmigkeit*, Leipzig, 1938).

Review of:

T. Arvedson, *Das Mysterium Christi: Eine Studie zu Mt. 11:25–30* ("Arbeiten und Mitteilungen aus dem NT Seminar zu Uppsala, VII"), Leipzig–Uppsala, 1937. In: *J.B.L.* LVIII (1939), 303–6.

M. Braun, *History and Romance in Graeco-Oriental Literature*, Oxford, 1938. In: *J.B.L.* LVIII (1939), 64f.

1940

An Introduction to Philo Judaeus, New Haven: Yale University Press, 1940.

* "The Fundamental Motif of Christianity," *The Journal of Religion*, XX (1940), 1–14. (Review-article on A. Nygren, *Agape and Eros*, London, 1938).

Review of:

R. O. Ballou et al., eds. *The Bible of the World*, New York, 1939). In: *J.B.L.* LIX (1940), 316.

S. Belkin, *Philo and the Oral Law: The Philonic Interpretation of Biblical Law in Relation to the Palestinian Halakah* ("Harvard Semitic Series, XI"), Cambridge, 1940. In: *J.B.L.* LIX (1940), 413–19.

A. Bertholet, *Über kultische Motivverschiebungen* (Reprint from the Sitzungs- berichte der preus. Akademie der Wissenschaften, phil-.hist. Kl., XVIII, 1938, 164–84), Berlin, 1938. *J.B.L.* LIX (1940), 83.

C. Clemen, *Lukians Schrift über die syrische Göttin* ("Der Alte Orient, XXXVII, 3–4"), Leipzig, 1938. In: *American Journal of Philology*, LXI (1940), 250.

T. Klauser and A. Rucker, eds., *Pisciculi: Studien zur Religion und Kultur des Altertums, F. J. Dölger dargeboten* ("Antike und Christentum, Ergän- zungsband I"), Münster, 1939. In: *The Journal of Religion* XX (1940), 403–7.

Comte Robert du Mesnil du Buisson, *Les peintures de la synagogue de Doura-Europas, 245–246 après J-C.* ("Scripta Pontificii Instituti Biblici, LXXXVI"), Rome, 1939. In: *J.B.L.* LIX (1940), 420–23.

Philo, with an English Translation, by F. H. Colson ("The Loeb Classical Library"), Cambridge, 1939, vol. VIII. In: *J.B.L.* LIX (1940), 57–59.

Philonis Alexandrini, In Flaccum, ed. and tr. H. Box, London, 1939. In: *J.B.L.* LIX (1940), 59f.

1941

Review of:

S. W. Baron, *Bibliography of Jewish Social Studies, 1938–39*, New York, 1941. In: *J.B.L.* LX (1941), 446f.

M. P. Nilsson, *Greek Popular Religion*, New York, 1940. In: *J.B.L.* LX (1941), 345–48.

H. M. Orlinsky, *An Indexed Bibliography of the Writings of W. F. Albright*, New Haven, 1941. In: *J.B.L.* LX (1941), 447.

A. Reifenberg, *Ancient Jewish Coins*, Jerusalem, 1940. In: *J.B.L.* LX (1941), 445f.

1942

* "Scientific Living," *The Humanist*, II (1942), 8–10.

Review of:

Philo, with an English Translation, by F. H. Colson ("The Loeb Classical Library"), Cambridge, 1941, vol. IX. In: *J.B.L.* LXI (1942), 305f.

1943

"Early Christian and Jewish Art," *The Jewish Quarterly Review* XXXIII 1942–43 (1943), 403–18. (Review-article on C. R. Morey, *Early Christian Art: An Outline of the Evolution of Style and Iconography in Sculpture and Painting from Antiquity to the Eighth Century*, Princeton, 1942).

1945

* "John a Primitive Gospel," *J.B.L.* LXIV (1945) 145–82.
"A Reply (to R. P. Casey, "Professor Goodenough and the Fourth Gospel," *J.B.L.* LXIV (1945), 535–42"), *J.B.L.* LXIV (1945), 543f.
* "The Mystical Value of Scholarship," *Crozer Quarterly* XXII (1945) 221–25.
* "Make-Believe," *The Deke Quarterly*, October 1945, 97f.

Review of:
W. L. Knox, *Some Hellenistic Elements in Primitive Christianity* ("Schweich Lectures on Biblical Archaeology, 1942"), London, 1944. In: *The Journal of Religion* XXV (1945), 297f.

1946

* "Philo on Immortality," *H.T.R.* XXXIX (1946), 85–108.
"The Crown of Victory in Judaism," *The Art Bulletin* XXVIII (1946), 139–59.

1947

"Religion and Psychology," (A seminar conducted at Columbia University, New York City, in 1947), mimeographed.
"The Old Conditioning" *in:* "Jewish Culture in this Time and Place, Symposium," *Commentary* IV (1947), 431.

1948

* "Needed: Scientific Study of Religion: How Long Will Free Inquiry Neglect This Basic Field?" *Commentary* V (1948), 272–77.
"Wolfson's Philo," *J.B.L.* LXVII (1948), 87–109 (Review-article on H. A. Wolfson, *Philo: Foundations of Religious Philosophy in Judaism, Christianity and Islam*, Cambridge, 1947, 2 vols.).

Review of:
Norman Brown, *Hermes the Thief*, Madison, 1947. In: *Crozer Quarterly* XXV (1948), 181f.

1949

Review of:
L. Delatte, *Les Traités de la royauté d'Ecphante, Diotogène et Sthenida* ("Bibliothèque de la faculté de philosophie et lettres de l'Université de Liège, fasc. 97"), Paris, 1942. In: *Classical Philology* XLIV (1949), 129–31.

1950

Review of:
A. J. Festugière, *L'Hermétisme* ("K. Humanistiska Vetenskapssamfun dets i Lund, Arsberättelse 1947–48, I"), Lund, 1948. In: *The Review of Religion* XIV (1949/50), 423f.

1951

"The Menorah among Jews of the Roman World," *The Hebrew Union College Annual* XXIII, 1950–51, part 2 (1951), 449–92.
"The Place of Religion in the Treatment of the Mentally Deficient," *Crozer Quarterly* XXVIII (1951), 120–26.

Review of:
C. Bonner, *Studies in Magical Amulets, chiefly Graeco-Egyptian*, ("University of Michigan Studies, Humanistic Series, XLIX"), Ann Arbor, 1950. In: *American Journal of Philology* LXXII (1951), 308–16.

G. Kisch, ed., *Pseudo-Philo's Liber Antiquitatum Biblicarum* ("Publications in Mediaeval Studies, The University of Notre Dame, X"), Notre Dame, 1949. In: *Speculum* XXVI (1951), 394f.

1952

"The Evaluation of Symbols Recurrent in Time, as Illustrated in Judaism," *Eranos-Jahrbuch* XX, 1951 (1952), 285–319.
* "The Inspiration of New Testament Research," (Presidential Address, Society of Biblical Literature and Exegesis), *J.B.L.* LXXI (1952), 1–9.

Review of:
M. Bodkin, *Studies of Type-Images in Poetry, Religion and Philosophy*, London, 1951. In: *The Review of Religion* XVII (1952), 69–71.
W. Wolff, *Changing Concepts of the Bible: a Psychological Analysis of Its Words, Symbols, and Beliefs*, New York, 1951. In: *The Review of Religion* XVII (1952), 71–73.

1953

Jewish Symbols in the Greco-Roman Period ("Bollingen Series XXXVII"), New York: Pantheon Books, 1953, vol. 1–3: *The Archaeological Evidence from Palestine and the Diaspora*.
* "Religious Aspirations," in *The Age of Diocletian: A Symposium, 1951*, New York, 1953, 37–48.
* "The Crown of Acanthus (?)," (with C. B. Welles), *H.T.R.* XLVI (1953), 241f.

Review of:
S. Aalen, *Die Begriffe, 'Licht' und 'Finsternis' im Alten Testament, im Spätjudentum und im Rabbinismus* ("Skrifter utgitt av det Norske Videnskaps-Akademi i Oslo, II, Hist.-Filos. Klasse, 1951, No. 1"), Oslo, 1951. In: *Journal of Theological Studies*, N.S. IV (1953), 63–68.
S. A. B. Mercer, *The Pyramid Texts in Translation and Commentary*, New York, 1952, 4 vols.. In: *Yale Review* XLII (1953), 440f.

1954

Jewish Symbols in the Greco-Roman Period ("Bollingen Series XXXVII"), New York: Pantheon Books, 1954, vol. 4: *The Problem of Method; Symbols from Jewish Cult*.

Review of:
Philo, *Supplement I: Questions and Answers on Genesis and Exodus translated from the Ancient Armenian Version of the Original Greek*, by R. Marcus ("The Loeb Classical Library"), London–Cambridge, 1953. In: *J.B.L.* LXXIII (1954), 169–71.

1955

Toward a Mature Faith, New York: Prentice-Hall, Inc., 1955 (reissued as a Yale Paperbound, Yale University Press, 1961).
"Our Faith and Doctor Freud," *The Saturday Review* XXXVIII, no. 20 (May 14, 1955), 9f., 40f.

Review of:
H. I. Bell, *Cults and Creeds in Graeco-Roman Egypt*, New York, 1953. In: *Jewish Social Studies* XVII (1955), 335.
G. Dix, *Jew and Greek: A Study in the Primitive Church*, New York, 1952. In: *Jewish Social Studies* XVII (1955), 334.

1956

Jewish Symbols in the Greco-Roman Period ("Bollingen Series XXXVII"), New York: Pantheon Books, 1956, vol. 5–6: *Fish, Bread and Wine.* "New Light from Stones," *America–Israel Bulletin*, Vol. I, no. 2, Dec. 1, 1956, 3f.

1957

"Pagan Symbols in Jewish Antiquity. The Vine, the Eagle, the Lion," *Commentary* XXIII (1957), 74–80.
* "The Bosporus Inscription to the Most High God," *The Jewish Quarterly Review* XLVII 1956–57, (1957), 221–44.

1958

Jewish Symbols in the Greco-Roman Period ("Bollingen Series XXXVII"), New York: Pantheon Books, 1958, vol. 7–8: *Pagan Symbols in Judaism.*
"The Paintings of the Dura-Europos Synagogue, Method and an Application," *Israel Exploration Journal* VIII (1958), 69–79.
* "A Jewish-Gnostic Amulet of the Roman Period," *Greek and Byzantine Studies* I (1958), 71–80.
"Communication" (Reply to H. Strauss' review of *Jewish Symbols in the Greco-Roman Period*, vol. 4–6, in *Judaism* VII (1958), 81–85), *Judaism* VII (1958), 177–79.

Review of:
C. H. Kraeling, *The Synagogue*, with contributions by C. C. Torrey, C. B. Welles and B. Geiger ("The Excavations at Dura-Europos conducted by Yale University and the French Academy of Inscriptions and Letters. Final Report, VIII, pt. 1"), New Haven, 1956. In: *American Journal of Archaeology* LXII (1958), 248–51.

1959

"Philo of Alexandria" in *Great Jewish Personalities in Ancient and Medieval Times*, S. Noveck, ed. (B'nai B'rith Great Books Series, I) New York: Farrar, Straus and Cudahy, 1959, 102–19.
* "Honest Doubt," *Yale Alumni Review* XXII, no. 7 (April, 1959), 19–21.
"Religionswissenschaft," *ACLS Newsletter* X, no. 6 (June, 1959), 5–19; also printed in *Numen* VI (1959), 77–95.
"Philo of Alexandria," *Jewish Heritage* I, no. 4 (Winter, 1959), 19–22 (reprinted in *Jewish Heritage Reader*, selected, with introduction by Morris Adler, New York: Taplinger Publishing Co., 1965, 173–77).
"Opening Remarks by the President," *Translations of the Connecticut Academy of Arts and Sciences* XXXVIII (1959), 154f.
"The Orpheus in the Synagogue of Dura-Europos: A Correction" (Reply to H. Stern's article in *Journal of the Warburg and Courtauld Institutes* XXI (1958), 1–6), *Journal of the Warburg and Courtauld Institutes* XXII (1959), 372.

1960

* "The Bible as Product of the Ancient World," in *Five Essays on the Bible*, Papers Read at the 1960 Meeting of the American Council of Learned Societies, New York, Published by the ACLS, 1960, 1–19.
* "A Yale Professor and Groton Parent Looks at the School," in *Views from the Circle: Seventy-five Years of Groton School*, Groton, Massachusetts, Published by the Trustees of Groton School, 1960, 335–46.

* "The Evaluation of Symbols in History," 519–25, and
"The Characteristics of Western Culture," 675–79, in *Proceedings of the IXth International Congress for the History of Religions, Tokyo and Kyoto, 1958*, Tokyo, 1960.

Review of:
M. Eliade and J. M. Kitagawa, eds., *The History of Religions: Essays in Methodology*, Chicago, 1959. In: *Ethics* LXX (1960), 343f.
V. Tcherikover, *Hellenistic Civilization and the Jews*. Philadelphia–Jerusalem, 1959. In: *Jewish Social Studies* XXII (1960), 105–8.

1961

"The Rabbis and Jewish Art in the Greco-Roman Period," *Hebrew Union College Annual* XXXII (1961), 269–79 (Julian Morgenstern Festschrift).
"Judaism at Dura-Europas," *Israel Exploration Journal* XI, (1961), 161–70.

1962

An Introduction to Philo Judaeus (second edition, revised), Oxford: Basil Blackwell, 1962; New York: Barnes and Noble, 1963 (sic).
"Philo Judaeus," in *The Interpreter's Dictionary of the Bible*, eds., G. A. Buttrick *et al.*, New York–Nashville, 1962, vol. 3, 796–99).
"The Scientific Study of Religion," Fourth Centennial Lecture, University of Denver Centennial, April 24, 1962 (mimeographed).
"A Rhyme on My Retirement," *The Spider's Web* XXVII, no. 2 (February, 1962), 5. (This issue of this publication of Jonathan Edwards College, Yale University was dedicated to the author at his retirement.)
* "Myths and Symbols for Children" (with Evelyn W. Goodenough), *Religious Education* LVII (1962), 172–77, 236.
"Catacomb Art," *J.B.L.* LXXXI (1962), 113–42 (Review-article on A. Ferrua, *Le Pitture della Nuova Catacomba di Via Latina*, Città del Vaticane, 1960 (Monumenti di antichita cristiana, Ser. 2, Vol. 8).)
"The New Synagogue at Woonsocket, Rhode Island," *Art International* VI, no. 10 (December 20, 1962), 26–29.

Review of:
Werner Jaeger, *Early Christianity and Greek Paideia*, Cambridge, 1961. In: *American Historical Review* LXVII (1962), 760.

1963

"Symbols as Historical Evidence," *Diogenes* XLIV (1963), 19–32; also printed in the French edition as "Les symboles et les preuves en histoire" (tr. M-.A. Béra), *Diogène* XLIV, 21–37.

Review of:
M. Avi-Yonah and E. G. Kraeling, *Our Living Bible*, New York, 1962. In: *J.B.L.* LXXXII (1963), 140f.
H. Rahner, *Greek Myths and Christian Mystery*, New York, 1963. In: *J.B.L.* LXXXII (1963), 444–48.

1964

Jewish Symbols in the Greco-Roman Period ("Bollingen Series XXXVII"), New York: Pantheon Books, 1964, vol. 9–11: *Symbolism in the Dura-Synagogue*.
* "Religionswissenschaft," in *Religion Ponders Science*, ed. E. P. Booth, New York: Appleton-Century-Crofts, Inc., 1964, 63–84.
"An Early Christian Bread Stamp," *H.T.R.* LVII (1964), 133–37.

1965

The Psychology of Religious Experiences, New York: Basic Books, 1965.
Jewish Symbols in the Greco-Roman Period ("Bollingen Series XXXVII"), New York: Pantheon Books, vol. 12; *Summary and Conclusions* (Vol. 13: General Index, with Maps, is in preparation).

1966

"Early Christianity in Acts," *Studies in Luke-Acts, Essays Presented in Honor of Paul Schubert*, eds. L. E. Keck and J. L. Martyn, Nashville: Abingdon Press, 1966, 51–59.
"The Greek Garments on Jewish Heroes in The Dura Synagogue," Philip W. Lown Institute of Advanced Judaic Studies, Brandeis University, *Studies and Texts*: Volume III, Biblical Motifs, ed. Alexander Altmann, Cambridge: Harvard University Press, 1966, 221–37.

1967

"A Historian of Religion Tries To Define Religion," *Zygon* 2 (1967) 7–22.

1968

"Life Purpose in View of the Past," in *Studies in Honor of Rudolph Willard*, ed. A. A. Hill, 1968.
"Paul and the Hellenization of Christianity," with A. Thomas Kraabel, in *Religions in Antiquity: Essays in Memory of Erwin Ramsdell Goodenough*.

INDEX